The
Southern
State of
Mind

The Southern State of Mind

Edited by
Jan Nordby Gretlund

With a New Afterword by the Editor

The University of South Carolina Press

© 1999 University of South Carolina
Afterword © 2010 University of South Carolina

Cloth edition published by the University of South Carolina Press, 1999
Paperback edition published in Columbia, South Carolina,
by the University of South Carolina Press, 2010

www.sc.edu/uscpress

Manufactured in the United States of America

19 18 17 16 15 14 13 12 11 10   10 9 8 7 6 5 4 3 2 1

The Library of Congress has cataloged the cloth edition as follows:
The Southern state of mind / edited by Jan Nordby Gretlund.
   p. cm.
  ISBN 1-57003-312-9 (alk. paper)
   1. Southern States—Civilization—20th century. 2. American literature—Southern States—History and criticism. I. Gretlund, Jan Nordby.
P216.2 .S64 1999
975'.043—dc21   99-6014

ISBN: 978-1-57003-899-0 (pbk)

Contents

Editor's Introduction	Present States of Southern Mind	vii

Part I: The Biracial South

Charles Reagan Wilson	The Myth of the Biracial South	3
Tony Badger	The Rise and Fall of Biracial Politics in the South	23
Paul M. Gaston	After Jim Crow: Civil Rights as Civil Wrongs	36
Dan Carter	A World Turned Upside Down: Southern Politics at the End of the Twentieth Century	49

Part II: The Changing State of Mind

Richard Gray	Recorded and Unrecorded Histories: Recent Southern Writing and Social Change	67
Lothar Hönnighausen	The Southern Heritage and the Semiotics of Consumer Culture	80
Walter Edgar	Beyond the Tumult and the Shouting: Black and White in South Carolina in the 1990s	95
Suzanne Jones	Refighting Old Wars: Race Relations and Masculine Conventions in Fiction by Larry Brown and Madison Smartt Bell	107
Dori Sanders	"After Freedom"—Blacks and Whites in the 1990s: The Facts and the Fiction	121

Part III: Reconstructing Southern Identity

James C. Cobb	"We Ain't White Trash No More": Southern Whites and the Reconstruction of Southern Identity	135
Russell Duncan	A Native Son Led the Way: Jimmy Carter and the Modern New South	147

Contents

François Pitavy	Let Us Now Praise Famous Women: Kaye Gibbons's Song for a Deceased Mother	161
Marcel Arbeit	Lies as the Structural Element in the Fiction of Lewis Nordan	175
Danièle Pitavy-Souques	Dancers and Angels: Communication in the Fiction of Josephine Humphreys	185

Part IV: Looking West and Back

Robert H. Brinkmeyer, Jr.	Westward, Ho!: Contemporary Southern Writing and the American West	203
C. Vann Woodward	Post-Reconstruction Periods Compared: 1890s and 1990s	212

Afterword   225

Index   227

Editor's Introduction

Present States of Southern Mind

As the "present state" is always by definition a state of flux, it is difficult to say something profound about the state of Southern letters and politics. "Southern identity," the Southernness of a multilayered culture, is forever in the making. But to avoid misinformation, fantasies, and delusions about the South, the opinions of historians and literary historians should be among the sources for the notions the public entertains about the present. These essays by internationally recognized experts on the South attempt singly and collectively to gauge the situation in the region today. The essays represent a collective effort at defining Southern identity and mind as they express themselves a hundred and thirty-four years after the War.

Gone are the ideas today of Southern history and literature as organic cultural continuities, in which an encompassing Southern culture flowered, bore fruit, and on the whole behaved in accordance with old horticultural metaphors. Yet these essays address both contemporary Southern history and its expression in fiction. The double vision is the strength of the collection. It seems that the attempt at defining "Southern identity today" inspires historians to consider *the origin* of the present ideas of Southern identity, whereas literary critics speculate about *the present and future* of the regional identity as they see it expressed in the literature of today's South. But both parties want to know how Southerners see themselves today, whatever the traditional stereotypical images. The rewarding dialogue between historians and literary historians demonstrates the interaction between the recording mind and the imagination in everyday Southern life, and it has helped shape the structure of the collection.

The essays combine a wide scope with detailed information. The book is not meant for a specific limited group and was certainly not written exclusively

Jan Nordby Gretlund

for academic readers. Nor are the writers just addressing each other or themselves; they obviously want to include the nonprofessional reader in the discussion. The essayists sum up the state of research in Southern history and literature with a general audience in mind, which does not make their historical views and literary comments less insightful or valuable; on the contrary, the approach makes the essays lively and accessible. The collection, as it now stands, is remarkably removed from the devotional, certifying, and celebratory view of the South that in the past dominated similar books. The present collection is focused on the theme of Southern identity. It is a volume designed to contribute to the discussion about Southern identity, and in this sense it is an expression of flourishing regionalism. Have the inherited values survived the modernization of recent decades? Or have they been bulldozed away now that the South is also a victim of interstate highways, chain stores, suburban life, and mass media advertising? By implication the region is simply seen as a Rorschach test for the state of American identity in general. The process in the South of ideological self-identification has enormous potential in the shaping of national attitudes, as the 1990s have proved, and this is what makes the essays relevant beyond their immediate subject.

Historians have mostly seen the theme as an invitation to write on the biracial South, seen in a historical perspective. In most of the contributions by historians the biracial relations dwarf every other subject in the contemporary South. That biracialism should be considered as a definition of Southern identity is, of course, significant in itself. The historians ask, when did a Southern identity develop? And how did that identity develop over the years? They are interested in how the present stereotypical images came out of the South's past. It is not that the historians are writing of a distant past, when race was indeed central to Southern identity; instead, they go back to look at recent decades in order to evaluate the present state of the biracial South. The life of the biracial myth from the 1970s until today is a constant presence in the volume. Biracial relations were regarded with a good deal of optimism two decades ago, according to most historians, but since then a growing pessimism has set in. Nevertheless some of the essays below argue that a reaching across the racial divide exists in certain areas that make up a true, if limited, biracial Southern identity.

Today's critics of Southern literature, on the other hand, are inspired by contemporary Southern novelists and have mostly chosen to focus on other aspects of Southern identity than biracialism. If we judge by the fiction of contemporary Southern writers, it is possible to travel through broad stretches of the South and find scarcely a black face in sight. If prejudice is a topic, it is usually through monologues exposing characters on the political right. The basic biracial problem is hardly ever in focus. Even Maya Angelou, Alice Walker, Toni Morrison, and Dori Sanders seem more interested in the black community and in the community of women, than in the black and white community. The writers of contemporary fiction seem to be living fully in a present where much is going on in Southern life *in addition to* racial and social changes. Surely, they seem to say, the African American presence is what distinguished the South in its various past avatars, but this is no longer important to the same degree.

The present South is about a lot of things, and race is but one of them; few of the younger novelists agonize over racial issues. To the novelists and their critics the historians seem too often to impose the familiar binary options of the past, by ignoring everything *new* that has been happening in the South during the last twenty years. Among the many exceptions in this collection is the essay by Walter Edgar about the changes in South Carolina. Are the novelists extra careful on the topic of race in the wake of William Styron's experience with his *Confessions of Nat Turner*? Or do the writings of white novelists today simply mirror the politicians who have been blinded to racial issues by the light of all those Republican conservative candles? Or are the novelists more in touch with the concerns and temper of their time? And are the issues they see and write about just as important in today's South as the biracial living? These are some of the issues raised in the collection.

The first section of the collection, "The Biracial Identity," opens with Charles Reagan Wilson's essay. He points out that it is the growing African American political strength that increasingly has led white politicians to acknowledge black aspirations in the South. Statistics show that the pattern of historic migration from the South was reversed in the 1970s, when many more African Americans moved to the South. (During the last five years of the decade they "returned" to the region at a rate of 100,000 a year.) Some consequences have been that more African Americans are now laying their claim to Southern culture, they are involved in the redefining of what it means to be Southern, and their endorsement is sought of the idea of a biracial South. Southerners do have a biracial heritage in music, language, foodways, religion, and other cultural features, and the ideology of the biracial South says the kinship between blacks and whites should be embraced. The welcome post–civil-rights-movement idea has been, Reagan Wilson notes, that the South has the potential to achieve an integrated society with harmonious race relations (which would have a meaning beyond the region). This sounds like a new version of the liberal dream of a racially converted South, washed in the blood of civil rights martyrs, which will eventually redeem the nation. But it is still just a myth, according to Reagan Wilson. Developments in the 1990s have under-

Jan Nordby Gretlund

mined the biracial myth. The assertion of black identity and their demands for the removal of "offensive" symbols have been met with a resurgence of the old myth of the Lost Cause. This is especially true among intellectuals and middle-class Southerners, who have rebelled against the African American demands. They do not see a need, Reagan Wilson maintains, to redefine the Southern identity from its historic meanings, which are associated with a white-dominated South. The significance of the older ideological perspective comes from these frustrated Southerners' active role in Republican politics.

In his consideration of the rise and fall of biracial politics Tony Badger examines moments in recent Southern history when it looked as if liberal racial ideas might be realized. He claims that the consequences of the failure of biracial politics in the 1950s meant more support among lower-income whites for segregationists. The long-term consequences were that the same white voters became conservative also on economic issues. Southerners adapted to racial change in the 1970s, Tony Badger argues, because defiance would have threatened the new-found prosperity in the region. But as the purchasing power of the median wage earner has declined since the mid-1970s, race relations have become competitive and racial violence has been revived. Liberal New South governors have been replaced in the 1980s and 1990s by politicians committed to a philosophy of low taxation, limited government, and opposition to any redistribution policy. The resurgent Republican Party is seen as a crucial element in the racial polarization of Southern politics by the historians writing on the present state of mind. It is almost exclusively a white party today, it is aided by the activities of the Christian Right, and it tries hard, Badger opines, to counter the impact of black voter registration. While he recognizes the increase in African American officeholding in the South and the responsiveness to the new political realities of elected sheriffs and appointed police chiefs, Badger is not optimistic about the prospects for biracial politics, for 90 percent of the registered black voters are Democrats and little is heard from the moderates who used to grace Southern Republicanism. The Democrats in the South are faced with the almost hopeless task of building a successful biracial electoral coalition.

Biracial efforts are undermined, Paul Gaston points out, by the ways the history of the civil rights movement is anaesthetized and sanitized in movies, documentaries, and textbooks. The argument is illustrated by a case study of the creation and the manipulation of the Martin Luther King, Jr., myth. Gaston argues that when the national holiday bill was proposed, it was the image of King as the great champion of *his country and its values* that was celebrated. The criticism that was obvious in the very existence of the civil rights movement and made specific by King in his last years was effectively silenced by a culture unwilling to face the existence of racism. The abolition of legal segregation and disfranchisement was a short-term objective, Gaston writes, whereas the greater challenge of an ethic of integration in a community is a long-term objective. As a molder of the historical imagination, the film industry is responsible for making freedom-struggle features that do not feature blacks and for its "white redemption" movies. In *Ghosts of Mississippi* (1996) the central figures are white people who are brought to an awareness of injustice. Although blacks were at the center of the freedom movement, not much is told of Medgar Evers and the freedom struggle he led. But Gaston finds some reasons for optimism in the striking success of *Eyes on the Prize,* a non-Hollywood version of civil rights history.

The first section of the collection ends with Dan Carter's attempt to sum up the biracial situation in the South. He sees the growth of the Christian schools as a manifestation of the complex racial, cultural, and religious fears of the growing evangelical majority. He also notes that Republicans dominate congressional delegations of the former Confederate States. In a generation the solid South has returned, but this time it is a solidly Republican South. Carter assumes that the Republicans have benefited from the increase in the region's suburban population, from the upsurge of religious fundamentalism in American politics, and from the number of predominantly "black" districts created under the Voting Rights Act. Even though the Southern levels of voter participation are the lowest in the nation, Carter sees the sweeping Republican gains of 1994, which led to the emergence of conservative Southern key figures in national politics, as a "Southernization" of American politics.

Some aspects of the South retain their grip on the imagination despite the economic metamorphosis of the region. On the matters of localism, attitudes towards violence, gun-ownership, and religion, white Southerners are still distinctive, according to John Shelton Reed. In those respects and others non-Southerners have gravitated toward Southern thinking. Richard Gray's discussion of Southern writing and social change is the opening essay of the second section of the volume, where the emphasis is on the changing state of mind in the South. The history of the way the South has been created through language is there in the written texts. Gray divides contemporary writers into "expatriates" who go away and write about the South in Faulknerian terms (Cormac McCarthy), "mavericks" who rebel but remember their childhood world (Harry Crews), and "homekeepers" (Josephine Humphreys) who react to the sudden pluralism of their Southern world by attempting a kind of recuperation and an examination of the degree to which moral continuity is still possible. But all the Southern writers tell us how their history is being altered and recovered. Over the past few decades the South has changed dramatically in terms of its day-to-day social and economic life, and its mental and moral habits have, at

Jan Nordby Gretlund

the very least, been challenged. Gray claims that if any group is likely to help us understand the exact forms that change has engendered in the contemporary South and the conflicting forces at work there, it must be the Southern writers. This is mainly due to the chance their writings give them to live both in and out of history and their urge to communicate their perspective.

The impact in the South of the conflicting tendencies toward nationalization and regionalization is recognized by Lothar Hönnighausen. He pays particular attention to the post–civil rights Southerner's impatience with the way the area is still portrayed in stereotypes. New Southern writers such as Barry Hannah, Bobbie Ann Mason, and Clyde Edgerton have launched parodic attacks on the Lost Cause rituals in an attempt to overcome the narcissism of their region. To make the Civil War the subject of irony, parody, and even farce would have been unthinkable for Margaret Mitchell and William Faulkner, but the new writers deconstruct the dead structures, revaluate regional values, and recode paralyzed cultural codes. The theme is rarely the Civil War itself, but the problem of coming to terms with it, historically and artistically. The new fiction reveals the urge to explode Southern myths with the aim of creating a usable past. But Hönnighausen's essay concludes that in spite of the obvious revisionist intentions, a specific awareness of history continues to inform the regional sensibility and remains a distinctive feature of Southern identity.

In South Carolina, the rancorous debate over one of the Lost Cause symbols, the Confederate battle flag, has overshadowed real changes. Walter Edgar points out that the media, probably distracted by the violence elsewhere, have tended to ignore South Carolina's progress. Despite the so-called Americanization of Dixie, relationships are still important to Southerners, and black and white Carolinians have begun, person to person, to reach out across the racial divide. At several levels South Carolina does have a biracial society. Not only do black and white children attend public schools together, but they also attend the same parochial and independent schools. And at the University of South Carolina black students comprise 18.7 percent of the undergraduate student body, and of the legislators in the state 21 percent are today black Carolinians. The progress is based on people dealing with other people, with individuals rather than races or groups. In spite of the progress made, Edgar acknowledges that South Carolina still has a long way to go, for racism still exists in the area. But how far they have come should be recognized, and very little attention has been paid to the quiet Carolina revolution. The Southern identity of 1962 is as dead as that of 1862. It took a generation for that to occur, but who in 1960 would have thought it possible?

Since the Civil War, white male writers of the South have created fictions about childhood friendships that crossed the color line. Suzanne Jones deals with the representations of friendships between adult blacks and whites that have only recently begun to appear in print. It is the reaching out across the racial divide that has become a topic in Southern fiction. Does the solution to the South's chronic racial problem reside in the building up of individual friendships? Southern novelists Larry Brown and Madison Smartt Bell have written interracial buddy novels that begin where earlier fiction about male friendships ended, i.e., when boys have become racially self-conscious men. Both novelists test the significance of the similar experiences of their black and white protagonists against histories of segregation and experiences of racial prejudice. With both *Dirty Work* and *Soldier's Joy* readers dwell momentarily in the tantalizing possibility of genuine friendships between adult black and white men. Brown does not test the relationship he creates in the larger context of Southern society; Bell does, but finally he cannot imagine how such a friendship will sustain itself in a society where hatred still lurks. In Southern fiction the conclusion seems to be that neither the Civil War nor the Vietnam War has made the South safe for cross-racial friendships, despite the readiness of some individuals of both races.

Dori Sanders is the right person to end the section on the changing state of mind in the South. She is a novelist, she is from South Carolina, and she is African American. In her essay she wants to address the present but finds she must first take a close look at the past; as she comments, "it is just a Southern thing." Sanders comments on black history in the South and on her own family history in particular. She maintains that, in fiction, the problem of race appears near the point of being resolved, but she is not sure it is the truth, as "racial tension is still with us." Sanders admits that on the whole she gave a very optimistic view of the present in *Clover,* her first novel. She observes that in spite of more than forty years of struggle for civil rights "the separateness of the races is self-evident for the least observant." On the other hand it is clear to her that the 1990s in South Carolina represent a South very different from that of forty years ago. Today, Sanders points out, the cultures have from all appearances blended, and it is an integrated South. But, she notes, the private lives of black and white still tend to be separate and "most beauty shops, funeral homes, and even churches are still separate, either black or white." But she recognizes that this is "usually a separateness dictated through choice."

The third section of the collection is focused on the reconstructing of Southern identity in the 1990s. James Cobb has written the lead essay, in which he concentrates on poor white Southerners. He notes that with the growing statistical evidence of the white South's assimilation into the American mainstream, interest in Southern cultural identity has soared. Southern whites, who have at last secured a full-scale participation in the national consumer culture, are now anxious to consume their own regional culture. Ironically, with the Southernization of America and the national embrace of conservative values, many experience difficulties in deciding just exactly what is Southern. But as Cobb points out, what could be more Southern than to obsess about being Southern? Southerners are haunted by the specter of cultural anonymity. As a result, obsession with everything remotely Southern, the "narcissism of small differences," threatens to turn the South of popular perception into a homegrown caricature of itself. Another irony, observed by Cobb, is that black Southerners seem considerably more confident in their Southernness than their white counterparts. But with the stream of black migration to the South and the improving economic circumstances, black Southerners may yet be plunged into an identity crisis of their own. But if white and black Southerners are to save themselves from being swallowed up in the American mainstream, Cobb argues, they will have to move past stereotyping and "cultural masturbation" and begin the building up of a new regional identity.

Russell Duncan outlines how one man, born a poor white, has constructed his identity. The life and myth of Jimmy Carter are considered. Duncan's interesting observation, as regards Southern identity, is that Carter's career, as invented and reinvented through numerous biographies and autobiographies, parallels the contemporary hopes of the South. Symbol, myth, and history are intertwined in the naive and profound recollections by Jimmy Carter and the equally paradoxical portraits by biographers. Nevertheless, Duncan argues, "this native son continues to embody the growing tolerance, influence, and ambivalence of the South."

Should we go on asking worn-out questions about the South and its writers, asks François Pitavy. Is there still a need for "slick and reassuring categorizing"? He notes that Kaye Gibbons has no reservation about being called "a Southern writer" and that her Southernness may well reside in her unerring and droll sense of language (which is possibly "the ultimate definition of place in an Americanized South"). What can the reading of Gibbons's fiction tell us about Southernness? In Gibbons's first novel a child's guilt about her mother's fate is compounded by her guilt over her own racism. So Ellen Foster's education as a Southern girl is also a racial coming of age, her own and that of the Southern psyche. It seems to Pitavy that except for comical effects Gibbons has, between her first and her fifth novels, steered away from traditional Southern topics. Her Southernness is, however, obvious in her revisiting of female genealogies. The burden in her fiction is no longer that of history, but that of individual memory. And the voice, Pitavy points out, is no longer "the Faulknerian masculine oratory" of the previous generation, but the toned down voice of private recovery, self-definition, and survival. The most profoundly enduring Southern concern has in this way become feminized and privatized.

Canonized versions of Southern identity are also the subject of Lewis Nordan's work. In his essay on Nordan's fiction Marcel Arbeit focuses on the writer's use of the imaginative lie to make our existence less incomplete and above all less dull. Through the use of the "lying" imagination Nordan gains the freedom to create metaphors that help dissolve the established monolithic "truths" of Southern life. The purpose is to remind us that every so-called "truth" about the Southern "reality" can and should be challenged. He also creates Southern characters who claim they are moral, but they obviously do not believe in the established moral standards of their community. In his fiction Nordan is optimistic, according to Arbeit, about the construction of a new Southern identity and suggests that the imagination will enable Southerners to extricate themselves from the burden of inherited moral demands and monolithic truths.

In the final essay of the third section Danièle Pitavy-Souques considers the notions that Southern writers are supposed to be more interested in moral problems, the survival of the family, and the existence of community life: old "truths" that are difficult to challenge as they have gained a mythical status and are identified with the South also outside the region. But the established myths are now balanced by modern Southern myths of a lack of belief in God and a society with no place for morals. It is, Pitavy-Souques points out, in the tension between the old and the new myths that the best of contemporary Southern writing has its origin. Like Kaye Gibbons and Lewis Nordan, South Carolina novelist Josephine Humphreys dramatizes the emptiness of myths. The static Old South of order and hierarchy is opposed by change and the very exuberance of today's Southern life. Humphreys is present in the margins of the Southern present and fills her fiction with angels, black doubles, ghost families, and unsuccessful yet kindly friends. In this way, Pitavy-Souques maintains, the writer constructs a network of positive relationships that effectively change the impression of Southern life. In this South the hopes raised by the civil rights movement could begin to be realized if only everyone would accept help of the other. The South could be rejuvenated by acceptance of its very idiosyncrasies, and as it happens for some of Humphreys's fictional Southerners, the traditional compartmenting imposed by class and prejudice could disappear.

Several contemporary Southern writers, such as Doris Betts, Clyde Edgerton, Barry Hannah, Rick Bass, Madison Smartt Bell, James Lee Burke, and most successfully Cormac McCarthy, have placed fiction in the American West. In the first of the two papers of the lagniappe section Robert Brinkmeyer speculates about what the move West in the Southern literary imagination tells us

Jan Nordby Gretlund

about the South. To go West is a move from place into space; the move represents an attempt to escape the traditional burdens of Southern identity and also the anxieties of suburban Sun Belt living. What was for James Dickey and others a desire to leave the responsibilities of home and work for the weekend has now, Southern fiction informs us, become a desire to step free of Southern identity altogether. In the tradition of Huck Finn modern Southerners light out for the territory, maybe to return, nobody knows. It is an imaginative trend that is "profoundly reshaping the Southern and the Western literary traditions." The West is where an individual, because he is no longer enmeshed in the web of Southern culture, can create his own ahistorical identity. For a consideration of Southern identity the interesting aspect of Brinkmeyer's essay is that the state of mind that comes with westerning involves an elaborate critique of the world left behind; and often the description of the fictional flights West are dwarfed by detailed thoughts on Southern culture.

The collection ends with C. Vann Woodward's essay on the two post-Reconstruction periods, the 1890s and the 1990s. His comparison is focused on racial disenfranchisement and segregation in the two periods. He reminds us that the Second Reconstruction was national rather than regional and that the South therefore faced new as well as old problems. He points out that it is an apparent paradox of Southern history that waves of democratic upheaval coincide with waves of extreme racism. This was the case in the history of disfranchisement and also in the history of Jim Crow segregation. Woodward argues that the common misreading lies not in the existence but in the causes of the paradox. The mistake is to attribute the outbursts of racism to lower-class whites.

It is no surprise to Woodward that optimism briefly soared in the 1860s after the legal end of slavery and again in the 1960s with some civil rights gained, but he notes that the optimists in both centuries shared the false assumption that the legal end of an institution meant the end of the abuse outlawed. Like most of the historians in the collection Woodward sees several negative developments in the South. By 1992 the black vote had begun to decline, which has made it difficult to gain a majority working with white Democrats. The creation of a number of minority districts through redistricting is now often seen as being at odds with the spirit of the civil rights revolution; besides, it drains strong Democratic votes from other districts. Whereas Dr. King's message of peaceful integration seems forgotten, just thirty years after his assassination, support for black nationalism, separatism, and racial hatred has grown. Woodward does not dismiss the achievements of the Second Reconstruction period, which swept away the legal foundations of segregation in schools, housing, and employment and which successfully banned Jim Crow in public places and accommodations. Nor does he exaggerate the importance of the minority called black separatists. It is the shift to the right in the courts and in the American electorate that makes the venerable historian less than optimistic about the future.

Southern studies have become a fertile area of intertextual relations, opposition, discontinuity, redeployment, and synthesis of cultural concerns. The results of the inquiry into the present state of Southern mind form a telling whole. They offer an exchange of opinions, bring to the fore some of the contradictions of Southern society, and reestablish the old common ground and traditional affiliation between history and literature. *The Southern State of Mind* makes it clear that history still matters and that great Southern fiction is still being written. On the topics addressed the essays offer a comprehensive view and yet are as various as the present states of Southern mind. When examined together, the contributions form contrasts, display overlapping, and invite suggestions. The general themes that tie the essays together refer to Southern identity as seen today and are all variations on that topic. The essayists bear witness to the pain of loss Southerners suffer as their region is rapidly losing its distinctive identity. Collectively they give us new insight into Southern cultural mythology and offer the provocative perspective of today's South as a nationally encompassing state of mind.

The Southern State of Mind

Part I

The Biracial South

The Myth of the Biracial South

Charles Reagan Wilson

Charles L. Black, a born-and-bred white Southerner, was teaching at the Yale Law School in 1957 when he wrote an article for the *New Republic* in which he outlined the legal and moral appeals that might be made to sympathetic whites to promote desegregation of the South. At the end of the essay, he revealed a dream he had long had, formed from pondering "my relations with the many Negroes of Southern origin that I have known, both in the North and at home." He noted "again and again how often we laugh at the same things, how often we pronounce the same words the same way to the amusement of our hearers, judge character in the same frame of reference, mist up at the same kinds of music. I have exchanged 'good evening' with a Negro stranger on a New Haven street, and then realized (from the way he said the words) that he and I derived this universal small-town custom from the same culture." Despite such cultural affinities, whites and blacks in the South, though, had failed to acknowledge them, these affinities that reflected a kinship. "My dream is simply that sight will one day clear and that each of the participants will recognize the other." If this happened, "if the two could join and look toward the future together—something would have happened uniquely beautiful in history. The South, which has always felt itself reserved for a high destiny, would have found it, and would come to flower at last."[1]

Black's words in 1957, when the black freedom movement was well underway, expressed a mythic view of Southern culture that would become in the 1970s a major ideological underpinning of the contemporary American South. The myth of the biracial South is the idea that the South has the potential to achieve a truly integrated society, harmonious race relations with meaning for American culture and beyond. Like a good evangelist, Leslie Dunbar, executive director of the Southern Regional Council, expressed this faith even more directly in 1961, testifying to his belief "that the South will, out of its travail and sadness and requited passion, give the world its first grand example of two races of men living together in equality and with mutual respect."[2] This essay will examine the historical origins of this myth of the biracial South, explore its full emergence in the 1970s, suggest its meanings for various Southerners, and briefly assess its development since the 1970s.

Charles Reagan Wilson

The South, of course, has long been the focus for myth making, both by Southerners themselves and by outsiders. Since George Tindall's seminal article "Mythology: A New Frontier in Southern History" (1964), scholars collectively have developed a framework for interpreting Southern history in terms of myth. The mythic perspective on Southern history would begin with the idea of a Colonial Eden, then portray the romantic Old South and the crusading Lost Cause, followed by the materialistic New South, and the twentieth century, with repeated expressions of a Savage South, but culminating seemingly in the idea of the Sun Belt, which mysteriously fused the South with the heart of darkness, southern California, in a prosperous world anchored by Disneyland and Disney World, before this summer's (1998) unlikely scenario of the Southern Baptists' symbolically casting those wholesome shrines into the nether regions. Racial myths have been prominent in this frame of mind, especially the myth of white supremacy, which became institutionally embodied in the Jim Crow laws from the 1890s to the 1960s. The South's distinctiveness in such myths was within a national context. Winthrop Jordan properly points out that "racial attitudes in the South have been peculiar not for their existence or their content but for their virulence, saliency, pervasiveness, and the predisposition of white people to overt action and of black people to fear, accommodation, resistance, and retaliation."[3]

One of the most enduring Southern myths has been that of the Savage South, which is the opposite of the myth of the biracial South. It traces back to the colonial era and flowered in full expression in the antebellum era of North-South conflict. The South appeared in the national culture as backward, sexually licentious, irreligious, alcohol drenched, and morally suspect. In an ironic reversal, the Menckenesque version of the Savage South in the 1920s saw the region as benighted for exactly the opposite reasons—it now seemed the prisoner of a Puritan worldview that made it too religious, too sexually inhibited, too morally uptight. In either event, race was central to the image of the Savage South—brutal public lynchings of African Americans, the sinister Ku Klux Klan, the legal outrages of cases like Scottsboro, the violent white resistance to desegregation in the 1960s at places like Birmingham, Oxford, Neshoba County, and Selma. All of these actual events take their place in a broader ideological view of the South as irredeemably evil. Fred Hobson, the historian of the myth of the Savage South, has traced its decline, noting that in the 1960s "the white South was taking its last racial stand." Since then, the nation's and the region's writers have continued to portray savagery in Southern places but it "appears, if not contrived, at least removed from the social base which gives rise to the fiction."[4]

Hobson speculated that "a powerful positive myth" of the racial interaction of blacks and whites, an example to the world of racial harmony, would succeed the myth of the Savage South. George Tindall, writing several years after Hobson, in 1989, pointed out that scholars had not studied "that newer version of the old religious myths that reserved the South for a high destiny—the Integrated South, purged by suffering and prepared to redeem the nation from bias and injustice."[5] For Tindall and Hobson, the issue is not whether the South actually is savage or integrated, but the cultural constructions that project these representations. The myth of the biracial South is thus one of the most recent representations of the South. What were the origins of this myth of the biracial South? When did it appear as an identifiable construct? How widespread has it become since the 1960s?

If the myth of the biracial South expressed the belief that the South had the nation's most harmonious race relations, one might trace its origins back to the region's traditionally conservative ideology. The paternalism of the slave system embodied the ways a social system of owner and slave functioned in a biracial context—with the owner wielding power but the slave influencing the working relationship and the broader culture as well. The biracial myth could be traced back to the conservative idea of the South as a hierarchical society, with society working smoothly when everyone understood and accepted his or her place. The racial radicals, whose frenzied rhetoric and wild violence periodically came to the fore, typically questioned blacks' having a place at all in Southern society, but conservatives understood the region's economic need for African Americans, if nothing else. Besides, the popular traditionalist metaphor of Southern society as a family writ large would suggest an ideological awareness of the need to keep a place at the supper table for blacks, even if their table was separate and in the kitchen.[6]

A variant of this outlook was the New South creed of the 1880s, which promoted the ideal of racial harmony, as essential to the good business climate necessary to lure Northern investment South after the Civil War. This view has surely remained an enduring justification for seeing Southern society as embodying harmonious race relations. Proponents of the New South praised the end of slavery but looked back fondly on the nostalgic prewar plantation and its interracial relationships. As Henry W. Grady wrote, "The Northern man, dealing with casual servants can hardly comprehend the friendliness that existed between the master and slave." Thomas Nelson Page sketched more fully this sentimental view of harmonious race relations in a biracial society. In his essay "Social Life in Old Virginia before the War," he portrayed an unpretentious plantation life, with honorable planters, joyous children, happy darkies, and devoted ladies. Grady went further as a booster of his society, insisting that the friendly relations between the races had "survived the war, and strife, and political campaigns." He concluded that "it is the glory of our past in the

South. It is the answer to abuse and slander. It is the hope of our future." White Southerners in the twentieth century became a cliché in the national culture, claiming that the South's race relations were better than elsewhere, and that racial harmony had been achieved, as long as outside agitators remained outside.[7]

The deeper source of the myth of the biracial South was not in the conservative ideology but in the South's liberal reform ethos. Antecedents could be found in the nineteenth century among advocates of biracial coalitions in Reconstruction and in the era of agrarian reform in the 1890s. These attempts at interracial cooperation had been limited by racial assumptions of white reformers, economic rivalries, and the chicanery of their opponents. In the twentieth century, organizations emerged that were more direct influences on the biracial ideology that flowered in the post-1960s. Women's groups like the Association of Southern Women for the Prevention of Lynching and the YWCA worked toward moderation on racial issues in the early twentieth century, fostering contacts between the races and promoting interracial ideals. More intentionally, organizers formed the Commission on Interracial Cooperation in 1919 and the Southern Conference for Human Welfare in 1938, both seeing Southern regional problems through an interracial lens. The Southern Regional Council succeeded the Commission on Interracial Cooperation in 1944 and thereafter served as the most effective agency for exchange of information and advocacy of interracial goals. While the SRC in its early years did not call for the overthrow of Jim Crow segregation but worked for African American betterment within the separate-but-equal system, the organization was surely in the forefront of biracial efforts in the middle decades of the twentieth century. Small numbers of Southerners lived out their interracial ideals in places like Clarence Jordan's Christian community, Koinonia, in South Georgia and the Providence Cooperative Farm in Tchula, Mississippi.[8]

Liberal reformers drew from democratic ideals in justifying racial moderation and eventually the end of Jim Crow, but they also reflected the South's religious culture, its evangelical character and aspirations toward salvation in a sinful world. This source was especially significant for the minority of Southern liberals in the 1930 to 1950 period who championed not just racial moderation but the end of Jim Crow segregation altogether. Such reformers came to believe that the caste system violated basic Christian ideals of brotherhood. As historian Morton Sosna has observed, "the importance of evangelicalism to Southern liberalism can hardly be overemphasized." Howard Kester, for example, who was a union organizer and antilynching crusader in the 1920s and 1930s, confessed his motivation was simply Christian love. "The kind of healing the region and the nation needed wouldn't come through politics or economic organization," he said; "there had to be an ethical orientation, a moral confrontation based on the teachings of Jesus." Another liberal reformer, Will Alexander, confessed in 1951, "I have never lost faith by what I seemed to glimpse in the New Testament. I have been influenced more by this than by anything I have ever known." Atlanta newspaper editor Ralph McGill revealed in his autobiography that his "Calvinist conscience was stirred by some of the race prejudice [he] saw." McGill, like other Southern liberals, used the language of evangelicalism, speaking of "shame" and "guilt," to describe how his feelings were led to change on racial issues. The Southern faith is one that knows of the wickedness of human nature, but believes in the possibility of conversion and ultimate redemption. These Southern liberals working most actively before the *Brown* decision for the end of Jim Crow knew of the South's sins but thought redemption possible. Racial healing could follow, resulting in the dream of racial harmony—the South then redeeming the nation.[9]

Southern blacks also advanced the idea of a redemptive South, especially the ministers of the civil rights movement. In a 1961 interview, Dr. Martin Luther King, Jr., spoke of "an intimacy of life" in the South that could become "beautiful if it is transformed in race relations from a sort of lord-servant relationship to a person-to-person relationship." He argued that the nature of life in the region would "make it one of the finest sections of our country once we solve this problem of segregation." King noted in 1963 that "when you find a white southerner who has been emancipated on the issue, the Negro can't find a better friend." King used the words "transformed" and "emancipated," but he might have substituted "converted," to catch the evangelical flavor of the personality change required in white Southerners to embrace the integrated society in his age. But it was possible. Even the state of Mississippi, he said in his "I Have a Dream" speech, "a state sweltering with the heat of injustice, sweltering with the heat of oppression, will be transformed into an oasis of freedom and justice."[10] The liberal dream, even in the 1950s and 1960s, was one of the racially converted South, washed in the blood of the civil rights martyrs, redeeming the nation.

But the nation saw the 1960s South, as the Savage South. Southern whites surely rejected King's lyrical vision as they defended segregation. With the end of Jim Crow legal segregation in 1964 and of voting disfranchisement of African Americans in 1965, Southern culture had to face new realities. As a public ideology, white supremacy had been vanquished. The Ku Klux Klan and the citizens' councils had been defeated, and rabble-rousing, old-time politicians had lost the battles and ultimately the massive-resistance war they had proclaimed in the 1950s. The hearts of Southern whites were not trans-

Charles Reagan Wilson

formed overnight on racial issues simply because of the changes the federal government mandated as a result of the pressures of their fellow black Southerners, but white Southerners would have to adapt their public culture. Beginning in the early 1970s, new ideologies came to the fore as emerging justifications for Southern public life and values.

The myth of the biracial South was another formative ideology in the post-segregation era. The L. Q. C. Lamar Society, organized in 1969, in Durham, North Carolina, was a good example of a new organization that actively promoted the new mythology. Named for a Mississippi secessionist who became a postwar advocate of regional reconciliation, the Lamar Society attracted a constituency of middle- and upper-middle-class professionals who advocated a vision of a still regionally distinctive South dedicated to transcending endemic problems of racial conflict, poverty, and environmental abuse. Like the Vanderbilt Agrarians four decades earlier, who championed a conservative vision of Southern traditionalism in the face of modernity, members of the Lamar Society worried about the survival of a distinctive regional culture in an industrialized modern world. Unlike the Agrarians, these Southern intellectuals and policy makers were reformers, wanting to use regional planning and government authority to preserve selective aspects from regional tradition. They pushed, in particular, for a new racial vision in the South. As writer Willie Morris said of the South in the introduction to the society's defining symposium volume *You Can't Eat Magnolias* (1972), "Racism was the primeval obsession. No longer is this so. It will hold out in places, but it will never again shape the white Southern consciousness." For generations, Morris wrote, racism had "misdirected the South from its other elemental problems of poverty and exploitation." The changes in the 1960s he foresaw having "a profoundly liberating effect" on the region.[11]

Alabama newspaperman H. Brandt Ayers, a founder of the Lamar Society, openly dismissed the continued attachment of the South to its old Lost Cause symbols, writing of the "viral weed of mythology" that "has been allowed to grow like kudzu over the South." Ayers urged the South to embrace a different heritage, symbolized not by the White House of the Confederacy but by reverence for "the symbols of Monticello or the Hermitage—houses built by white Southerners who led the nation" and represented egalitarian ideals. Ayers saw contemporary Southerners within the long perspective of Southern history: "Southerners, black and white, locked together in yet another uniquely Southern experience, should be addressed with the humanity that teaches wise and just men to hate the sin, but love the sinner." Ayers also saw history overcoming the separation of the regions. "North and South," he wrote, "we have now been reduced to the same historical dimension." The frustrations of

The Myth of the Biracial South

the Vietnam War and the nation's recognition of racial problems extending beyond the South had "shattered the Yankees' innocent illusions that they have been ordained by God to trample out immorality and that His truth marches with them into every war."[12]

Just as the older racial myths of white supremacy were institutionally supported in a structure of the Democratic Party, the Ku Klux Klan, Protestant churches, state laws, and racial etiquette that virtually all whites enforced against all people of color, so now the myth of the biracial South was reinforced by institutions like the Lamar Society and its periodical *Southern Journal,* the Institute for Southern Studies in Durham and its *Southern Exposure,* the Southern Growth Policies Board, and academic regional studies centers such as the University of Mississippi's Center for the Study of Southern Culture. Like other such institutes in the South, the Mississippi center, which the university set up in 1977, had a pronounced interracial theme. African American artist Romare Bearden's painting of black musicians adorned the cover of its first publication, *Southern Journal,* a glossy annual report issued in 1980. Inside, photographs of black blues singers and basket makers were interwoven with illustrations of white quilting ladies and people enjoying a dinner on the grounds after church. The center, located in the benighted state of Mississippi, symbolically embraced the new recognition of biracialism by picturing Alex Haley and Eudora Welty side by side in its annual report.[13]

Southern politics also reflected the impact of the myth of the biracial South in the early 1970s, just as African Americans were becoming a major force in Southern politics. The most racially obsessed states, those of the Deep South, dramatically changed from supporting prosegregation candidates in the pre-1970 era to supporting those who did not use racial rhetoric or campaign on the segregation issue. In 1976, African Americans represented between 17 and 26 percent of the electorate in the Deep South states, and by then politicians were openly courting black votes. This was not a sentimental gesture on the part of white politicians. The growing power of African American political strength led Southern white politicians to increasingly acknowledge black aspirations. As Congressman Andrew Young noted in 1976: "It used to be Southern politics was just 'nigger' politics—a question of which candidate could 'outnigger' the other. Then you registered 10% to 15% in the community, and folks would start saying 'Nigra.' Later you got 35% to 40% registered, and it was amazing how quick they learned how to say 'Nee-grow.' And now that we've got 50%, 60%, 70% of the black votes registered in the South, everybody's proud to be associated with their black brothers and sisters."[14]

Progressive young governors symbolized the change in Southern politics that would make it a prime carrier of the new racial mythology in the early

Charles Reagan Wilson

1970s. Dale Bumpers in Arkansas, Jimmy Carter in Georgia, John West in South Carolina, Reuben Askew in Florida, William Waller in Mississippi, and Edwin Edwards in Louisiana, followed by politicians like William Winter in Mississippi and Bill Clinton in Arkansas, all were committed to new interest-group politics that promoted biracial coalitions and a new rhetoric of the South as the chosen place. They did not appeal to traditional Southern defensiveness about the federal government or fears about outside agitators, nor did they throw around racial code words. They overtly repudiated traditional Southern mythology, distancing themselves from the past and expressing hope and optimism for the future. George Busbee, elected governor of Georgia in 1974 with black support, stated in his inaugural address that "the politics of race has gone with the wind," using an especially evocative term in Margaret Mitchell's home state to dismiss past racial ideology. Edwin Edwards spoke directly to blacks in his 1972 inaugural address, pledging that "the old imaginary barriers no longer exist. My election has destroyed the old myths, and a new spirit is with us."[15]

Dramatic new images came along with the rhetoric. Eugene "Bull" Connor could be seen singing "We Shall Overcome" in a black church while campaigning unsuccessfully. George Wallace crowned a black homecoming queen at the University of Alabama. The governor of Georgia, Jimmy Carter, dedicated a portrait of Martin Luther King, Jr., in a prominent spot in the Georgia state capitol building. When Forrest "Fob" James was inaugurated governor of Alabama in 1979, he boldly linked two central symbols of a newly emerging rhetoric of biracialism: "I believe if Robert E. Lee and Martin Luther King, Jr., were here today, their cry to us—their prayer to God—would call for 'The Politics of Unselfishness'—a people together—determined to climb the highest plateau of greatness."[16] The imagery of Lee and King praying together to God projected explicitly an image of civil religion, both Southern heroes blessing the region. Their photos would soon be linked in a new iconography within Southern public institutions.

The revealing gestures of even segregationists like Connor and Wallace to seek black political support reflected the political aspects of a broader redefinition of the symbolic Southern community in the 1970s. Whites had shaped the imagery and meaning of previous outcroppings of the Southern instinct for mythology, and white-dominated organizations had institutionalized and promoted traditional myths. Just as blacks in the older South had been politically disfranchised, racially segregated, and economically exploited, so they had been virtually powerless in influencing the South's public culture. They did not have a vote on the symbols the South's culture projected or on the civic rituals its people acted out. The process underway in the 1970s represented the beginnings of a redefinition of a new Southern community, reflecting black influence. While the changed political rhetoric of a George Wallace could be attributable simply to his craven instinct for political success, he was part of a broader society grappling with the need for a new ideological foundation to give a sense of purpose and direction. Myths last only if they unify and can evoke feelings of a broad range of citizens, who may identify with the myths for differing reasons. The myth of the biracial South filled the void represented by the decline of older Southern myths at a time when the racial basis of Southern society had shifted dramatically.[17]

At the heart of the myth of the biracial South stood a moral earnestness that enabled the South to make claims upon national idealism that were far removed from the region's civil rights disgraces of the 1960s. Reuben Askew stated the idea of Southern moral superiority in 1972: "For many years now, the rest of the nation has been saying to the South that it is morally wrong to deprive any citizen of an equal opportunity in life because of his color. I think most of us have come to agree with that. But now the time has come for the rest of the nation to live up to its own stated principles. Only now are the other regions themselves beginning to feel the effects of the movement to eliminate segregation." He insisted that "the rest of the nation should not abandon its principles when the going gets tough." Just as the nation had "sought to bring justice to the South by mandate and court order" so now "perhaps it is time for the South to teach the same thing to other regions in a more effective way—by example."[18]

New England, the moral center of antebellum abolitionism and other reform movements, became the counterpoint of the new Southern racial mythology, lending weight to new Southern moral claims in the 1970s. Violence and disorder accompanied efforts to desegregate Boston schools from 1973 to 1975, bringing national condemnation. At the same time, schools desegregated with far less turmoil in Charlotte and countless smaller communities. Of course, this desegregation was not voluntary but the result of federal court orders. Southern schools, nonetheless, became the nation's most desegregated schools in the 1970–71 academic year. In any event, these developments led Texas writer Larry L. King to chastise Northerners for their hypocrisies: "Do you good Boston folk—who once sold slaves on Boston Common—wanna step over here in the pea patch and talk to me about Louise Day Hicks and the violence heaped on your kids while they were being bussed to school? Naw, I expect you'd rather talk about George Wallace or busing violence in South Carolina a decade ago."[19] King linked present New England woes to its past sins, reversing the usual Yankee saint, Southern sinner expectation.

Southerners were, nonetheless, not the only Americans proclaiming the myth of the biracial South. The national culture rediscovered the South during the Jimmy Carter presidential campaign in 1976, and one of its fascinations was with race relations in what seemed a new South indeed, compared to the national news media's last barometric reading of the region, in the South of massive resistance to desegregation in the 1960s. The nation no longer saw the South as the Savage South but in favorable terms as a storehouse of valuable qualities seemingly threatened in the rest of the nation. *Time* magazine's special edition on Carter in September of 1976 was typical in its representation of the South in the post–civil rights era. "The Spirit of the South" was the lead article, portraying the South as "a place apart," "the last American arena with a special, nurtured identity, its own sometimes unfashionable regard for the soil, for family ties, for the authority of God and country." The South was a place apart, not the cloud-cuckoo-land of W. J. Cash but rather "a redoubt of old American tenets, enshrined for centuries by the citizenry."[20]

The *Time* magazine article portrayed a progressive South, vitalized by the coming of industry, thanks to air-conditioning. "Tyrannical heat," the article surmised, "delirious summers, dog days that breed flies and sloth, squabbles and morbid introspection are gone with the vent." The writer of the piece stressed the continuities between the New South and the older, in religion, patriotism, attachment to family, and respect for the law. "Could it be that in many ways it can now teach the nation something about how to live?" it asked, reflecting recognition now of a superior South. Recognizing that "the idea can easily be exaggerated," it saw hope in a redemptive South because of race relations, reflecting that "the harshly segregated South showed the rest of the nation that it was possible to change despite deeply held prejudices—and to achieve at least the beginnings of racial amity." A national culture that had discovered its own racism now began looking hopefully to the South as embodying perhaps a way out. The myth of the biracial South is here anchored in broader Southern virtues: "Other parts of the U.S., without consciously turning to the South, began to long for some of its values: family, community, roots."[21]

By the middle 1970s, not only had the South rejoined the nation, it was beginning to dominate it. A generation after Confederates lost their crusade against the nation (a century before Carter's election), the nation's culture enthusiastically embraced the Lost Cause, as Southern writers became popular in American magazines, theatrical plays with Southern heroes and heroines dominated Northern theater, and American popular music projected appealing romantic lyrics of the lazy, hazy South. Similarly, having lost their massive-resistance Lost Cause, Southern whites now found themselves influencing the national culture more profoundly than at any time since the late nineteenth century. Country music, evangelical Protestantism, films and television shows about Southerners, Southern literature—all were in vogue. Even in politics, the nation turned south, electing the first Deep South politician since the Civil War as president.[22]

If Southern politicians endorsed the myth of the biracial South and the national culture was fascinated with it, black Southerners were, if anything, even more enthusiastic promoters of the myth in the 1970s. The new ideology reflected real, dramatic changes in the region that began in the aftermath of the civil rights movement, the epochal event in the new mythology equivalent to the Civil War in the myth of the Lost Cause a century before. In 1975 the Reverend Frederick Reese, a veteran black leader, concluded that "we've come a long way." His evidence was largely the change in white behavior toward blacks. "Whites who wouldn't tip their hats have learned to do it. People who wouldn't say 'Mister' or 'Miss' to a black have learned to say it mighty fine. We've got black policemen, black secretaries, and we can use the public restrooms. The word 'nigger' is almost out of existence." His words evoked the older South of racial etiquette that the region's public culture had indeed finally rejected. Jessie Campbell, a black store manager on the Mississippi Gulf Coast, insisted that race was "almost nonexistent now." He saw a "new generation of people, black and white, here," again suggesting behavioral changes associated with the end of old racial ways. Campbell also pointed to economic developments, noting that "there's been a pretty big rise in the standard of living of the black people." Andrew Young told a meeting of Southern black mayors that "we can't help but be people who believe in doing the impossible, because we've already done so much of it." Young in 1974 overtly summoned the image of the redemptive South: "I strangely think we're going to be able to deliver in the South. . . . I think the direction of this nation is going to be determined by the direction that comes from the southern part of the United States."[23]

Migration patterns suggested the demographic basis to rhetoric. In the 1970s, for the first time, more blacks moved from the North to the South than were leaving the South for other parts of the United States. In the first three years of the 1970s, 80,000 more blacks came to the South than left it, and in the last five years of the decade 500,000 African Americans moved to the region, reversing the historic outward migration. Writing in 1972, North Carolinian Mary E. Mebane remembered that "the names Alabama and Mississippi aroused something akin to terror." She had always viewed blacks from there "with awe" and wondered "how they could possibly have survived." The North, on the other hand "seemed the Promised Land." When blacks from New York City came home to visit, "the men drove big cars and

13

the women dressed in fine clothes and wore false eyelashes." New York was "where everybody wanted to go." But in the previous few years, she had begun noting that "blacks in the Northern cities were coming home, down South." Mebane admitted that "disenchantment caused by the disorder in Northern cities" was one reason that some African Americans left the North for the South, as were new job opportunities, but she concluded that "the primary reason for the influx of blacks into the South is the Civil Rights Acts of 1964–65." The key to the North's losing "much of its allure" was the removal of "the overt signs of racial discrimination" in the South and the discontinuance of "some of the most vicious racist practices."[24] To Mebane, blacks seemed waiting for the South to welcome them home.

The South in the 1970s and 1980s became home to more black elected officials than any other part of the United States, also contributing to Southern blacks' affirming the ideology of the biracial South, because of its potential in terms of the exercise of power in the region they shared with Southern whites. The South represented about 50 percent of the nation's African Americans in 1987, but it had 62 percent of elected black officeholders, as compared to the next largest region, the North Central census states that had 19.2 percent. Mississippi led all states with 548 officials in 1987, and four of the five states with the most black officeholders were in the South. Curtis M. Graves, a black representative in the Texas Legislature and a vice president of the Lamar Society, pointed out that many of these electoral successes were because of black numerical strength, not attraction of white votes. But he looked to the biracial South for the future of black political success in the South. "Our real strength lies in coalition politics," he wrote. He himself had been elected as a result of such a coalition. "For the first time, whites and blacks in the South are working together in mutual trust. Realizing that things in the South are not as they should be for either blacks or whites, the two groups are beginning to talk over their common problems; they are joining forces to see that a better South is created." He suggested in his optimistic scenario that the South's "biggest problem today, our mutual problem" was replacing "the centuries of hatred and suspicion with a new era of respect and trust." Graves went beyond the then-present realities of Southern coalition politics in the early 1970s to project a hopeful scenario for the future.[25]

Black endorsement of the biracial South became part of a process of African Americans' redefining what "the South" means. As Thadious M. Davis has argued, the recent return of African Americans to the South, both physically and spiritually, represents "a laying of a claim to a culture and to a region that, though fraught with pain and difficulty, provides a major grounding for identity." She goes further, speculating "that this return to the South is a new form of subversion—a preconscious political activity or a subconscious counteraction to the racially and culturally homogeneous 'sunbelt.'" Rather than a "nostalgic turning back to a time when there were 'good old days,'" this embrace of the South "is gut-wrenching revisioning of specifics long obscured by synoptic cultural patterning." As part of the redefinition of "the South," black writers tried to evoke the texture of black culture and to understand the nature of black history in the South—its distinct character apart from issues of white supremacy. Alex Haley, Ernest Gaines, Margaret Walker, Clifton Taulbert, and Alice Walker are only a few of the best-known figures exploring the Southern black community from within. "No one could wish for a more advantageous heritage," writes Alice Walker, "than that bequeathed to the black writer in the South: a compassion for the earth, a trust in humanity beyond our knowledge of evil, and an abiding love of justice." Walker evoked the spirit of the biracial South in insisting that black Southerners had to "give voice to centuries not only of silent bitterness and hate but also of neighborly kindness and sustaining love." Davis evoked that nurturing spirit of the myth of the biracial South as well in arguing that African American contemporary creative works illustrate "the creative power of telling about the South and the healing power of uniting with another story in order to weave a necessary future."[26]

Out of this effort to understand the black community has come an insistence on whites' acknowledging the black role in the region as part of formal public culture in the South. This imperative among black Southerners to revision the South has figured in the recent conflict over Southern public symbols. The traditional symbols and images that public institutions projected often had associations with the Old South and the Lost Cause of the Confederacy. Beginning in the 1970s, black Southerners have pressured to remove symbols they regard as offensive. "To appreciate the differences in feelings about the South by white southerners and black southerners," wrote Paul Delaney, the deputy national editor of the *New York Times* in 1983, "one need only play 'Dixie' or wave a Confederate flag. Whites, many of them, respond with rebel yells; blacks, almost unanimously, flinch, finding the old symbols detestable." Black protests in the 1970s did lead to the removal of Confederate battle flags from many Southern universities and public schools, which had once flown them as symbols of school spirit that tied contemporary sporting events to white regional tradition. The observance of Confederate Memorial Day, a once vibrant ritual that brought out white celebrants each spring, has continued its decline, which began well before the civil rights movement, to where it is a marginal activity in most Southern communities, if it is held at all.[27]

As the commemoration of the Old South and the Lost Cause declined, the memory of the civil rights movement has been freshened. Maya Lin's dramatic memorial to the martyrs of the movement is at the Southern Poverty Law Center in Montgomery, Alabama. Jackson, Mississippi, has its monument to Medgar Evers; a University of Mississippi student group is raising funds for a monument to civil rights efforts on the campus where one of the most violent confrontations of the 1960s took place; and Arthur Ashe now stands in statue on Richmond's resonant Monument Boulevard, near the images of Lee, Jackson, and Davis. The celebration of the Martin Luther King, Jr., federal holiday is the most obvious example, however, of the commemoration of the people and events of the civil rights movement, which is no longer honored simply in the black community but by the broader Southern public as well, making these occasions into rituals of the myth of the biracial South. King is often honored in the South, for example, in schools, universities, community centers, and at church services for blacks and whites; but often the commemoration of his memory is at the same time as that for Robert E. Lee, whose birth date is close to King's.[28]

This joint celebration of a King-Lee holiday is surely a ritual triumph of the myth of the biracial South—one holiday that blacks and whites can celebrate for differing reasons. Arkansas newspaper editor Paul Greenberg argues that the South will never achieve racial peace until "Southerners, black and white, accept the same symbols." He rejects the idea of "hauling down the Confederate battle flag at Montgomery," when the better solution is to "erect a statue of Martin Luther King, Jr., on the Capitol grounds, and celebrate both." Writing in 1988, Greenberg showed the continuing power of the biracial ideal. "The South will rise again," he said, "when it rises as one—when we rise together, not against each other." Looking into the future, he predicted that "the South will be one when a march celebrating King's birthday is led by some brave and discerning soul carrying the Confederate battle flag."[29]

African Americans might admire the grandness of Greenberg's millennial vision, but their skepticism about its plausibility would be understandable given the worsening of American race relations in the 1980s, which suggested the millennium was not at hand and challenges were questioning the myth of the biracial South. The economic and civil rights policies of the Ronald Reagan administration worsened race relations. "I am not the optimist I was twenty years ago as a young reporter in Atlanta," wrote black editor Paul Delaney in 1983. "I see the future of race relations in the South, and the nation, as bleak," with Reagan policies suggesting that "white racism still lies just beneath a thin veneer of racial civility." Despite this pessimistic view, even Delaney allowed himself to grasp the hope of the redemptive South at the heart of the biracial ideology: "If the South can counter that psychology, it will have made an everlasting contribution to racial understanding. Perhaps the

South can solve the problem, for its heritage of person-to-person relationships, its aversion to abstractions, and its commitment to good manners suggest that people should be respected as individuals." In 1984, the year after Delaney's words, Republican candidates in several Southern states earned the condemnation of black leaders for their use of racial code words in campaigning, and by the late 1980s David Duke's prominence as a Southern politician drawing on a white racial constituency symbolized the opposition to the biracial myth from at least a sizeable number of Southern whites.[30]

The last five years have witnessed a surprising development in terms of regional mythology, which has further undermined the myth of the biracial South. In the two decades since the rise of the biracial myth, African Americans have steadily escalated their demands for the removal of public symbols they regard as offensive. White Southerners, in turn, increasingly have rebelled against these demands. Despite black protests, the Confederate battle flag still flies above the South Carolina capitol in Columbia. The state flags of Mississippi and Georgia still project the Confederate flag as part of their designs. The University of Mississippi band still plays "Dixie" at football and basketball games while many of its fans still wave the Confederate battle flag. The frustrations of black efforts have been a cultural setback to the goal of redefining the Southern identity in order to make it feasible for black Southerners to fully embrace the region and the myth of the biracial South.[31]

The assertion of black identity has been met with a resurgence in the 1990s of an older Southern myth among contemporary whites—the myth of the Lost Cause. White working-class culture probably never affirmed the myth of the biracial South, but that culture lost much of its influence on Southern public culture as a result of the changes of the 1960s, leading to the white populist rage that politicians from George Wallace to David Duke have exploited. But it has been intellectuals and middle-class Southerners who have reasserted the Lost Cause, beginning at the end of the decade that gave birth to the biracial myth. In 1979, the magazine *Southern Partisan* appeared, steadily expanding to its present circulation of 15,000. Peter Applebome has pointed out that "even most Southerners are not familiar with its somewhat schizoid mix of Old South gun-and-musket lore, scholarly Burkean-Calhounian political philosophy, and contemporary hard-right politics." Articles explore many facets of Southern white culture, but stress the centrality of the Confederacy to the Southern identity. As one recent cover story concluded, "This storm-cradled nation has much to teach us—as does the terrible war by which it lived and died." Southerners interested in the neo-Confederate identity can now also subscribe to *Southern Heritage, Confederate Underground,* the *Journal of Confederate History,* the *Confederate Sentry,* and *Counterattack.* They can join organizations such as the Confederate Society of America, the Culture of the South Association, the Southern Heritage Association, and the Sons of Confederate Veterans, one of whose chapters publishes a newsletter called the *Rebel Yell,* whose motto is "If at first you don't secede, try, try again." The neo-Confederacy received a boost in June 1994 when organizers formed the Southern League as "an activist organization of unreconstructed Southerners pursuing cultural, social, economic and political independence for Dixie." None of these organizations is large in itself and none of these publications has an impressive subscription list, but together they represent a new organizational structure pushing for an older ideological perspective on the South. Their significance comes from their active role in Republican politics in the South and their tapping into the frustrations of white Southerners who do not see a need to redefine the Southern identity from its historic meanings associated with a white-dominated South.[32]

The Southern psyche is thus deeply divided, again, judging by its mythological outcroppings as the millennium nears. As long as the South's population remains biracial, as long its people have to struggle to live together and to make a common culture and society that both blacks and whites can acknowledge, rooted in the bitter realities and soaring hopes of the past, the myth of the biracial South will likely remain a relevant one—especially for a world that in the twenty-first century faces increasing interaction between differing ethnic and cultural traditions, as the Western World faces the Third World. This Southern myth tells about what happened in one isolated area of the world when such people met and continued to struggle with each other for centuries. As Charles Joyner, Mechal Sobel, and others have shown, Southerners do indeed have a biracial heritage, seen in the music, language, foodways, religion, and many other cultural features of the traditional South.[33] The ideology of the biracial South says this should be acknowledged, the kinship between blacks and whites—as Charles Black long ago dreamed—should be embraced.

The religious aspect of the contemporary myth of the biracial South is crucial because it suggests that the Southern story still has moral meanings, that the struggle in the end will signify more than just sound and fury. The moral meanings projected in this contemporary myth are not the same that the antebellum proslavery advocates thought, believing the South was the last noncapitalist hope against a materialistic wave that had conquered Europe and the Northern United States. The myth of the biracial South does not embody the same moral meaning that the Lost Cause did for its true believers, nurturing its supposed wisdom from wartime defeat and purification. It does not embody the same redemptive meanings that Southern evangelicals have long cherished—the South as the last enclave of spirit-filled religion that must send missionaries to the world to con-

The Myth of the Biracial South

vert it. Common to all of these expressions of what Lewis Simpson calls the Southern spiritual community is the belief that Southern experience has spiritual-moral meaning. The myth of the biracial South embodies the same aspiration, although no longer with conservative content. Oscar Carr, Jr., a white Mississippian who headed the national Office of Development for the Episcopal Church in New York City in the 1970s, argued that "once Southerners can jump into the economic mainstream they will be more liberal than people in Connecticut," but in doing that "the greatest thing the South can offer the nation is its religious and moral sense."[34] It was the same contribution that earlier generations of Southerners had claimed as a potential for the region's people within the nation.

Today, despite recent challenges, the myth of the biracial South still abides. *Washington Post* columnist William Raspberry, a native of Okolona, Mississippi, wrote in 1991 of his home state, once the epitome of the Savage South, as now the embodiment of the biracial South. He praised "the infectious friendliness of the bigger towns" in Mississippi, whose racial practices had earlier driven him out as a young man. He gloried now in the friendly folk of his hometown and the "laid back sophistication" of the Mississippi Gulf Coast, marveling "at how seldom this pervasive graciousness is spoiled by racial rudeness." Raspberry was clear-eyed about Mississippi failures, noting the segregation academies that were white racial islands, the "places where a black stranger in town walks with care," and the state's governor, Kirk Fordice, "who had shown a willingness to play the race game." Still, he lauded the "easiness to relationships, a mutual respect and a willingness to move beyond race that," as he concluded, "quite frankly didn't exist during my years in the state."[35] His words indeed reflected real changes that fifty years ago represented a revolution in the Southern way of life. The danger of Raspberry's viewpoint, however, is Southerners' concluding that the myth has been achieved. We may be at the same point as New South advocates after the 1880s. Having proclaimed their ideology, they soon came to believe it had become reality, though the South remained provincial, economically underdeveloped, and racially divided. The myth of the biracial South in the 1970s had especially rested on the idea of behavioral changes in the aftermath of the epochal civil rights movement, and Raspberry framed his vision of his reformed home state in that same image, suggesting that this behavioral change was the myth's compelling insight. If human behavior could be so dramatically changed in what had seemed a morally evil society, in Mississippi, the most savage of the South, perhaps the myth's redeeming hopes still could be achieved.

The best judgment about what will happen with the myth of the biracial South may be found in the tentative words of one of the wisest of Southerners, black critic Albert Murray. Back in 1976, at the peak of the Carteresque embodiment of the biracial South, Murray wrote, "I hope the changes are permanent," but he foresaw that "there could be a counterthrust." He added, "As a Southerner, my main response is through the blues. The nature of the blues is improvisation . . . you must be ready for all eventualities."[36]

Notes

1. Charles L. Black, Jr., "Paths to Desegregation," *New Republic,* October 21, 1957, p. 15.

2. Leslie W. Dunbar, "The Annealing of the South," *Virginia Quarterly Review* 37 (Autumn 1961): 507.

3. George B. Tindall, "Mythology: A New Frontier in Southern History," in *The Idea of the South: Pursuit of a Central Theme,* ed. Frank E. Vandiver (Chicago: University of Chicago Press, 1964), pp. 1–15. The "Mythic South" section of the *Encyclopedia of Southern Culture,* ed. Charles Reagan Wilson and William Ferris (Chapel Hill: University of North Carolina Press, 1989), pp. 1093–145, provides an overview of the South's mythic history. The Jordan quote is on p. 1119. See also Patrick Gerster and Nicholas Cords, *Myth and Southern History,* 2 vols. (Urbana: University of Illinois Press, 1989).

4. Fred C. Hobson, "The Savage South: An Inquiry into the Origins, Endurance, and Presumed Demise of an Image," in *Myth and Southern History,* eds. Gerster and Cords, pp. 133–40 (quotes vol. II, pp. 145, 146).

5. Ibid.; George B. Tindall, "Mythic South," in *Encyclopedia of Southern Culture,* ed. Wilson and Ferris, p. 1098.

6. Joel Williamson, *The Crucible of Race: Black-White Relations in the American South since Emancipation* (New York: Oxford University Press, 1984), pp. 6, 82–86, 507–10.

7. Thomas Nelson Page, *Social Life in Old Virginia before the War* (Freeport, N.Y.: Books for Libraries Press, [1897] 1970). The Grady quote is in Henry W. Grady, *The New South* (New York, 1890), pp. 146–52.

8. John Egerton, *Speak Now against the Day: The Generation before the Civil Rights Movement in the South* (New York: Knopf, 1994); Morton Sosna, *In Search of the Silent South: Southern Liberals and the Race Issue* (New York: Columbia University Press, 1977).

9. Sosna, *In Search of the Silent South,* pp. 173–74; Ralph McGill, *The South and the Southerner* (Boston: Little, Brown, 1963), pp. 58, 217.

10. Martin Luther King, Jr., *The Wisdom of Martin Luther King in His Own Words* (New York: Meridian, 1968), pp. 23, 64, 75; Martin Luther King, Jr., *Why We Can't Wait* (New York: Harper & Row, 1964), pp. 80; *New York Times,* August 28, 1983, p. 16.

11. Willie Morris, introduction, *You Can't Eat Magnolias,* ed. H. Brandt Ayers and Thomas H. Naylor (New York: McGraw Hill, 1972), p. xi. See also Karen McDearman, "L. Q. C. Lamar Society," in *Encyclopedia of Southern Culture,* ed. Wilson and Ferris, pp. 694–95.

12. Ayers and Naylor, *You Can't Eat Magnolias*, pp. 5, 19.

13. Stephen A. Smith, *Myth Media, and the Southern Mind* (Fayetteville: University of Arkansas Press, 1985), pp. 74–78; *Southern Journal* (Oxford, Miss., 1980).

14. "Out of a Cocoon," *Time*, September 27, 1976, p. 40.

15. Busbee and Edwards quoted in Waldo W. Braden, "The Speaking of the Deep South Governors, 1970–1980," in *A New Diversity in Contemporary Southern Rhetoric*, ed. Calvin M. Logue and Howard Dorgan (Baton Rouge: Louisiana State University Press, 1987), pp. 198. See also Smith, *Myth, Media, and the Southern Mind*, chap. 4, pp. 62–93.

16. Braden, "The Speaking of the Deep South Governors, 1970–1980," p. 200; David R. Goldfield, *Promised Land: The South since 1945* (Arlington Heights, Ill.: H. Davidson, Inc., 1987), pp. 173–74.

17. James C. Cobb, "Community and Identity: Redefining Southern Culture," *Georgia Review* (Spring 1996): 9–24.

18. Reuben Askew quoted in Smith, *Myth, Media, and the Southern Mind*, p. 89.

19. Larry King quoted in ibid., 89–90.

20. "The Spirit of the South," *Time*, September 26, 1976, pp. 30–31.

21. "The Spirit of the South," pp. 30–31.

22. Jack Temple Kirby, *Media-Made Dixie: The South in the American Imagination*, rev. ed. (Athens: University of Georgia Press, 1986), chaps. 8 and 9.

23. Quoted material from David R. Goldfield, *Black, White, and Southern: Race Relations and Southern Culture 1940 to the Present* (Baton Rouge: Louisiana State University Press, 1990), pp. 220, 225–26.

24. Mary E. Mebane, "And Blacks Go South Again," *New York Times*, July 4, 1972, p. 17. See also for the black migration southward, Goldfield, *Black, White, and Southern*, p. 221; and "Race and the South," *U.S. News and World Report*, July 23, 1990, p. 22.

25. Curtis M. Graves, "Beyond the Briar Patch," in Ayers and Naylor, *You Can't Eat Magnolias*, pp. 41–42.

26. Thadious M. Davis, "Expanding the Limits: The Intersection of Race and Region," *Southern Literary Journal* 20 (Spring 1988): 6–7; Alice Walker, "The Black Writer and the Southern Experience," in *In Search of Our Mothers' Gardens* (New York: Harcourt Brace Dovanovich, 1983), p. 21.

27. Paul Delaney, "A New South for Blacks?" in *Dixie Dateline: A Journalistic Portrait of the Contemporary South*, ed. John B. Boles (Houston: Rice University Studies, 1983), pp. 37–47. See also Charles Reagan Wilson, "Unifying the Symbols of Southern Culture," in *Judgment and Grace in Dixie: Southern Faiths from Faulkner to Elvis* (Athens: University of Georgia Press, 1995), pp. 159–63; and Kevin Thornton, "The Confederate Flag and the Meaning of Southern History," *Southern Cultures* 2 (Winter 1996): 233–45.

28. Wilson, "Unifying the Symbols of Southern Culture," pp. 159–63; "In Virginia, King Shares His Day of Honor with Confederate Heroes," *Atlanta Journal and Constitution*, January 15, 1989, sec. A, p. 14.

29. Paul Greenberg, "Blacks, Whites Must Accept Common Past, Symbols," *Jackson Clarion-Ledger*, February 17, 1988, p. 7A.

30. Delaney, "A New South for Blacks?" pp. 44–46.

31. Nadine Cohodas, *The Band Played Dixie: Race and the Liberal Conscience at Old Miss* (New York: Free Press, 1997).

32. Peter Applebome, *Dixie Rising: How the South Is Shaping American Values, Politics, and Culture* (New York: Times Books, 1997), chap. 5, especially pp. 118–19, 131.

33. See Ted Ownby, ed., *Black and White: Cultural Interaction in the Antebellum South* (Jackson: University Press of Mississippi, 1993), for a consideration of the South's biracial cultural history.

34. Oscar Carr, Jr., quoted in "The Spirit of the South," p. 30.

35. William Raspberry, "Return Home Proves State of Mississippi Is, Finally, a Good Place to Be," *Jackson Clarion-Ledger,* November 21, 1991, p. 21A.

36. "Other Voices," *Time,* September 26, 1976, p. 99.

The Rise and Fall of Biracial Politics in the South

Tony Badger

In 1949 V. O. Key surveyed the factionalized politics of the South and argued that in such a disorganized politics "over the long run, the have-nots lose." He identified four devices that perpetuated conservative control in the region: one-party rule, a restricted electorate, notably the disfranchisement of blacks, the malapportionment of state legislatures, notably the vast overrepresentation of the Black Belt, and racial segregation. If these devices were eliminated, Key believed, the "underlying Southern liberalism will be mightily strengthened." He envisaged a vigorous democracy in which party competition for popular, biracial support would bring long-overdue benefits to the have-nots, the mass of Southern whites.[1]

The obstacles to a liberalized South identified by Key have all been eliminated. De jure segregation has been expunged, the Voting Rights Act of 1965 made possible full-scale black political participation, the vibrant Southerner Republican Party has almost turned on its head the notion of a solid South, loyal to the Democratic Party, and one man, one vote court decisions have forced legislatures to be scrupulous in apportioning political representation. Key, however, would surely have been surprised, almost fifty years on, to see the politicians of his own time, the late 1940s, wield so much influence in the contemporary South. The Dixiecrat presidential candidate of 1948, Strom Thurmond of South Carolina, threatens to become the first hundred-year-old United States Senator. Jesse Helms, who ran the race-baiting, red-baiting campaign that defeated Frank Porter Graham in 1950, presides over the Senate Foreign Relations Committee in his idiosyncratic way and, through the Congressional Club, bankrolls mean-spirited Republicans throughout the region. William Colmer of Mississippi, who chaired the committee of Southerners in the House in the 1940s and 1950s that coordinated the regional resistance to civil rights legislation, is dead. But his longtime legislative assistant, Trent Lott, is now a Republican and the Senate majority leader. Why was Key's optimism misplaced? This paper will examine the moments in the postwar South in the

1950s and 1970s when it looked as if Key's vision of a biracial, liberalized politics might be realized to see what went wrong and examine the bleak contemporary prospects for a biracial politics.

In the 1940s and early 1950s liberal politicians were elected in the South by a biracial alliance of lower-income whites and the small, but steadily increasing black electorate. Politicians in the state houses like Kerr Scott, Jim Folsom, and Sid McMath and those in Washington like Lister Hill, John Sparkman, Estes Kefauver, and Albert Gore offered voters a New Deal–style economic program that promised the welfare and public services long denied lower-income voters by the conservative elites. In response to the voter-registration campaigns in black urban communities that had quadrupled the percentage of voting age blacks registered to vote, they adopted a stance of racial moderation, protecting the black right to vote, improving services to black communities, seeking increased appropriations for black institutions and appointing blacks to state government jobs.[2]

But these liberal, biracial politics were not the force of the future in the South. Voters increasingly supported instead the conservative candidates, some before *Brown,* some after, who most vociferously protested their loyalty to segregation and their determination to resist racial change. Numan Bartley has blamed the failure of the biracial politics on national cold war liberals. American liberalism, he argued, abandoned its vision of economic reform and redistribution aimed at the biracial lower-income coalition and instead embraced the politics of antiracism and desegregation. It substituted a moralistic concern for symbolic opportunity and the elimination of de jure segregation, for the substance of a drive to tackle the problem of black and white economic disadvantage. Liberalism "became increasingly fixated on race relations," it lost "most of its substance and direction" and left white workers with "little aside from contempt and the right to compete for scarce jobs with black workers."[3]

Bartley is right to see the race issue as crucial to the failure of Southern liberalism in the 1950s, but he points the finger of blame at the wrong targets. To blame Northern liberals for the downfall of popular front liberalism in the South is perverse. Southern conservatives race-baited and red-baited the Southern Conference for Human Welfare for its own indigenous combination of economic and racial radicalism, not because of any new national liberal agenda imposed on the conference from outside. Bartley underestimates, I believe, the extent to which social democratic, redistributionist politics persisted amongst mainstream white Southern politicians into the 1950s. His argument appears also to be based on a mistaken assumption that tackling de jure segregation was a goal that somehow had nothing to do with the aspirations of Southern blacks active in the voter-registration and union-organizing drives of the 1940s.[4]

The Rise and Fall of Biracial Politics in the South

Bartley's explanation of the failure of biracial politics links to a common argument that anticommunism, part of Bartley's cold war liberalism as well a conservative device, silenced dissent in the South and ended biracial cooperation. There is no doubt that anticommunism played a part in marginalizing black and white radicals in the Southern Conference and in left-led unions. But Michael Heale's new study of McCarthy's Americans will show that opponents of racial change, for example in Georgia, did not need anticommunism to justify violent racial repression in the 1940s. It was later during massive resistance in the late 1950s and early 1960s, after the national McCarthy tide had ebbed, that Southern anticommunism really flourished and stifled dissent. Many of the liberal politicians espousing biracial politics were red-baited in the 1940s and early 1950s, but survived.[5]

Biracial politics failed in the 1950s because white conservative leaders set out to undercut the cross-race alliance by stirring up the racial animosities of lower-income whites and by throwing roadblocks in the path of increased black political participation. In response, white liberal politicians were paralyzed by their fear of mass white racism and were more attuned to that white sentiment than to the view of Southern blacks whose support they traditionally sought at a distance. As a result, biracial politics simply did not deliver the policy outcomes that blacks desired, and they turned instead to direct action protest.

White conservative elites in the South were convinced that ordinary white Southerners were not alert to the dangers of racial change posed by the *Brown* decision and the threat of federal government intervention. They determined to show whites that desegregation was not inevitable, and they waged a righteous crusade to stir up white opinion. Apart from sponsoring massive-resistance legislation, they also took steps to check the increase in black political participation. In part, they continued the delaying tactics of rural voting registrars; in part, they resorted to violence and physical and economic intimidation, particularly in Mississippi and Alabama; in part, they gerrymandered; in part, they threatened black leadership; in part, they systematically removed blacks from the voting rolls, as in Louisiana. Effectively they halted, especially after 1956, the steady increase in black voting, almost entirely preventing any significant black registration outside the Southern cities.[6]

The effectiveness of this conservative drive to arouse the white citizenry was demonstrated by the response of most Southern liberal politicians. Most of them were paralyzed by their belief that the mass of whites, especially in the Black Belt, would not tolerate school desegregation and racial change. Their sense of the overwhelming force of popular white racism sent them running for cover, particularly after 1956; those who held out were sufficiently often defeated to convince white liberals and moderates that prudence was justified.

As a result, white liberals refused to campaign to build up white support for gradual racial change or compliance with the Supreme Court.[7]

White politicians were much more attuned to the demands of their white constituents than to the demands of their black supporters. White moderates were unable to penetrate the ritual of condescension and deference that characterized their relations with black leaders. Their relationships with the African American community were conducted at a distance. While we do not know enough about how Southern politicians actually secured black support in this first postwar era of biracial politics, it is clear that they rarely campaigned directly for this support. Instead they approached, usually through intermediaries, local leaders in the black community who delivered their community's vote as a bloc. Kerr Scott used a funeral director in Winston-Salem and a janitor at East Carolina Teachers' College. Folsom used his chauffeur. These black leaders were often, as Numan Bartley describes them, "racial diplomats" who told white politicians what they thought the politicians wanted to hear. In 1956, for example, I. S. McClinton in Arkansas assured Fulbright's aide that the black community recognized that the Arkansas senator had no alternative but to sign the manifesto blasting the Supreme Court.[8]

Dante Fascell in Miami was a rare candidate who did campaign directly for black support. The local state senator did not think that Fascell could win in 1954 because he was too short, the wrong race, and had a name that voters could not pronounce. When Fascell still seemed determined to run, the senator as a former sheriff promised to help him out with black support. Fascell was driven out into the countryside to a small black church to meet a group of black ministers who, he was told, could deliver him the black votes. He made it clear that he could not offer them any money. What was also different was that Fascell became the first candidate in Miami to campaign for the black vote "in daylight" taking his three-piece band into black neighborhoods and actively canvassing the black community.[9] But most white politicians were shielded from the growing sense of grievance in the black community: they did not have the same personal feel for the humiliations and impatience of the black community that they had for the fears of the white community. Consequently, they espoused policies of acquiescence and gradualism that simply could not satisfy the demands of black voters.

Montgomery was a classic example of what biracial politics had brought the African American community and why those gains were not enough. Blacks in Montgomery constituted 37 percent of the population by the mid-1950s. They made up only 7.5 percent of the electorate but they did, as Mills Thornton has shown, hold the balance of power in the battle between two white factions in the city. They were identified as responsible for the election of a supporter of

Jim Folsom to the city commission. Black leaders, as in other Southern communities, used this leverage to secure concessions from white politicians on the appointment of black policemen, representation on the parks board, and better treatment on the buses. When Mrs. Parks was arrested on December 1, black leaders saw the boycott initially simply as a temporary method of increasing that leverage and putting pressure on the city authorities. But the intransigence of the white community, which led to the boycott and then led to failed negotiations, convinced black leaders that they had to go to the courts and stay off the buses to secure their goals. Biracial politics in its 1950s variant increasingly could not deliver the changes in segregation that black community leaders and their supporters wanted. Direct action, rather than electoral politics and negotiation, and demands for the immediate, rather than gradual, end to segregation increasingly became the tactics of the black community.[10]

The short-term consequences of the first postwar failure of biracial politics was that lower-income whites who potentially supported liberal candidates on economic issues, increasingly supported segregationists in the late 50s and 60s who combined a "common man good ol' boy appeal" with the staunchest rhetorical defense of white supremacy. The long-term consequence was that the conservatism and suspicion of government intervention that characterized these lower-income white voters' racial views would be translated into conservatism on economic issues as well.[11]

The racial polarization of the politics of the 1960s was held in check: first, by the massive increase in black voter registration after the 1965 Voting Rights Act and, then, by the belated recognition by Southern business elites that desegregation was inevitable and that the economic cost of defying the federal government was unacceptable. The first manifestation of this change was the development of biracial coalitions—that cut across class—of blacks and affluent whites who had shared interests in peaceful racial change. One such coalition behind the candidacy of Albert Brewer almost defeated George Wallace in 1970. The second was the failure of some of the good ol' boy segregationists, like Lester Maddox and Orval Faubus, to win elections on the old messages. The third testimony to the new importance of the black vote was the transmogrification of some of the old segregationists as they sought at least to make their peace with their old black enemies and to recognize patronage and pork barrel needs of their black constituents. Thus, George Wallace would eventually be rewarded by an honorary degree at Tuskegee Institute and Strom Thurmond would receive the Distinguished Service Medal from the South Carolina Conference of Black Mayors.[12]

The manifestation of a new biracial politics that attracted national attention was the rise of New South politicians: young, attractive candidates who were conservative enough on social and economic issues to appeal to white voters and moderate enough on racial issues to satisfy their black constituency. Across the South there were new white faces who seemed adept at this coalition building: Reuben Askew in Florida, Dale Bumpers in Arkansas, William Winter in Mississippi, James Hunt in North Carolina. If Jimmy Carter attracted most interest it was in part because, as veteran segregationist Roy Harris lamented, he campaigned by saying he was just like Lester Maddox and yet he turned out to be the most liberal governor ever. In part it was because he slew the Wallace dragon in the 1976 presidential primaries and won the presidency as a Southern white man whose decisive votes came from Southern blacks.[13]

The policy outputs of the biracial politics should not be underestimated. There was a dramatic increase in black officeholding in the South. Mississippi became the state with the most elected black officials in the country. Black mayors took control of cities like Atlanta, Richmond, Birmingham, and Charlotte. Overt racism was largely eliminated from the South's politics. Public desegregation became a routine part of civic life. Day to day race relations were significantly less tense as whites accepted "visible blacks" in positions of authority. There were significant black employment gains in the public sector. Basic public services for the black community were transformed. Voting is not, as John Dollard reminded us, merely an honorific function. Perhaps the most dramatic consequence of biracial politics was the improvement in law enforcement that came from the responsiveness of elected sheriffs and appointed police chiefs to the new political realities and their newly empowered black constituents.[14]

Yet the policy gains of the biracial politics were precisely circumscribed. New South governors were very much in the "business progressive" tradition: they concentrated on efficient and honest government and measures designed to create the infrastructure for a modern South that would continue to attract outside investment and the in-migration of skilled, managerial, and professional workers. Roads, airports, education, and racial harmony were the targets. Spending on welfare or measures designed to reduce the still persistent economic and racial inequality or to protect workers were not part of their agenda. But constrained though these New South governors were, they tended to be replaced in the 1980s and 1990s by politicians who were even more committed to a philosophy of low taxation, limited government, and hostility to any redistributionist government policy. Liberal biracial coalition builders were not to be the dominant force of 1980s and 1990s Southern politics. Carter's electoral success in 1976 turned out to be the only election since 1960 when the Democrats won a majority of Southern states in a presidential election, and even then, Carter did not receive a majority of the votes of his fellow white Southerners. Exemplars of New South politics like William Winter and James Hunt were defeated in early 1980s elections. Locally successful black coalition builders, like Harvey Gantt and Andrew Young, were either defeated in bids for statewide office, or deterred from even running, like Richard Arrington and, most recently, John Lewis.[15]

What has happened to those dreams of a biracial liberal politics? To a certain extent what has happened in the South can be placed in the context of the national phenomenon of the Culture of Contentment, diagnosed with such acuity by John Kenneth Galbraith. He argued that middle-class taxpayers preferred the short-term benefits of tax cuts, even if upper-income voters benefited from those cuts more than they did, because the alternatives either incurred short-term costs for benefits that could only be seen in the long-term (attempts to deal with structural poverty or the environment) or short-term costs for benefits that would go to others and people who did not vote (welfare spending programs). In the South, white taxpayers were, in addition, reluctant to incur additional costs to pay for programs designed primarily to benefit blacks, and white Southerners have been historically suspicious of the efficacy of government intervention and collective action, suspicions that since the 1960s have been joined to the decline in faith in government to do the right thing, which polls show has dramatically declined nationally. In the Southern context, the Culture of Contentment is manifested in a willingness to tolerate the most mouth-watering incentives to attract industry, as long as the middle-class taxpayers' bill does not increase, and a reluctance to raise taxes to tackle the problems of a region where per capita income still lags some 20 percent behind the national average and where over 30 percent of black families live in poverty.

There are few signs of a willingness to marshal sufficient resources to tackle the problems of the urban underclass that Jimmy Carter is attempting to solve with Project Atlanta or to address the problems of the Third World poverty that exists in communities like Tunica in the Mississippi Delta, in the heavily black-populated counties that are shunned by outside investors. Casino gambling is the Southern answer to these problems: an apparently painless revenue raiser for the state that may delay tax hikes, at least in Mississippi, if not Louisiana, but which takes its money disproportionately from the poorer sections of the community and leaves little of the benefits in the communities where the casinos are located. All riverboat gambling will leave Tunica is a spanking new four-lane highway to enable visitors to get in and out of the community as quickly as possible.[16]

The tax-cutting climate is, of course, grist to the mill of the modern Republican Party. In 1980 they won six Southern Senate seats and demonstrated that the party could elect colorless candidates even over Democrats with impeccable conservative credentials like Robert Morgan and Herman Talmadge. But the party was still heavily reliant on presidential coattails (all six incumbents were defeated in 1986) and on the voter recognition of high-profile figures like Jesse Helms and Strom Thurmond. At the local level, the party often failed to compete. In 1997, however, the Republican Party is firmly bedded down in the South holding a majority of the region's governorships, and seats in the U.S. Senate and House. It is close to gaining control of some state legislatures. Even though it does not always contest all elections, it now wins a majority of the races it does contest.[17]

This resurgent Southern Republican Party is a crucial element in the racial polarization of Southern politics. It is almost exclusively a white party: its voter-registration drives are conducted in white communities only. Its agenda is racially defined. There is little trace these days of the racial moderates who used to grace Southern Republicanism: Winthrop Rockefeller, Linwood Holton, or those courageous judges like Elbert Tuttle, Frank Johnson, and John Minor Wisdom (even though Newt Gingrich's media consultant attempted to convince people that, at heart, the Speaker was a Nelson Rockefeller Republican). Recent work on the Republican Party shows that the desire to capture the segregationist white vote in the South predates Goldwater's famous dictum that the party should "go hunting where the ducks are," that is, among the Southern racists. Operation Dixie run by Lee Potter in the late 1950s targeted precisely those voters. Dan Carter reminds us that the newly elected chair of the Harris County Republican Party in 1963, George Bush, emphatically opposed Kennedy's civil rights legislation. Carter, of course, has brilliantly shown how the Republican Party nationally and regionally went after the Wallace vote, successfully tapping the rage and frustrations of ordinary white voters. The party specialized in "demonizing and scapegoating the powerless." Racially nuanced targets, affirmative action and welfare, became central to the Republican appeal. Affirmative action and minority set-asides, many believed, deprived well-qualified whites of jobs and gave those jobs to less qualified members of the new black middle class. Welfare created an underclass of dependents, mainly black. Hard-earned taxpayers' dollars, so the argument went, were supporting idle and irresponsible welfare mothers. As one white hospital technician at Louisiana State University put it, "We work so that they can have baby after baby."[18]

The Republican Party nationally and regionally does, of course, disown explicitly racist candidates like former klansman and nazi sympathizer David Duke, or Charles Davidson, who put his speech advocating the return of slavery on the Internet. But there is no escaping the racially exclusionary nature of the party and its success. When Duke ran for governor of Louisiana in 1991, he still secured 55 percent of the white vote. At exactly the same time next door Kirk Fordice was elected governor in Mississippi with national Republican acclaim on exactly the same platform as Duke, targeting welfare mothers and affirmative action, acting tough on law and order, and advocating lower taxes. Fordice was reelected in 1995. On the eve of that election, the late Frank Smith, veteran Mississippi white liberal, told me that they may have cleaned up his act a bit and polished him up, but "he's still the same racist reactionary . . . he always was." That year Mike Foster was elected governor as a Republican in Louisiana, referring to New Orleans as "the jungle" and running on a platform almost identical to Duke's four years earlier. Duke endorsed him. Foster defeated black congressman Cleo Fields overwhelmingly.[19]

The Republican rise was aided by the activities of the Christian Right, responding to the new lifestyle issues of the 1970s, most notably the issue of abortion. The Religious Right has given a zeal to Republicanism that is difficult to counter, even if sometimes difficult for the Republicans to contain. When half the white voters in South Carolina identify themselves as evangelicals, there can be little doubting the power of religious wing of the Republican Party. Nowhere was this more vividly shown than in Louisiana where evangelicals, in the state that is the base of Jimmy Swaggart and the Catholic bishops, pushed for the toughest antiabortion law in the country. Abortion would be second-degree murder punishable by ten years of hard labor, with only one exception in the event of danger to the life of the mother. Advocates of the law argued that other exceptions in the case of rape or incest would be tantamount to abortion on demand. Legislators received telegrams from Mother Theresa and phone calls from the Vatican. Mother Theresa turned out to be a priest in Lafayette and the Vatican had a 504 area code number. No one, however, should ignore the segregationist origins of most of the leading television evangelists, and there is little evidence that the racial views of the Religious Right have softened over the years. It is difficult to know whether the promise of the governor of Alabama to stand in the courthouse door and to call out the National Guard to protect the Ten Commandments is an advance on his predecessor's promise over thirty years ago to stand at the schoolhouse door and mobilize the National Guard to halt school desegregation.[20]

The religious and partisan dimension of racial polarization should not obscure the fact that racial amelioration tends to come when it is relatively cost-free to the dominant majority. The federal civil rights legislation of the 1960s was cost-free to Northern whites who saw the cost being born in the South; they were less sympathetic to measures that threatened jobs, schools, or house prices in their Northern suburbs. Southerners adapted to racial change in the 1970s, in part, because the alternative of defiance threatened the newfound prosperity of the Sun Belt. Since 1980 the South has slipped back from the rest of the country in per capita income. Its particular regional difficulties—declining oil revenues in Texas and Louisiana—have been compounded by the general factor identified by Dan Carter: the decline in real terms of the purchasing power of the median wage earner since the mid-1970s. Race relations in such an economic climate tend, in C. Vann Woodward's formulation, to become competitive, and whites balk at measures designed to assist blacks and seek to distance themselves socially and physically from them. Revived racial violence, church burnings, resegregation of the schools, and controversies over the Confederate flag speak to that competitive pattern of race relations.[21]

To sustain biracial politics, historical circumstances and white strategies have rendered the black vote less powerful than it might have been. Southern blacks acquired the vote on a large scale precisely at the moment they were leaving the region in large numbers. Even with black return migration from the 1970s onwards, the increase in black population has been offset by faster rates of white in-migration. Even in black-majority areas it has been hard to shake off the effect of a history of violence and intimidation. The difficulty of securing black control in black-majority Mississippi Delta counties testifies to that persistent fear and apathy. White voter registration has increased just as fast, if not faster than black voter registration. First the citizens' councils then the Republican Party sought to counter black registration by their own registration efforts in the white community. Efforts to dilute the impact of black voting through at-large elections and multimember constituencies have had to be challenged consistently by the Justice Department. Both black registration figures and turnout figures consistently lag ten points behind those of whites.[22]

Given the attitude of the majority of white voters, black leaders have faced an unenviable choice between a moderate policy aimed at coalition-building with moderate white Democrats and a racially exclusionary policy concentrating on black power. Sometimes, with Jim Hunt in North Carolina, Zell Miller in Georgia, and Lawton Chiles in Florida, the former tactic seems to promise a return to the New South politics of the 1970s. But the hopes aroused by Douglas Wilder's success in Virginia in 1989 that such coalitions might lead to statewide success for black candidates have proved chimerical. All too often, it seems to black leaders, white politicians who courted the black vote, ignore their concerns once elected and pursue policies primarily designed not to upset white sensibilities. On the other hand, an emphasis on black racial solidarity can bring local power but at the cost of wider influence, with blacks attaining power in inner cities and rural districts where they do not have access to the resources to solve the problems of their black constituents. This dilemma was sharply summed up by Stephen Holmes in an article on the controversy over black-majority districts.

Republicans championed such districts because removing blacks from other districts made those other districts more white and more susceptible to Republican control. "Which is better," asked Holmes, "concentrating black voters and thereby maximizing the number of black lawmakers, or dispersing black voters so that they can be a liberalizing influence in predominantly white districts and enhance the prospects of Democratic candidates there?" Republicans and blacks largely opted for the first strategy in the 1991–92 redistricting exercise. Black leaders remained committed to the black-majority strategy on the whole, even after the Supreme Court ruled out one such redistricting plan in Georgia in 1995. The issue was complicated by the 1996 success of black incumbents of formerly black-majority seats in newly created white-majority constituencies. But Cynthia McKinney, one such successful congresswoman, pointed out that it was easier for incumbents who had built up a visible record of constituency service for both races to win re-election in such circumstances than for a new black candidate to win in such a seat.[23]

The prospects for biracial politics are not encouraging. The Republican Party is overwhelmingly white. Ninety percent of registered black voters are Democrats. In 1992 and 1996 the Democratic Party, with two moderate white Southern candidates, could only win a majority of the votes in the presidential election in two Southern states and a plurality in two others. Clinton's relative failure suggests the formidable obstacles to any coalition builder of a biracial politics of, on the one hand, maximizing the black turnout and, on the other, securing 35 to 40 percent of the white vote necessary to win. A similar dilemma faced Radical Republicans in the South under Reconstruction. While there may well now be a more favorable federal presence than in the 1870s and fraud and terror may play a lesser part, the task of building a successful biracial electoral coalition demands political skills that were lacking in the 1860s and 1870s and are not obviously in evidence today.

Notes

1. V. O. Key, Jr., *Southern Politics in State and Nation* (New York: Knopf, 1949), pp. 307, 670.

2. Tony Badger, "Fatalism, not Gradualism: The Crisis of Southern Liberalism, 1945–1965," in *The Making of Martin Luther King and the Civil Rights Movement*, eds. Tony Badger and Brian Ward (London: Macmillan, 1996), pp. 75–79, 85–86. Tony Badger, "Whatever Happened to Roosevelt's 'New Generation' of Southerners?" in *The United States in Depression and War* (Edinburgh: Edinburgh University Press, forthcoming).

3. Numan V. Bartley, *The New South, 1945–1980: The Story of the South's Modernization* (Baton Rouge: Louisiana State University Press, 1995), pp. 68–70, 73.

4. I have developed these arguments at greater length in "The Constraints of Southern Liberalism," a paper delivered before the Southern Intellectual History Circle, February 1997, at Samford University.

5. Adam Fairclough, *Race and Democracy: The Civil Rights Struggle in Louisiana, 1915–1972* (Athens: University of Georgia Press, 1995), pp. xiii,135–47. Michael Heale, *McCarthy's Americans: Red Scare Politics in State and Nation* (London: Macmillan, 1998), pp. 214–76.

6. Numan V. Bartley, *The Rise of Massive Resistance* (Baton Rouge: Louisiana State University Press, 1969), pp. 82–107, 190–231. Steven Lawson, *Black Ballots: Voting Rights in the South, 1944–69* (New York: Columbia University Press, 1976), pp. 116–39.

7. Badger, "Fatalism, not Gradualism," pp. 85–90.

8. On Folsom's chauffeur, Winston Craig, and his role in the Montgomery black community, see Fred Gray, *Bus Road to Justice: Changing the System by the System* (Montgomery, Ala.: Black Belt Press, 1995), pp. 42–45. Bartley, *The New South*, pp. 175–76. Randall Bennett Woods, *Fulbright: A Biography* (New York: Cambridge University Press, 1995), p. 211.

9. Interview with Dante Fascell, February 27, 1997.

10. J. Mills Thornton, "Challenge and Response in the Montgomery Bus Boycott of 1955–56," *Alabama Review* 33 (1980): 163–235.

11. Numan V. Bartley and Hugh Davis Graham, *Southern Politics and the Second Reconstruction* (Baltimore: Johns Hopkins Press, 1975), pp. 51–135.

12. Bartley and Graham, *Southern Politics*, pp. 136–83.

13. Bartley and Graham, *Southern Politics*, pp. 136–83. Jack Bass and Walter deVries, *The Transformation of Southern Politics: Social Change and Political Consequences since 1945* (New York: Basic Books, 1976), pp. 41–56.

14. John Shelton Reed, "Up from Segregation," *Virginia Quarterly Review* 60 (1984): 373–99. Margaret Edds, *Free at Last: What Really Happened When Civil Rights Came to Southern Politics* (Bethesda, Md.: Adler and Adler, 1987), pp. 51–76, 95–123, 193–238. John Dollard, *Caste and Class in a Southern Town* (New Haven: Yale University Press, 1937), p. 211. Frank Parker, *Black Votes Count: Political Empowerment in Mississippi after 1965* (Chapel Hill: University of North Carolina Press, 1990), pp. 197–209.

15. Bartley, *The New South*, pp. 398–416. James C. Cobb, *The Selling of the South: The Southern Crusade for Industrial Development; 1936–80* (Baton Rouge: Louisiana State University Press, 1982), pp. 179–268. Earl Black and Merle Black, *Politics and Society in the South* (Cambridge, Mass.: Harvard University Press, 1987), pp. 125–51, 175–94.

16. John Kenneth Galbraith, *The Culture of Contentment* (London: Sinclair-Stevenson, 1992), pp. 13–29, 144–53. Black and Black, *Politics and Society*, pp. 195–231.

17. Richard K. Sher, *Politics in the New South: Republicanism, Race and Leadership in the Twentieth Century*, n.e. (Armonk, N.Y.: M. E. Sharpe, 1997), pp. 132–36.

18. Interview with James Farwell, November 20, 1997. Dan T. Carter, *The Politics of Rage: George Wallace, the Origins of the New Conservatism, and the Transformation of American Politics* (New York: Simon and Schuster, 1995), pp. 451–68. Dan T. Carter,

From George Wallace to Newt Gingrich: Race in the Conservative Counterrevolution 1963–94 (Baton Rouge: Louisiana State University Press, 1996), pp. xi-xiii. Tyler Bridges, *The Rise of David Duke* (Jackson: University Press of Mississippi, 1994), p. 218.

19. Peter Applebome, *Dixie Rising: How the South Is Shaping America's Values, Politics, and Culture* (New York: Times Books, 1996), pp. 298–302. Interview with Frank Smith, November 1, 1995.

20. Applebome, *Dixie Rising,* pp. 7, 52–55. Tod A. Baker, "The Emergence of the Religious Right and the Development of the Two-Party System in the South," eds. Tod Baker et al., *Political Parties in the Southern States: Party Activists in Partisan Coalitions* (New York: Praeger, 1990), pp. 135–47. John Maginnis, *Cross to Bear: America's Most Dangerous Politics* (Baton Rouge: Dark Horse Press, 1992), p. 138.

21. Dan T. Carter, "Legacy of Rage: George Wallace and the Transformation of American Politics," *Journal of Southern History* 62 (1997): 13–17.

22. Sher, *Politics in the New South,* p. 251. Chandler Davidson, "The Recent Evolution of Voting Rights Law Affecting Racial and Language Minorities," *Quiet Revolution in the South: The Impact of the Voting Rights Act, 1965–1990,* eds. Chandler Davidson and Bernard Grofman (Princeton, N.J.: Princeton University Press, 1995), pp. 21–37. James Cobb, *"The Most Southern Place on Earth": The Mississippi Delta and the Roots of Regional Identity* (New York: Oxford University Press, 1992), p. 273. Parker, *Black Votes Count,* pp. 201, 203. For a more upbeat assessment of the potential for effective representation of black interests, see Carol M. Swain, *Black Faces, Black Interests: The Representation of African Americans in Congress* (Cambridge, Mass.: Harvard University Press, 1993), pp. 193–225.

23. Sher, *Politics in the New South,* pp. 150, 254–58, 389–90. Steven A. Holmes, "For Very Strange Bedfellows, Try Redistricting," *New York Times,* July 23, 1995.

After Jim Crow

Civil Rights as Civil Wrongs

Paul M. Gaston

The black freedom struggle of the 1960s unleashed a searing critique of American values and institutions. It subverted the nation's treasured claim of moral rectitude. Its subversive effect was enlarged by liberation movements it inspired, all of them threats to received truths and ways of behavior. Hostile reaction set in before the decade was out, in time finding its battle flag carried by three Republican presidents; an exuberant band of right-wing politicians, pundits, and think tanks; a popular culture seeking assurance and approval; and a population of ordinary people crying out that enough is enough. The counterrevolution entered nearly every aspect of public and private life in the nation, and the mopping up operation shows few signs of abatement. A historian with Yogi Berra's literary talents might call this déjà vu all over again. Reminiscent of the counter-Reconstruction of the last century, it brings haunting reminders of the long era between *Plessy* and *Brown,* between the crushing of the Populist Revolt and the birth of the civil rights movement.

To sort out the complex interacting forces underlying the reactionary mood of the past thirty years will be no easy task. The opportunity to bring clarity to one of the murkiest and most disappointing eras of American history, however, ought to be a powerful inducement. One part of the task is to explain how conceptions of the past, especially of the civil rights movement itself, have served to justify the reaction. We may be guided in this direction by Santayana's familiar warning that "those who cannot remember the past are condemned to repeat it."[1] We may also recall Willie Lee Rose's reminder, in her lyrical book about the rehearsal for Reconstruction in the Carolina sea islands, that "revolutions may go backward."[2] Revolutions may more easily go backward when those who thwart them control the past, another aphorism of the historian's profession: those who control the past control the present and the future. What follows is a tentative exploration of a small part of that subject, an inquiry into the ways in which civil rights history has been anaesthetized and sanitized. Case studies of the creation and manipulation of the King myth and of Hollywood's role as a molder of the historical imagination are followed by brief estimates of the roles played by documentary films, high school textbooks, and the works of scholars.

Since the moment of his death, the image of Martin Luther King, Jr., has been manipulated to turn back radical social change and to underwrite reactionary political and economic policies. At memorial ceremonies all over the country in April of 1968 he was lauded as the twentieth century's greatest black liberation leader. Some of the white speakers may have praised him for leading the war against Jim Crow, but their favored theme was his philosophy and practice of nonviolence. In the violent year of 1968, however, that philosophy and practice were manipulated to become a weapon to douse flames burning in American cities and to turn back the angry protests of brick-throwing black Americans. King's nonviolence, at the moment of his death, meant repression of the ongoing, now often violent, black freedom movement. Following his death, King moved quickly to the role of martyred hero. There is no record, however, of anyone's hoisting James Agee's flag of warning, telling what it meant to praise famous men: "Every fury on earth has been absorbed in time, as art, or as religion, or as authority in one form or another. The deadliest blow the enemy of the human soul can strike is to do fury honor. Swift, Blake, Beethoven, Christ, Joyce, Kafka, name me a one who has not been thus castrated. Official acceptance is the one unmistakable symptom that salvation is beaten again, and is the one surest sign of fatal misunderstanding, and is the kiss of Judas."[3]

The absorption of King's fury, begun so pointedly at the moment of his death, has deepened ever since. Long before a national holiday was established in his honor, most official celebrations of his civil rights leadership routinely began with selections from his "I Have a Dream" speech that climaxed the 1963 March on Washington. His dream, he said, was "deeply rooted in the American dream." Incessant repetition of this phrase gave birth to the myth of King the reformer who wanted nothing more for his people than to win admission to a fundamentally sound society, one whose values, ideals, and economic order were flawed only by its practice of racial exclusion. Racism, according to this myth, was an independent variable that could be excised without disturbing the basic architecture of the society in which it flourished or altering the nature of its dream. Thus was the fury of America's most charismatic and influential warrior against racism tamed and the nation's image of itself as fair, just, and superior vindicated.

It was this image of the furious nonviolent warrior who was nonetheless a great champion of his country and its values that was celebrated when the national holiday bill was proposed and established. Ronald Reagan, on whose watch the deed was done, was a reluctant supporter of the inevitable, but he predictably turned it to his advantage by praising King as a good man who believed in brotherhood and harmony. "Such a carefully cropped portrait," as Robert Weisbrot writes of Reagan's manipulative characterization, "enables the nation to create a comforting icon."[4] That has been the familiar presidential line ever since, as witnessed even by Bill Clinton who begins King holiday speeches with a question: "Remember what Martin Luther King said?" And then he answers: "My dream is deeply rooted in the American dream."[5]

It has not been enough for the King myth to serve as an authoritative endorsement of the American social order. Pundits and politicians of the right have pressed it into service as a weapon to brandish against affirmative action and other Johnson-era efforts to right social wrongs. George Will, conceding the existence of continuing poverty and disadvantage in the land, explains them as the "terrible price" blacks have been made to pay "for the apostasy of today's civil rights leaders from the original premise of the civil rights movement." That premise, he declares, was that "race must not be a source of advantage or disadvantage." Will's fellow journalist Rush Limbaugh wonders how "the vision that Dr. Martin Luther King, Jr., had for a color-blind society has been perverted by modern liberalism." Newt Gingrich and Ward Connerly, blasting what they call "the failure of racial preferences," begin their broadside by recalling what they call King's "heartfelt voice" calling for a time when people would be judged by "the content of their character rather than the color of their skin."[6]

The "content of their character rather than the color of their skin" excerpt from the "dream" speech has become the incantation of choice for much of the nation, including virtually everyone on the right. It drapes the King mantle over the most unlikely partisans of the civil rights movement and uses the most famous voice of that movement to condemn policies to which it gave birth. Ward Connerly, the Sacramento businessman and University of California regent, launched a personal crusade to win votes for the California anti-affirmative action referendum on King's birthday with the announcement that "Dr. King personifies the quest for a color-blind society." Understanding of the King legacy should help the nation "resume the journey" he started and stop the terrible "drift from the ideal of a color-blind society"[7] The drift, as conservative Arch Puddington puts it, widened into a powerful rush "to the current environment of quotas, goals, timetables, race-norming, set-asides, diversity-training, and the like." No champion of King pledging fealty to civil rights history could possibly support such things.[8]

King's "dream" speech, the primary text of those who would cast him as an ally of the contemporary right wing, has a memorable passage about a promissory check returned for insufficient funds, and his other speeches and actions are full of ideas about and demands for many forms of what are now called "race-based" policies to begin the long process of undoing the effects of the "race-based" policies of the previous three centuries. In the last three years of his life he greatly expanded on these themes. It was time to move beyond the reformist tactics of the previous decade. Having cleared away the debris of Jim Crow it was easier to see the fundamental tasks yet to be accomplished. "We must recognize," he said," that we can't solve our problem now until there is a radical redistribution of economic and political power." Among other things, this would require facing the truth that "the dominant ideology" of America was not "freedom and equality," with racism "just an occasional departure from the norm." Racism was woven into the fabric of the country, intimately linked to capitalism and militarism. They were all "tied together, and you really can't get rid of one without getting rid of the others," he said.[9] What was required was "a radical restructuring of the architecture of American society."[10]

The King reflected in these remarks has pretty much disappeared from American history. In fact, he hardly entered it. His radical critique was drowned out from the beginning by angry White House rejections, white fear of the Black Power movement, escalating riots in Northern cities, and liberal integrationists' continuing loyalty to their reformist principles of social change. Even before the thermadorian reaction of the Nixon Administration set in, the King who would remake the "architecture of American society" was absent from school books, anniversary celebrations, and political oratory. Julian Bond put it well a few years ago when he declared that "we do not honor the critic of capitalism, or the pacifist who declared all wars evil, or the man of God who argued that a nation that chose guns over butter would starve its people and kill itself. We do not honor the man who linked apartheid in South Africa and Alabama; we honor an antiseptic hero." William Buckley, the dean of right-wing pundits who quoted these words of Bond's, agreed. "That is absolutely correct," he wrote. King's "kindergarten socialism" had no place in America. "Many Americans who objected strenuously to positions taken by Dr. King," Buckley wrote, "agreed to suspend their reservations in order to celebrate King the Civil Rights Leader." Generosity on the part of the right wing along with a clear separation between civil rights and radical restructuring thus constituted the bargain that underlay the holiday bill and, as Bond put it, the making of an "antiseptic" hero.[11]

King's radical prescription for remaking America extended beyond economic and foreign policy to embrace a call for a "revolution in values," specifically a rejection of market-place mentality and its obsessive fealty to the profit motive.[12] But he did not apply his "revolution in values" and rejection of market-place mentality to the nation's entertainment and cultural life where values, assumptions, and beliefs about history are formed and perpetuated.

Paul M. Gaston

Hollywood's portrayal of the civil rights movement is a major example of how tightly popular filmmaking is woven into the architecture of American society and is a largely unexamined instance of how the movement's deeper meaning has been obscured. Its conservative power sanitizes the history of the movement and leaves believing viewers with a sense of complacency about the present. The stunning lack of awareness of this process was demonstrated on the popular television program *Nightline* in January of 1989. Guests Julian Bond and Gene Hackman were on camera to discuss the recently released *Mississippi Burning*, the most ambitious and influential Hollywood feature film on the civil rights movement yet made. Director Alan Parker aimed for it to be seen by millions of people in fifty countries—to instruct, he said, "an entire generation who knows nothing" of the civil rights struggle. When the *Nightline* conversation turned to what Dr. King might have thought of the film, Hackman, who had proudly played a starring role, was shaken by Bond's characterization of it as a betrayal of the movement. Genuinely surprised and disappointed, Hackman weakly replied that he had been in New York during Freedom Summer and therefore did not know what had been going on in Mississippi.[13]

An avalanche of strident critics enumerated the film's many failures as a representation of history.[14] Its popularity, however—it grossed $34.6 million—and its almost unique status as Hollywood's major effort to portray civil rights history make it a good choice for a case study.[15] Scriptwriter Chris Gerolmo, who conceived the story, came out of a documentary history tradition and was an admirer of Frederick Wiseman. The script he produced, however, strayed badly from the Wiseman tradition. With little knowledge of the civil rights movement and only a slim reading list to guide him, Gerolmo fell easily into simplistic Hollywood formulas. His subject matter was the search for the bodies and the killers of the three civil rights workers in Mississippi during Freedom Summer. He told it in a melodrama that centered on a fictional battle of wills and might between the Ku Klux Klan and the Federal Bureau of Investigation. The Hollywood formula he turned to was the reliable western. His two FBI agents were modeled on two leading men in *The Man Who Shot Liberty Valance*. In that film, a peace-loving Jimmy Stewart, committed to achieving justice in the gun-toting West through books and the law, is finally outraged enough by bad-man Lee Marvin to reach inexpertly for a borrowed six-shooter. Men must be killed to make justice reign. John Wayne is the Gene Hackman character whose fast draw and manly ways actually save his friend.[16]

In director Alan Parker's hands, the Klan members are portrayed more as caricatures than as the frighteningly everyday persons they were. Their violent behavior is so gross that the film undermines belief in the reality of the violence that in fact did take place. The FBI, representing the forces of good that will triumph over evil, is presented in a way that is an even greater distortion of historical truth. Gene Hackman's superb acting (who can't believe him?) achieves the preposterous result of persuading innocent viewers that this FBI man, a one-time Mississippi sheriff now teamed in the service of J. Edgar Hoover with a button-down bureau man, is the one person who knows how to outsmart the redneck enemy, using a formulaic mixture of sex and violence. His gentle romancing of the deputy sheriff's wife leads her to tell him where the bodies are buried, and when his own tough talk and hands are not enough to get the names of the murdering Klansmen from the men who know, he calls in a bureau specialist whose violent ways succeed.

In the original script, Gerolmo created a Mafia character, beholden to the FBI, who stuck a pistol in the mayor's mouth to extract the needed information. Parker rewrote this scene (as he did many) so that we see a black FBI agent menacingly fingering a razor blade, threatening the mayor with castration. Somehow Parker thought this reversal of the black-white sex and cut scenario would give his audience a cathartic release. The mayor sweats and cringes; the black agent quickly gets him to name names. He then flies off into the night, mission accomplished. Innocent viewers may walk out of the theater never suspecting that the only blacks who worked for Mr. Hoover in 1964 were the men who drove his limousine and mowed his lawn.

Critics have scored the film for its many distortions, including especially its presentation of the FBI as the triumphant ally of the civil rights movement. They have properly complained that African Americans are seen almost without exception as deferential to whites—docile and easily intimidated. In one of the many departures from reality, Parker has the character based on Chaney riding in the back seat of the sedan, the two whites in the front, on the night they were overtaken and murdered. In fact, Chaney was driving the car. The film is set in Freedom Summer, but summer volunteers, though referred to contemptuously by the white locals, are virtually invisible. Underlying the critics' complaints is an implied belief in the possibility of a symbiotic relationship between film and history. Through fiction, they believe, it should be possible to present deeper truths, without slavish fidelity to historical detail. Thus, according to this view, the fault with *Mississippi Burning* lies in the personal and artistic failures of Parker and Gerolmo and their associates. There is plenty of blame to parcel out to the filmmakers, to be sure, but the deeper problem lies elsewhere—in the cultural architecture of American society.

As in *The Man Who Shot Liberty Valance,* good triumphs over evil in *Mississippi Burning* because only violence can prevail against violence. It is an ancient Hollywood custom, deeply rooted in American values and assumptions. Reformed gunmen who have hung up their pistols always reach for them in the end; peace-loving Quakers, sworn never to resort to violence, always hunt up the squirrel rifle when their women have been violated. One critic observed that "Hollywood believes . . . the secret glory of such movies is the violence itself."[17] The convention is so deeply rooted that neither Parker nor Gerolmo understood that it was they who were doing violence to their subject. Nonviolence, the philosophical basis and strategic weapon of the civil rights movement, was what brought Jim Crow to heel and inspired the nation to insist on a law and order that would diminish the violence. (And as for the FBI, it parceled out $30,000 in bribe money—good and legal detective procedure—to find the bodies and learn the names of the murderers.) It was precisely the belief that might does *not* make right that guided the movement.

Crippled by its vision of violent behavior as a social good, Hollywood is unable to see the power of nonviolence. It also requires that films about social issues have resolutions that do not weaken faith in the nation's ability to solve its problems without altering its architecture. Parker and Gerolmo have the established authorities solve the problem and in so doing erase from the record entirely the fact that it was the grassroots demand for a new concept of justice that mobilized an otherwise reluctant federal government to act. *Mississippi Burning*, fitting the formula, has its viewers believe that America is an automatically self-correcting nation. It is a comforting, conservative view and one that uses civil rights history to support the opposite of what the movement was about. Finally, the story of the black freedom struggle in *Mississippi Burning* is told by white men, leading King's widow, along with many others, to wonder, "how long will we have to wait before Hollywood finds the courage and the integrity to tell the stories of . . . black men, women, and children who put their lives on the line for equality?"[18] Asked why blacks were pushed to the sidelines, Parker replied that "our heroes are still white." A film with black heroes had little chance of box-office success, he believed, and in Hollywood "the film industry is about the pursuit of the dollar." Ruing the damage to artistic integrity such a value system inflicts, he nonetheless moved in its orbit because "if you want to reach the largest possible world audience, it's the only place to work."[19] He might have said he would not try to change the architecture of American society.

Parker's fellow director Richard Attenborough agreed. *Cry Freedom*, his extravaganza about the South African freedom struggle, preceded *Mississippi Burning* and raised many of the same questions. Based on a book by white journalist Donald Woods, *Cry Freedom* was more the story of Donald Woods than Steve Biko. Both Woods and Attenborough believed that the film would not succeed if Biko were the central figure, as he was in real life. When Biko's comrade Mamphela Ramphele went to Harare during the screening to protest, she reduced Attenborough to tears but failed to change his mind.[20] Only with a white hero, he believed, could white viewers be moved to sympathy and support for the South African liberation struggle. A film centered on Biko could not accomplish that purpose. Denzel Washington, who played Biko, agreed: "because of the reality of economics of a $22–million film," he said, "it would be mostly the story of the journalist, Donald Woods." Whites could, however, identify with Woods's transformation under Biko's tutelage.[21]

Mississippi Burning and *Cry Freedom,* the two most notable freedom struggle films up to the time of their release a decade ago, were not films that featured blacks, but they inaugurated a genre of "white redemption" that has characterized works of the 1990s. The best of these are *The Long Walk Home* (1990) and *Ghosts of Mississippi* (1996). The central figures in both are white people whose personal involvement in civil rights issues brings them to an awareness of the injustice of white supremacy. Redeemed from their inherited prejudices, they stand up for the oppressed, braving the hostility of society and the alienation of their spouses. *Ghosts of Mississippi* tells the story of the recent successful retrial of Byron de la Beckwith, featuring the redemption and courage of District Attorney Bobby DeLaughter, without telling much about Medgar Evers and the freedom struggle he led. *The Long Walk Home,* set in Montgomery during the bus boycott, portrays the awakening of a middle-class housewife. "We just didn't know any better," she tells her black maid. "The rest of the world's living that way, so you don't question it."[22]

The white housewife, the white district attorney, and the white FBI agent all begin to question. As they do they arouse in moviegoers anger against white oppression of blacks and hold out the example of people who could stand against the system. Ironically, such a formula meshes nicely with the sensibilities of both contemporary liberals and the dominant conservative ideology. For today's audiences, the end of segregated buses, assassination of civil rights leaders, and Klan brutality are so widely accepted as to be almost irrelevant to daily life. Viewers can identify with the whites who took a stand beside the blacks without being moved to question anything about their own lives or society. The past that these films cause to live in the present is therefore an anaesthetized one, free of the challenge, burden, and rebuke that was present in the movement as a whole, made specific by King in the last years of his life, and silenced by a culture unwilling to question the givens of its society.

Alan Parker's aim, he said, was "to reach an entire generation who knows nothing" of the history he would bring to life. Factual accuracy was the domain of the documentary, and he thought many of them had appeared on PBS. "But nobody watches them," he said, "and that's enough of a reason, a justification, for fictionalizing."[23] Almost two years before the release of

Mississippi Burning, Henry Hampton's six-part documentary, *Eyes on the Prize: America's Civil Rights Years,* appeared on PBS. An eight-part sequel covered the next two decades.[24] Some twenty million people have watched the series on television.[25] How many more have seen it in school and university courses we do not know, but we can safely conclude that no Hollywood film on the civil rights movement has been seen by so many people.[26]

The striking success of *Eyes* does not suggest that Parker, Attenborough, and their Hollywood colleagues are wrong to believe that truth-in-history must be compromised to gain popularity and profits. It does suggest, however, that there is a very large segment of the population receptive to a non-Hollywood version of civil rights history—a version fundamentally different from Hollywood's. Blacks, not whites, are at the center of the freedom movement. Their growing strength and influence, not the beneficent leadership of the federal government or the redemption of white people, is the main story. The impetus for change comes from grassroots protest, not from federal government initiative. The *Brown* decision is the fruit of two decades of NAACP litigation; the Civil Rights Act of 1964 results from the mass protests culminating in the Birmingham demonstrations; the Voting Rights Act is inspired by the confrontation at Selma. Even the burial of Jim Crow, momentous though it is, appears less important in the film than the growing power and confidence of blacks in the movement. Finally, each of the six episodes in *Eyes I* is crafted to end on a note of doubt, presaging further battles ahead. Optimism and pride in achievement are always soberly balanced by expanding awareness of the obstacles to freedom yet to be removed. Eyes remain on a prize yet to be won. Slaying Jim Crow is not the prize.

No one has yet made an authoritative study of the impact of *Eyes on the Prize* on its viewers. We have anecdotal evidence and some teachers have recorded the reaction of their students. My students—primarily my white students, Southern and Northern—responded first of all with surprise and horror at what they saw. No sense of history had prepared them for the evil deeds that took place before they were born. Their next response was to heave a sigh of relief, secure in the belief that those shocking crimes against humanity happened a long time ago and that the laws passed by the federal government had resolved this ugly American dilemma.[27] A professor at Bridgewater College in Virginia characterizes his students more bluntly. They still prefer "the mint julep version of history," finding it "comfortable," and "they don't seem especially interested in racism. . . . Their assumption is that the past was racist and that was bad, but racism is over, except for a few crazies."[28] Where these ideas and reactions come from is not easy to trace out. Some of the reaction may have to do with the American history textbooks they read in high school.

James Loewen, reviewing a dozen widely used texts, concludes that they tell an essentially Parkeresque history of the movement, showing the federal government as the principal agent for constructive change, punishing racists and enacting civil rights legislation. Loewen believes that this approach is part of a worldview nurtured by what King called the architecture of American society. Consequently, they are bound to present a benign view of America's past and an optimistic one of its future. Looking to maximize profits through adoptions, they steer clear of "acknowledging that anything might be wrong with white Americans, or with the United States as a whole."[29]

Even when the teaching and the reading are more to our liking, the obstacles are formidable. Loewen tells the story, for example, of a university student who said to him: "You'll never believe all the stuff I learned in high school about Reconstruction—like, it wasn't so bad, it set up school systems. Then I saw *Gone with the Wind* and learned the truth about Reconstruction." Robert Coles, a shrewd judge of both history and humanity, would understand. In a poignant note on Southern history books, he once wrote: "One can only wonder how it has been possible for so many extraordinarily eloquent and powerful books, all so carefully written and meticulously documented, to avail so little against what I once heard a white tenant farmer in Alabama call 'the powers that be.'"[30] Coles is right that "extraordinarily eloquent and powerful books, all so carefully written and meticulous documented," have been published about the South. Historians of the civil rights movement, however, ought not go unexamined in this brief and tentative foray into the mythmaking that has turned civil rights history into a conservative endorsement of reaction. A full-scale review must await another occasion, but a starting point might be with our focus and periodization. Many of us, in our writings and in our teaching, think of the movement as beginning in the mid-1950s, with *Brown* and the bus boycott, and culminating in 1965, with the Voting Rights Act; the sudden acknowledgment of racism as a national, not regional, problem; and the rapid fracturing of the principal civil rights organizations. We speak of the achievement of the "limited aims" of the movement, usually meaning the abolition of legal segregation and disfranchisement. In this way we may unintentionally give succor to those who would turn civil rights history against its champions and intended beneficiaries.

In fact, the aims only appeared to be limited because of the media attention to public policy demands and the fierceness with which the Jim Crow system was imposed and defended. Its destruction—one of the great triumphs of this century—was nonetheless a short-term objective. Movement participants announced the real prize on which they had their eyes when they sang of "freedom overhead" and marched for dignity, opportunity, and equality.

Paul M. Gaston

Radical economic thought was there, too, though little noticed and not systematically presented. Student Nonviolent Coordinating Committee (SNCC) workers, for example, all received the same salaries, opposing hierarchy and the profit motive as bases for social organization. Many movement participants exemplified an ethic of integration in a beloved community that was a greater challenge to the nation than the assault on Jim Crow. Should we shift our focus to movement culture and to a consequently evolving set of tactics, we might better provide a corrective to some of the myths and mischief that have been the subject of this essay.

Notes

1. George Santayana, *The Life of Reason; or, The Phases of Human Progress* (New York: Charles Scribner's Sons, 1911), p. 284.

2. Willie Lee Rose, *Rehearsal for Reconstruction: The Port Royal Experiment* (Indianapolis: Bobs-Merrill, 1964), p. 408.

3. James Agee, *Let Us Now Praise Famous Men* (New York: Houghton Mifflin, 1941), p. 15.

4. Robert Weisbrot, "Celebrating Dr. King's Birthday: A Legacy of Confrontation and Conciliation," *New Republic*, January 30, 1984.

5. Bill Clinton, "Remarks Honoring Martin Luther King, Jr.," *Weekly Compilation of Presidential Documents*, January 23, 1995.

6. George F. Will, *The Leading Wind: Politics, the Culture, and Other News, 1990–1994* (New York: Viking, 1994), p. 143; Rush H. Limbaugh III, *See: I Told You So* (New York: Pocket Books, 1993), p. 244. Newt Gingrich and Ward Connerly, "Face the Failure of Racial Preferences," *New York Times*, June 15, 1997.

7. Jack E. White, "I Have a Scheme: Ward Connerly's Effort to Hijack Dr. King's Legacy Is Full of Black Humor," *Time*, February 3, 1997, p. 46; for a fascinating account of Connerly's tangled racial history and identity, see Barry Bearak, "Questions of Race Run Deep for Foe of Preferences," *New York Times*, July 27, 1997, pp. 1, 20–21.

8. Arch Puddington, "What to Do about Affirmative Action," *Commentary*, June 1995.

9. Quoted in David J. Garrow, *Bearing the Cross: Martin Luther King,, Jr., and the Southern Christian Leadership Conference* (New York: William Morrow, 1986), pp. 536–39.

10. "Federal Role in Urban Affairs": *Hearings before the Subcommittee on Executive Reorganization of the Committee on Executive Reorganization of the Committee on Government Operations, U.S. Senate*, 89th Cong., pt. 14: 2981.

11. William F. Buckley, Jr., "The Other Dr. King," *National Review*, May 20, 1993, p. 62.

12. He told a Senate committee, "The values of the marketplace supersede the goals of social justice. We narrowly define economic cost and ignore social costs. We rely on

the unseen hand of economic growth to do the task of social justice. The theme of 'efficiency' overwhelms the need for equity." *Hearings before the Subcommittee on Executive Reorganization,* pt. 14: 2969.

13. The Parker quote appears in Robert Brent Toplin, *History by Hollywood: The Uses and Abuses of the American Past* (Urbana: University of Illinois Press, 1996), p. 27. Toplin's chapter on the film is a helpful overview. The information on the *Nightline* episode comes from Toplin, p. 35, and an interview with Julian Bond, June 26, 1997.

14. For a good sampling of unfavorable reviews, see Julian Bond, "A Movie with Eyes on the Wrong Prize," *Southern Changes,* December 1988, pp. 22–23; William H. Chafe, "Mississippi Burning," in *Past Imperfect: History According to the Movies,* eds. Ted Mico, John Miller-Monzon, and David Rubel (New York: Henry Holt, 1995), pp. 274–77; Thulani Davis, "Civil Rights and Wrongs," *American Film,* December 1988, pp. 33ff; Pauline Kael, "The Current Cinema: Love/Hate," *New Yorker,* December 26, 1988, pp. 72–75; Stanley Kauffmann, "Matters of Fact," *New Republic,* January 9 and 16, 1989, pp. 24–25; Harvard Sitkoff in *Journal of American History* 76 (December 1989): 1019–20; Jeremy Larner, "Violence for Fun and Profit," *Dissent* (Spring 1988): 268–70; Gavin Smith, "Mississippi Gambler," *Film Comment* 24 (November–December 1988): 26–30; "Facts for Burning," *Economist,* January 7, 1989, p. 79; "Mississippi Burning," in *The Motion Picture Guide: 1989 Annual* (Evanston, Ill.: Cine Books, 1989), pp. 110–11; "Mississippi Morass: When Hollywood Messes with History Everyone Stands to Lose," *Quill,* March 1989, pp 20ff; review in *Time,* January 9, 1989, p. 57. Two magazines—*Newsweek,* December 12, 1988, p. 73, and *People,* December 12, 1988, p. 18—have short, unsigned favorable reviews. The film is favorably reviewed also by Vincent Canby, "3 Murders, 2 Agents, One Long Hot Summer," *New York Times,* December 9, 1988, p. 399, and by Stuart Klawans, "Films," *Nation,* January 2, 1989, pp. 24–26.

15. Toplin writes that the film was a box-office success and that it "aroused the audiences' curiosity about an important subject from American history that had received very little from Hollywood. The motion picture reached many people who were not going to read about racial violence or watch *Eyes on the Prize* on PBS." Toplin, *History by Hollywood,* p. 43.

16. "The idea," Gerolmo reportedly said, "was a working-through of a Western-type conflict like *The Man Who Shot Liberty Valance,* where the rule of law needs the rule of force." Quoted in Gavin Smith,"'Mississippi' Gambler," *Film Comment* 24 (November–December 1988): 28. The same point is made by Toplin, *History by Hollywood,* p. 31.

17. Jeremy Larner, "Violence for Fun & Profit," *Dissent* (Spring 1988), 268.

18. Quoted in Toplin, *History by Hollywood,* p. 35.

19. The quotations are from Toplin, *History by Hollywood,* p. 42, and "Dialogue on Film: Alan Parker," *American Film,* January–February 1988, pp. 12–15.

20. Conversation with Mamphela Ramphele in Cape Town, South Africa, July 1986.

21. The Denzel Washington quote, from the Chicago *Tribune,* January 7, 1990, is from Patrick Rael, "Freedom Struggle Films: History or Hollywood?" *Socialist Review* 11 (July 1992): 123.

22. The quote is from Rael, "Freedom Struggle Films," 121.

23. Quoted in Toplin, *History by Hollywood*, p. 42.

24. *Eyes on the Prize: America's Civil Rights Years* (1987); *Eyes on the Prize: America at the Racial Crossroads* (1989).

25. Interview, Judy Richardson of the Blackside staff, July 28, 1997.

26. *Mississippi Burning* grossed $34.6 million. A rough estimate would translate that into about five million box-office customers. How many more have seen it on television reruns or on videos is not possible to determine, but it is safe to say that *Eyes on the Prize* has been seen by four or fives times as many people as have seen *Mississippi Burning*. Box-office statistics for *Mississippi Burning* come from *Internet Movie Data Base*.

27. This disconnect between past and present stood out sharply in questionnaires I distributed to roughly three hundred students over a period of three years in the early 1990s. One of the most striking discoveries was that, for 75 percent of the white students, the civil rights movement was not part of their oral history; it was seldom, if ever, discussed in their homes when they were growing up.

28. Steve Longenecker, *H-South Posting* on the Internet, July 12, 1997.

29. James W. Loewen, *Lies My Teacher Told Me: Everything Your American History Textbook Got Wrong* (New York: New Press, 1995), pp. 227–28.

30. Loewen, *Lies My Teacher Told Me,* p. 154; Robert Coles, *Migrants, Sharecroppers, Mountaineers,* vol. 2 of *Children of Crisis* (Boston: Little, Brown, 1971), p. 629.

A World Turned Upside Down

Southern Politics at the End of the Twentieth Century

Dan Carter

In mid-July of 1995, I sat in a downtown restaurant in Birmingham, Alabama, eavesdropping on two old college friends catching up on their careers in the years since they had graduated together from university. One was a lifelong resident of Birmingham, a well-connected financial adviser living in Vestavia, one of the city's most exclusive suburbs. The other—born in the Midwest—had gone on to become the vice president of a Jacksonville, Florida, furniture manufacturing company and was in town on business. The furniture executive was bubbling with excitement. The new president of his firm had abandoned the usual weekly meetings in which department heads and junior level executives discussed production quotas and marketing plans. Instead, he had told his team, it was important that they read serious analyses of current economics and society in order to understand the basic forces that would shape their company's future. As their first assignment, the Jacksonville businessman told his friend, they had read an exciting and revelatory book, *The Bell Curve* by Charles Murray and the late Richard J. Herrnstein.

Murray had become one of the most provocative intellectuals of the new conservatism in 1984 when he published *Losing Ground,* his brief against the welfare state. The only hope for a declining America, Murray had argued, was to scrap the "entire federal welfare and income-support structure for working-aged persons, including AFDC, Medicaid, Food Stamps, Unemployment Insurance, Worker's Compensation, subsidized housing, disability insurance, and the rest," since government welfare programs inevitably rewarded the "least law-abiding," the "least capable," and the "least responsible" among the poor.[1] By the mid-1990s, the arguments of *Losing Ground* were no longer so outlandish; indeed, they represented a wish list for the Republican Party's right wing.

But *The Bell Curve* was a bit more politically risqué. Murray and fellow author Richard Herrnstein argued that twentieth-century liberal ideologues had conspired to conceal the uncomfortable reality that genetically inherent

I.Q. limited the capabilities of some racial (and ethnic) groups. To put it more bluntly, a racial hierarchy of intelligence existed with East Asians at the top (along with Ashkenazi Jews), most American "whites" just below, Hispanics further down the scale, and blacks at the absolute bottom.[2] What the Florida executive found so fascinating about this book, however, was that it explained more than simply the inferiority of most blacks, for Herrnstein and Murray had argued that at least 10 percent—probably more—of whites were genetically stunted and incapable of functioning in an increasingly complex postindustrial society. It explained why liberalism was doomed to failure, he told his friend with excitement as he rattled off the absurd positions taken by the national Democratic Party. Take the continuing effort of liberal Democrats to raise the minimum wage, he said. If they suddenly started paying $10 an hour to those men working in their assembly plant, "do you think they would go out and open a 401-K plan?" he asked. "No," he said. "They would go out and buy a case of beer and sit on the stoop of their trailer house and drink till it was time to go inside and get their wives pregnant again."

Here I was in the middle of a New South city with a black mayor whose main tourist attraction was a civil rights museum. Eugene "Bull" Connor and the racial turmoil of the 1960s seemed very far away. Clearly some things had changed. But as I listened to this business executive outline a social philosophy that melded pseudoscientific racism and eugenics, Social Darwinism, and New South country club arrogance, the past seemed very near. The next day as I sat in the library of my father's retirement home in Birmingham, I pulled off the shelf a copy of V. O. Key's book, *Southern Politics in State and Nation*.[3] Perhaps, I thought, this is as good a place to begin as anywhere to unravel this story.

When the Texas-born political scientist published his landmark account of the American South in 1949, he looked back upon a seventy-year political tradition in which the white South had created a political nation within a nation characterized by its almost unbroken devotion to the Democratic Party. Between 1880 and 1944, the former states of the Confederacy voted Democratic 95 percent of the time. Once one excludes the 1928 campaign in which New York Catholic Al Smith led the Democratic ticket, the term "solid South" is literally true for the seven decades after Reconstruction.[4] History, economics, culture all combined to create that unbroken political allegiance, but Key had no hesitation in pointing to the central factor in this peculiar political orientation. "In its grand outlines," he concluded, "the politics of the South revolves around the Negro." And the most salient aspect of this obsession with maintaining white supremacy was the leverage that it historically gave to the small minority of Southern whites in the Black Belt, particularly the planter elite that had rebounded from the war and replaced a system of cotton and slavery with one of cotton and sharecropping.[5]

In the years leading up to the Civil War, these whites "persuaded the entire South that it should fight to protect slave property," said Key. Later, in a conservative alliance with emerging industrial interests, Black Belt–led reactionaries crushed the populist movement and convinced whites of all classes that their best interests lay in subordinating all interests to the cause of white supremacy. Politically, this meant not simply the disfranchisement of blacks, but the restriction of voting to a manageable number of whites. When all else failed, Southern elites felt no compunction in resorting to overt fraud and corruption. While rural Black Belt planters established and shaped this system, emerging business and corporate interests found that—whatever their divisions—they were united on the main outlines of conservative politics.[6]

Over the next generation, that Black Belt elite had to make a few strategic retreats and adjustments. In the upcountry of the Piedmont and in a few urban centers, an emerging business/middle class promoted the rise of industry and commerce. In their quest for improved transportation, better educational facilities (for whites), and a state government based upon models of "business efficiency," these bourgeois reformers sometimes modified the region's time-honored commitment to governmental laissez faire. At the same time there was little predisposition to move beyond this "business progressivism." Good schools, good roads, and good government may have become the mantra of this new business and professional class, but these house-broken reformers were a far cry from the Populist radicals of the 1890s. The center of political gravity within the state remained overwhelmingly conservative. As historian-journalist John Egerton so aptly summarized the credo of the large-scale landowners, small town elites, corporate leaders and utility executives who continued to dominate the politics of the region, their faith remained in "low taxes, low wages, high profits, and balanced budgets, states' rights, limited government, and selective federal aid without interference from Washington; a cheap, plentiful labor force without unions; and always, unfailingly, an abiding devotion to segregation and white supremacy."[7]

As Key finished his manuscript, he was well aware that he was on the cusp of a transformed region. The Dixiecrat revolt of right-wing racists in the 1948 presidential campaign had sounded a warning to traditional Democrats; over the next three presidential elections, the number of Southern states voting Republican increased steadily. Still, the core of state and local politics remained Democratic for another fifteen years. When V. O. Key died in 1963, only sixteen of the 106 members of the Southern house delegations were Republican; there was only one Republican senator and one Republican state governor, and Democrats—albeit conservative Democrats—held more than 95 percent of all state and local offices.

Today, however, the South is well on its way to becoming solidly Republican. A Democrat has not won a majority of the region's electoral votes for the presidency since Jimmy Carter in 1976. Republicans dominate the congressional delegations of the former Confederate States, two to one in the Senate and three to two in the House. In the Senate, Mississippi's Trent Lott is the majority leader while Old South turncoat Democrats like South Carolina's Strom Thurmond and North Carolina's Jesse Helms hold key committee chairmanships. In the United States House of Representatives, the dominance of the region is even more extraordinary. House Majority Leader Newt Gingrich represented a suburban Atlanta congressional district, his two top congressional lieutenants were Texas congressmen, Tom DeLay and Dick Armey, and three of the most important committees of the House of Representatives—Judiciary, National Security, and Appropriations—were chaired by conservative Southern Republicans.

The Republican ascendancy, while less advanced in state and local politics is well on its way. Democrats hold only three of the eleven state governorships, and Republicans are within striking distance of taking control of the North Carolina, Virginia, and South Carolina legislatures. Even more critically, GOP candidates now dominate the growing suburbs of the South and have won two-thirds of the contested local elections over the last six years.[8] In a generation, the solid South has returned. But this time it is a solidly Republican, rather than a solidly Democratic South.

This was not the way it was supposed to work. V. O. Key, and most members of his academic generation, were shaped by their own experience with the class-interest politics of the New Deal. The way to bring the South into the mainstream of American life was to enfranchise Southern blacks and expand the level of political participation by poorer whites in the region. This would make possible the emergence of Southern liberal politicians who would defend the economic interests of working- and middle-class Southerners against the predatory policies of conservative elites. In that process, the fledgling labor movement would play a key role in liberalizing the region. Eventually, in some way not yet foreseen, the intensity of race feelings would subside and a solution to the vexing color line would gradually evolve. Key was not alone in reaching that conclusion; it represented the thinking of most liberals in the late 1940s, South and North. But a number of interconnected developments derailed their assumptions. First came the political emasculation of the emerging labor movement in the South. Because of the prominence of McCarthyism outside the region and the role that a handful of Southern politicians played in opposing the Wisconsin politician, we have often underestimated the powerful weapon that the rise of anticommunism gave to Southern conservatives. Sometimes unconsciously, but often with deliberate forethought, reactionary elements in the region skillfully linked fears of Soviet expansionism and internal subversion with traditional hostility toward radicalism and "socialism."[9]

By the late 1950s, the labor movement's effort to organize the South had collapsed under the fierce assault of conservative business leaders and their political supporters, and any possibility for a black-white working-class coalition had ended as white Southern workers enlisted as soldiers in the war for white supremacy.[10] While conservatives throughout the nation found anticommunism a convenient rhetoric to attack the labor movement, Southern defenders of the status quo usually placed a far greater emphasis upon the communist efforts to promote racial "amalgamation." And in the late 1930s and 1940s, racial issues moved to the forefront of Southern politics. Even during the United States Supreme Court's conservative heyday in the mid-1930s, the tide began to turn. In 1935, in one of the Scottsboro trial appeals, the Court set aside the conviction of black defendant Clarence Norris on the grounds that the consistent absence of African Americans from Southern jury pools was prima facie evidence of racial discrimination.[11] Over the next fifteen years the high court moved to open law and professional schools to blacks and to probe the outer political defenses of white supremacy. Between 1944, when the Supreme Court struck down the white Democratic primary in *Smith v. Allwright,* and 1954, when *Brown v. Board of Education* overturned the "separate but equal" doctrine, decisions came almost every year, striking down some aspect of the old system.[12]

Superficially, these court decisions might be described as a development from the top down, but it more accurately reflected the dialectical process of reform from above and below. For it was black litigants who instigated the court suits, and it was the National Association for the Advancement of Colored People that furnished the legal expertise and arguments that carried the day. More importantly, the entire legal campaign reflected broader undercurrents within the black community. For years, a handful of black activists and visionaries had organized a variety of community civic-uplift and voter-registration organizations as well as NAACP chapters that tied this grassroots constituency to a larger national movement, always hammering home to a disfranchised people their central message: change would never come without access to the political process. It was the shifting mood of the black community of the South and its unwillingness to passively wait for deliverance that formed the foundation of the modern civil rights movement. In the thirty-six

Dan Carter

months after the *Allwright* decision, the number of black registered voters in the South tripled from 150,000 to nearly half a million and then doubled again over the next five years.[13]

This still left 80 percent of the potential black electorate unregistered and for over a decade, racist politicians across the region mobilized the power of the state to bully and intimidate black citizens in an effort to return to the days of unquestioned white supremacy. In large part their failure stemmed from the courage and resourcefulness of the region's African Americans. Using the non-violent tactics of Mohandas Gandhi and the traditional moral arguments of the American religious community, African American leaders mobilized a broad national coalition directed at destroying the institution of legal segregation. The Civil Rights Act of 1964 and the Voting Rights Act of 1965, by destroying the legal structure of segregation and enfranchising the region's black citizens, marked one of the great reform achievements of the twentieth century. Still, it was a victory that inevitably led to heightened racial tensions in the region, tensions reflected in the political process as white Southerners angrily denounced the party of their fathers and turned first to third-party candidate George Wallace and then to an increasingly conservative Republican Party. We are all familiar with the story of white backlash. Nearly thirty years ago Numan Bartley first described the process in his study *The Rise of Massive Resistance*.[14] In tantalizing previews of his own forthcoming study of white Southern moderates Anthony Badger has described the weakness and ultimate capitulation of those Southern "liberals" to the forces of racial reaction. And in my own biography of George Wallace I have tried to describe some of the ways in which the race issue mobilized whites in a way unseen since the 1850s.[15]

The transformation of Southern politics stemmed from economic and demographic factors as well as race. By the 1950s, an emerging Southern suburban middle and upper middle class was disenchanted with the national Democratic Party on economic as well as racial grounds. This was not simply a Southern phenomenon. Throughout the nation, isolated from the escalating demands of the growing urban underclass, residents of America's suburbs could control their own local governments, and they could buy good schools and safe streets (or at least better schools and safer streets than those of the inner city.) They were also free to turn their back on the increasingly unruly public spaces of decaying central cities by creating a "secure and controlled environment" in malls and private automobiles (as opposed to public transportation). The advent of cable television and video rentals even ensured private entertainment space within their homes. All of this inevitably reinforced the "privatization of American life and culture" and strengthened a conservative political ethos.[16] But the South had always been a bulwark of low taxes and limited government services and suburbanization strengthened this tradition and created some of the most conservative constituencies in American politics. It goes without saying that racial fears were interwoven with these economic concerns. Suburbanization had a particular appeal to middle- and upper-income families in the region who had often lived—in small and medium-sized cities at least—in relative proximity to blacks. White flight allowed them to escape the economic costs of urban deterioration and the demands of integration.

While Dwight Eisenhower showed surprising strength in the growing suburban precincts of New South cities in the presidential elections of 1952 and 1956, it was Arizona's Barry Goldwater who was most successful in laying the foundation for the modern Republican Party within the South with his 1964 campaign for the presidency.[17] Goldwater's Southern support stemmed from a mixture of racial and economic factors. Much of the general support within the white South came as a consequence of his decision to vote against the Civil Rights Act of 1964. But his economic emphasis upon lower taxes and a limited federal government had particular resonance with the New South suburban voters. Of the region's 375 Republican delegates who went to the party's convention in San Francisco in 1964, 366 cast their votes for the senator from Arizona. This new generation of ideologically committed Southern Republicans was white, overwhelmingly male, far wealthier than the typical delegates of either party, and economically as well as racially on the far right of the political spectrum. In a postconvention survey response, 80 percent of the Southern delegates rejected *any* federal action on civil rights, even when blacks were denied the right to vote, and 90 percent opposed federal funding for unemployment insurance, medical care, housing, or education.[18]

By the 1980s Southern Republicans not only profited from the racial backlash of the 1950s and 1960s and the general increase in the region's suburban population, they also benefited from the growing number of predominantly "black" districts created under the Voting Rights Act. With Democratic black voters siphoned from the constituencies of "moderate" white Democrats the stage was set for the sweeping Republican gains of 1994 and for the emergence of Southern Republicans as the key figures within a transformed Republican Party. In many ways the "Contract with America" was little more than a wish list for this New South suburban constituency.

In reviewing the factors that shaped a new Republican majority, it is clear that many of these operated North and South.[19] There was one additional factor in the shaping of a Republican South that did seem particularly (if not uniquely) "Southern": the critical role of a politicized religious constituency. The full story of the growing role evangelicals—particularly Southern evangelicals—played in the transformation of regional politics in the 1970s and 1980s is complex. One thing is clear: this political development caught most pundits by surprise. Beginning with the publication of William Buckley's scathing attack on irreligious liberalism in the Ivy League (*God and Man at Yale*, 1954) and particularly after the establishment of the flagship conservative magazine the *National Review* in 1955, mainline "secular" conservatives appeared on the radar screen of political pundits and journalists, even if they were often dismissed as marginal gadflies. As late as the mid-1970s, however, sophisticated Americans tended to dismiss religious ultraconservatism as a part of America's cultural past. Hadn't Clarence Darrow finally put that nonsense to rest in the 1925 Scopes trial?

But even in the case of Billy Graham, the father of modern American evangelism, political pronouncements—particularly anticommunist rhetoric—had often preceded the altar call for repentance and conversion. During the 1950s Graham laced his sermons with warnings of the dangers of Godless communism. Karl Marx, he told a California crusade, was a "degenerate materialist" whose perverted philosophy had culminated in the "filthy, corrupt, ungodly, unholy doctrine of world socialism." He called for "internal security" investigations to expose the "pinks, the lavenders and the reds who have sought refuge beneath the wings of the American Eagle."[20] Even further to the right than Graham were Joseph Welch's John Birch Society, the Reverend Carl McIntire's Twentieth Century Reformation Hour, Dr. Fred Schwarz's Christian Anti-Communism Crusade, the Reverend Billy James Hargis's Christian Crusade, Edgar Bundy's Church League of America, and other lesser lights. In rallies, revivals, "seminars," sponsored radio and television broadcasts, and dozens of magazines and newsletters, they promoted the theme elaborated by Joseph McCarthy in his heyday: America was under moral siege from the threat of communism that had crept into this nation under the guise of liberalism. Over and over they hammered away at their main argument: liberalism equaled socialism; socialism equaled communism; therefore, liberalism was only two precarious steps away from a treasonous embrace with the communist menace.

The right-wing televangelists foreshadowed the coming upsurge of religious fundamentalism in American politics. In a movement almost ignored by academics and journalists, these resurgent religious fundamentalists had begun to overtake mainline Protestant denominations in numbers even as they created their loose-knit network of orthodox "Bible" colleges, publishing houses, and radio and television media outlets. Although most Southern Protestants, fundamentalist and "moderate" alike, were still conditioned to avoid active involvement in politics, those restraints weakened through the 1960s. There were many factors that led these religious leaders and their followers to enlist in the cause of political conservatism. As the civil rights movement expanded in the 1960s to inspire the women's rights movement, the antiwar movement, and the politics of sexual liberation, journalists might greet this growing counterculture with curiosity, even approval, but millions of deeply conservative religious Americans, North and South, despised the civil rights agitators, the antiwar demonstrators, and the sexual exhibitionists as symbols of a fundamental decline in the traditional cultural compass of God, family, and country.

White evangelicals in the South were already angry with Northern liberals and federal authorities over their role in promoting integration. By the mid-1970s it was no longer politically correct to complain of the courts' role in promoting racial amalgamation. But with court decisions sanctioning abortion, forbidding prayer in the public schools, and protecting the rights of foul-mouthed exhibitionists like Larry Flynt, religious Southerners found it easy to shift their grievances to complaints that the national government, dominated by secular liberals, promoted godlessness and immorality. But there was another precipitating incident, often overlooked, that seems to have been equally important in promoting evangelical political activism: the United States Internal Revenue Service's 1978 proposal to challenge the tax exempt status of the growing number of Christian academies on the grounds of racial discrimination. Between 1970 and 1980, while public school enrollment in the South declined over 10 percent, the number of students in "independent" Christian schools doubled. By 1985, 2.5 million students attended 17,000 Christian academies. Most of these schools were in the South; most were all-white.[21]

It is not fair to say that the growth of the Christian schools can only be explained as a manifestation of racism, but this development certainly represented the complex blending of racial, cultural, and religious fears that drove this growing evangelical majority. As English journalist Geoffrey Hodgson summarized these events, the IRS challenge to the evangelical school movement "shattered the Christian community's notion that Christians could isolate themselves inside their own institutions and teach what they pleased." As they came to realize that there was no safe haven—at least not one that was tax-exempt—their anger fused with their longtime conviction that "government is too powerful and intrusive." This linkage, argues Hodgson (and other observers), is what made evangelicals active.[22] Within weeks the Internal Revenue Service received over 120,000 letters of protest, more complaints than on any subject in history. The Congress—responding to the political pressure—moved to strike down the IRS proposals. Within a year a half dozen evangelical political action committees had emerged, led by Jerry Falwell's "Moral Majority."

These groups played an important role throughout the nation in supporting Ronald Reagan in 1980, and, thereafter, they were overwhelmingly committed to the conservative wing of the Republican Party. But their greatest impact was in the South. Through the 1980s and into the 1990s the number of individuals who defined themselves as "evangelicals" or "fundamentalists" never reached more than 10 percent outside the region, but they amounted to over 40 percent of the Southern electorate. Moreover, while these evangelicals were much less likely to take an active role in politics, under the leadership of Pat Robertson's "Christian Coalition" their level of registration and political participation steadily climbed during the 1980s until it substantially exceeded that of the population as a whole.

To summarize: racial conflict, the emergence of a dominant cultural secular ethos, and the creation of a new suburban conservative constituency reinforced an earlier tradition of ultraconservatism within the South. Given the critical role that these regional Republicans came to play in the national party, it would seem logical to see this development as a major force in pushing the GOP toward an increasingly conservative, even reactionary, stance in American politics: in short, the "Southernization" of American politics. It is certainly a theme with longstanding appeal. From antebellum abolitionists' fear of the slave power to Northern liberals' 1960s lament over the role of white Southerners in exporting racism to the rest of the country, this is a longstanding tradition. In a broader context, I used it myself in attempting to describe the impact of Alabama Governor George Wallace upon American politics.[23] But John Egerton, who initially coined the phrase, was more accurate when he linked two developments: the "Americanization of Dixie and the Southernization of America." In viewing Southern politics during the last quarter century we can see a dialectical process in which the broader currents of modern political conservatism have moved back and forth across the Mason and Dixon line, much like the old college roommates in Birmingham. The network of right-wing publications (the *National Review,* the *Spectator, Commentary*) and the foundations and think tanks established since the 1960s (the Manhattan Institute and the Heritage, John Locke, Bradley, Smith Richardson, Olin, Earhart, and Carthage Foundations) have formed one stream of the new conservatism, and the vast network of evangelical institutions the other, symbolized by such groups as the Moral Majority and the Christian Coalition. Flowing together, they have reshaped the face of American politics, North and South.

For that shrinking band of liberals, particularly Southern academic liberals, there is a longing to imagine a history that might have taken a different course. In his recent survey of the South from 1945 to 1980, for example, Numan Bartley argues that the civil rights movement made a fundamental mistake in following Gunnar Myrdal's emphasis upon racism as a "matter of right and wrong—rather than the product of socioeconomic and ideological forces." In the late 1940s and early 1950s, argues Bartley, national liberals abandoned their previous emphasis upon their concerns for "economic reform and for the redistribution of wealth" and increasingly identified "national and international corporate expansion with the growth of democratic values." The South, which had been considered the nation's number one economic problem in the 1930s, became the nation's number one "moral problem" in the context of the cold war. The end result was to link civil rights with a "comprehensive hostility toward the South," which was increasingly seen as the root of all violence and racial bigotry in American society.[24]

Unfortunately, desegregation often placed the greatest demands upon the white Southern working class, (middle- and upper-middle-class suburban whites were safely out of harm's way). Almost inevitably, this beleaguered group became the villains of the moral tableaux that played out on national television. The central tragedy, concluded Bartley, was that "many lower-income whites blamed blacks rather than the system."[25] Implicit in Bartley's analysis is the suggestion that, if liberals had maintained their emphasis on class rather than racial solidarity, the divisions between black and white within the region might have been minimized. However appealing this analysis might appear, it is hard to avoid a sense of fatalism in viewing the events of the 1940s and 1950s. Labor advocates of class solidarity were never very successful in bridging racial division in the modern South, and the labor movement itself had already gone into decline well before the heyday of the civil rights movement.

This is not to say that the new conservatism is not without internal tensions. For years, analysts of the new right have predicted the break up of this ungainly coalition of moral zealots and advocates of right-wing economics, what one journalist has called the clash between "traditionalist-authoritarians" and "libertarian-capitalists."[26] As recently as 1988 Steve Bruce, a religious sociologist at the Queen's University of Belfast, went so far as to title his book, *The Rise and Fall of the New Christian Right*.[27] And, whatever the continuing strength of the so-called "social" issues, circumstances would seem ripe for a swing of the political pendulum away from the economic dogmas that have dominated the thinking of American policy makers since the Reagan years. After all, during the twelve years of the Reagan-Bush administrations, the median wage earner in the United States saw his or her income decline 5 percent in real dollars after adjustments for inflation. During the same year, taxpayers in the top 5 percent saw their income increase nearly 30 percent, while the top 1 percent fared even better: their earnings rose 78 percent.[28] By the time of the 1994 election, the top 20 percent of American households received 55 percent of after-tax income and owned 85 percent of the country's marketable wealth. And the closer to the top of the income pyramid, the greater the increases. Between 1983 and 1994 national net worth rose $6.5 trillion dollars; the top .5 percent of America's population received over half this amount. By the mid-1990s, the top 1 percent of Americans controlled over 40 percent of the nation's wealth, an imbalance in national income and resources not seen since the 1930s.[29]

While these gloomy developments were first noted by a dwindling handful of traditional liberals, even conservatives like Robert Heady, publisher of one of the nation's largest banking magazines, has warned fellow-conservatives to take their eyes off the Wall Street bull market and focus instead on the "biggest economic threat" facing the nation: "the widening gap between the haves and have-nots."[30] The growing awareness of that imbalance was reflected as well in the three to one support Americans—North and South—gave to the United Teamsters' Union in their August 1997 strike against the United Parcel Service. (When the flight controllers went on strike in 1981, less than 20 percent of the American people backed the controllers' union, PATCO, and Ronald Reagan felt free to destroy the union, setting a pattern for the rest of the decade). Despite these straws in the wind, the prospects for a political shift to the left seem more remote than ever. Perhaps the leading Republican strategist of the 1994 campaign was right when he said: "Newt grasped the essential cultural revolt [of the 1980s and 1990s]. Middle-class people are not against rich people—they're against funding poor people."[31] And that is a view particularly consistent with the suburban constituencies of the New South. Nor is there much evidence of a rising political upheaval in the working-class and lower-middle-class white communities of the region where racial, cultural, and social issues have often played a more important role than economic self-interest. For white religious conservatives there is also the possibility for enlisting black Southerners—who share many of these conservative social positions—into their crusade to restore "traditional" values.[32]

The greatest force for conservatism may be the political cynicism that runs throughout American society, a cynicism that is nowhere more pervasive than in the American South where levels of voter participation are the lowest in the nation. In the 1880s and 1890s Southern conservatives used violence and various legal maneuvers to truncate the electorate. In the 1980s and 1990s much the same has been accomplished without the need for legal or extralegal activities. Less than half of the Southern electorate bothers to go to the polls. What is striking is the makeup of the current electorate. According to data gathered in the 1996 election, the most prosperous 20 percent of Southern voters made up 34 percent of the electorate, only 1 percent less than the economic bottom half of voters within the region.

A World Turned Upside Down

Tensions there will undoubtedly be, and the national political pendulum may swing back from the right, but the firm foundation of a Republican South is likely to act as a ballast tilting American politics away from the liberal activist state of the 1933–1968 era. As the politics of the American South have turned upside down, it has helped to insure that those of the nation will land right-side up.

Notes

1. Charles Murray, *Losing Ground: American Social Policy, 1950–1980* (New York: Basic Books, 1984), pp. 227–28.

2. Charles Murray and Richard J. Herrnstein, *The Bell Curve* (New York: Free Press, 1994), pp. 360, 549.

3. V. O. Key, *Southern Politics in State and Nation* (New York: Alfred A. Knopf, 1949).

4. The one exception is 1920, when the border state of Tennessee narrowly voted Republican. Key, *Southern Politics,* p. 10.

5. Key, *Southern Politics,* pp. 7–8.

6. Key, *Southern Politics,* p. 9

7. John Egerton, *Speak Now against the Day: The Generation before the Civil Rights Movement in the South* (New York: Alfred A. Knopf, 1994), p. 339.

8. Figures on the shifting congressional and state political tide have been compiled from the *Congressional Quarterly, Washington Information Directory, 1997–1998;* from R. R. Bowker's, *Who's Who in American Politics, 1995–96;* and from Earl Black and Merle Black, *Politics and Society in the South* (Cambridge: Harvard University Press, 1987).

9. The best account of this linkage is in Wayne Addison Clark, "An Analysis of the Relationship between Anti-Communism and Segregationist Thought in the Deep South, 1948–1964" (Ph.D. diss., University of North Carolina at Chapel Hill, 1976).

10. In their book, *Who Rules Georgia,* Calvin Kytle and Jamie Mackay publish an extensive series of interviews they conducted in 1948. Collectively, these interviews offer a revealing insight into the receptive attitudes most white Georgians had to these arguments. (Athens: University of Georgia Press, 1998). Patricia Sullivan best describes the consequences of this devastating attack throughout the region in the last chapter of her book *Days of Hope: Race and Democracy in the New Deal Era* (Chapel Hill: University of North Carolina Press, 1996).

11. *Norris v. Alabama,* 294 US 589–98 (1935). As I note in my study of the Scottsboro case, the ruling had little immediate effect in the wake of Southern officials' continued resistance, but it marked a turning point in the Court's attitude. Carter, *Scottsboro: A Tragedy of the American South,* 2d ed. (Baton Rouge: Louisiana State University Press, 1979), pp. 322–24.

12. The best general account of the court's shifting movement on race remains Richard Kluger, *Simple Justice* (New York: Alfred A. Knopf, 1976).

13. Black and Black, *Politics and Society in the South,* p. 85. Almost every recent study of the civil rights movement points to the 1940s as a critical period in the movement.

See Charles Payne, *I've Got the Light of Freedom: The Organization Tradition and the Mississippi Freedom Struggle* (Berkeley: University of California Press, 1995). For a southwide view, the best account is John Egerton, *Speak Now Against the Day*.

14. Numan Bartley, *The Rise of Massive Resistance* (Baton Rouge: Louisiana State University Press, 1969).

15. Dan T. Carter, *The Politics of Rage: George Wallace, the Origins of the New Conservatism and the Transformation of American Politics* (New York: Simon and Schuster, 1995).

16. William Schneider, "The Suburban Century Begins," *Atlantic Monthly*, July 1992, p. 37.

17. Bernard Cosman and Robert Huckshorn, eds., *Republican Politics: The 1964 Campaign and Its Aftermath for the Party* (New York: Praeger, 1968).

18. Cosman and Huckshorn, eds., *Republican Politics*, pp. 242–43.

19. That was one of the main themes of the influential study of recent politics in Thomas Byrne Edsall and Mary D. Edsall, *Chain Reaction: The Impact of Race, Rights, and Taxes on American Politics* (New York: W. W. Norton, 1991).

20. Graham's anticommunism and his vague hints of internal subversion always remained within the American mainstream. Like other twentieth-century evangelicals, he used the rise of communism as an object lesson, showing America's fall from grace and its descent from a lost arcadia of small towns and small town values to the "cesspool" of modern secularism. Marshall Frady, *Billy Graham*, (Boston: Little, Brown, 1979), 235–37.

21. There are dozens of works on the rise of the religious right. Some of the more useful are Steve Bruce, *The Rise and Fall of the New Christian Right: Conservative Protestant Politics in America, 1978–1988* (New York: Oxford University Press, 1988); Gillian Peele, *Revival and Reaction: The Right in Contemporary America* (Oxford: Oxford University Press, 1984); Leo P. Ribuffo, *The Old Christian Right: The Protestant Far Right from the Great Depression to the Cold War* (Philadelphia: Temple University Press, 1983); Michael Lienesch, *Redeeming America: Piety and Politics in the New Christian Right* (Chapel Hill: University of North Carolina Press, 1993); and Alan Crawford, *Thunder on the Right: The "New Right" and the Politics of Resentment* (New York: Pantheon Press, 1980).

22. Godfrey Hodgson, *The World Turned Right Side Up: A History of the Conservative Ascendancy in America* (Boston: Houghton Mifflin, 1996), p. 178.

23. As English journalist Godfrey Hodgson recently concluded: white Southerners in general and white Southern Republicans in particular have reshaped national politics so that "the rest of the country has become more like the South." Hodgson, *The World Turned Right Side Up*, p. 297.

24. Numan V. Bartley, *The New South, 1945–1980* (Baton Rouge: Louisiana State University Press, 1995), pp. 66–69.

25. Bartley, *The New South*, p. 279.

26. Hodgson, *The World Turned Right Side Up*, p. 312.

27. Steve Bruce, *The Rise and Fall of the New Christian Right: Conservative Protestant Politics in America, 1978–1988* (New York: Oxford University Press, 1988).

28. John Cassidy, "Who Killed the Middle Class?" *New Yorker,* October 16, 1995, p. 113. Ironically, Kevin Phillips, one of the most influential Republican strategists of the 1960s and 1970s, became the most unsparing critic of the economic consequences of the Republican revolution in his book *The Politics of Rich and Poor: Wealth and the American Electorate in the Reagan Aftermath* (New York: Random House, 1990).

29. *New York Times,* April 17, 1995, p. 1; Paul Krugman, "What the Public Doesn't Know Can't Hurt Us," *Washington Monthly,* October 1995, p. 8.

30. In his nationally syndicated business column, Heady pointed out that, over the past twenty years, the "average income of the wealthiest 5 percent of Americans soared more than 54 percent," while the bottom rungs of the nation's ladder barely stayed even. *Atlanta Journal-Constitution,* September 7, 1997, sec. E, p. 6.

31. Connie Bruch, "Profile: The Politics of Perception," *New Yorker,* October 9, 1995, p. 62.

32. I am skeptical that black Southerners—however conservative in their social views—are going to support the full panoply of far-right economic positions taken by the Christian Coalition and other right-wing religious activists. Still, it is worth noting that a recent poll of black and white Americans found that more blacks than whites supported the "voucher" educational program under which public monies would be channeled into private schools—a pet project of the religious right.

Part II

The Changing State of Mind

Recorded and Unrecorded Histories

Recent Southern Writing and Social Change

Richard Gray

In 1983, the critic Fred Hobson complained that, "if pondering and examining the mind and soul of Dixie had seemed a Southern affliction before 1945," since then it had "assumed epidemic proportions." The historian George Brown Tindall agreed. During the sixties, seventies, and eighties, he suggested, conferences and symposia on the "changing South" had become "one of the flourishing minor industries of the region."[1] I have no great desire to add to the deluge of books variously titled *The Lasting South, The Everlasting South, Why the South Will Survive*—or, alternatively, *The Changing South, An Epitaph for Dixie, Look Away from Dixie,* or *The Americanization of Dixie: The Southernization of America.* Still, it is perhaps necessary to emphasize a few fundamental points. It has always been difficult to talk about the South in singular, monolithic terms (no matter how hard some Southerners have tried to do so) because, like any culture, the South was always plural, made up of a number of conflicting classes, castes, and interests and was hardly frozen in time. Now, with the growth of cultural pluralism and the accelerating nature of social and economic development, it has become impossible. Over the past few decades, the South has changed dramatically in terms of its day-to-day social and economic life and its mental and moral habits have, at the very least, been challenged. The nature of the material alterations is, perhaps, clearer now than it was twenty or even ten years ago. "Prior to 1940," Leonard Reissman has written, "the South could fairly be described, with one or two states excepted, as a predominantly rural region here and there dotted with cities." By the 1980s, by contrast, the South could be defined by another historian, James Cobb, as a "conservative capitalist's dream come true."[2] By then the Southern workforce was just under one-half white male, just over one-third white female, just under 10 percent black male and just under 10 percent black female.

Richard Gray

The collapse of the plantation system, the dispersal of the mill villages, and the breakdown of other places of settled employment left white males exposed to the demands of the market. The civil rights movement and consequent federal legislation allowed blacks to become a more active and fluid—if still significantly disadvantaged—part of the labor force. And the women's movement, together with the crumbling of traditional structures, opened up female access to the marketplace. In effect, the changes in the material fabric of Southern society between the 1940s and the 1980s confirmed the transfer to the market economy and completed the commodification of most of the adult population of the South. In the words of one Southern historian, writing in 1995: "A dynamic free-flowing work force unburdened by labor union membership, unity, or much in the way of state protection or social legislation complemented the drive for economic growth while it undermined family, community, and the spiritual aspects of religion."[3] One does not have to agree with the assumptions evident in this description (for example, the implication that union membership is a "burden") in order to accept its assessment of the way things have gone. For good or ill, the Southern economy has become part of the global marketplace. Or, as one unsympathetic commentator has put it, "the South has been laboring mightily to re-create itself into a tinfoil-twinkling simulation of Southern California."[4]

Laboring mightily, it may be, but not too hard: the paradox remains that, despite exposure to the marketplace and material change, many Southerners—and, in particular, many *white* Southerners—continue to resist, are still entrenched in difference. The figure of entrenchment is chosen advisedly. "Southerners feel," the historian Charles Lerche observed in 1964, "that they are struggling against an open conspiracy and a totally hostile environment." Five years after this another commentator, Sheldon Hackney, added the comment that "the Southern identity has been linked from the first to a siege mentality."[5] And when, in 1986, the sociologist John Shelton Reed came to write a concluding note to a new edition of his seminal book, *The Enduring South,* he found similar feelings of being marginalized, and even threatened, still at work among white Southerners. More to the point, the data accumulated for the new edition only confirmed what he had claimed when *The Enduring South* first appeared fourteen years earlier. "Cultural differences that were largely due to Southerners' lower incomes and educational levels," Reed explained, and "to their predominantly rural and small-town residence," these differences, he said, "were smaller in the 1960s than they had been in the past, and they are smaller still in the 1980s." "A few" of the differences, he added, "have vanished altogether."

On the other hand, the differences that Reed labeled "quasi-ethnic," because of their putative origins in the different histories of the American regions—these, or many of them, persisted. On the matters of localism, attitudes towards violence, gun ownership, and religion, *white* Southerners still revealed themselves to be different. In fact, if there appeared to be any significant change in mental maps between the 1960s and the 1980s, Reed commented, it was among non-Southerners. "Non-Southerners are becoming more like Southerners," Reed concluded, "in their tendency to find heroes and heroines in the local community, or even in the family," in "the conviction that individuals should have the right to arm themselves," and in their tendency "to have had the sort of religious experience that is theoretically central to Southern Protestantism."[6]

What has been called the "Southernization of America" over the past two or three decades suggests that one response to commodification, the globalization of the material life, is resistance and even a kind of cultural reversion: Americans, and not just Southerners, react to the blanding of America by subscribing to cultural values that simultaneously register their anxiety about change and measure their difference from the corporate ethos. A recent article in the *Economist* even claimed that "the 'primitive' values that east-coast liberals used to sneer at are now those of America."[7] This is surely too sweeping, but it underlines the point that surrender to the consensual values of the global village is not the only available option. On the contrary, Southerners have always shown how one viable response to feelings of being marginalized is to *build* on the margins, to root one's thinking precisely in the sense of being disempowered and different; and some non-Southerners, at least, appear now to be imitating them. John Shelton Reed put it more wryly. "I do not want to suggest that Americans are becoming privatistic, born-again, gun-slingers," he declared, "or that Southerners are." Nevertheless, he added, "perhaps there is a pattern here"[8]—a pattern of convergence, that is, quite different from the one that anticipated the South's simply becoming more like the rest of America.

Even a phrase like "the Southernization of America" is too simple, however, and in the end no more satisfactory than "the Americanization of the South." Non-Southerners have certainly gravitated towards Southern thinking in many ways. And those non-Southerners range from the anonymous people surveyed in *The Enduring South* to a distinguished historian of the political left, Eugene Genovese, who, in a recent book *The Southern Tradition,* appears to see the tradition of Southern conservatism as the only serious challenge now—with the collapse of communism—to what he terms "market-oriented bourgeois ideologies."[9] The situation is immensely complicated and enriched, however, by two factors: the selling of the South, sometimes as a kind of giant theme park or American version of the heritage industry, and our increasing sense of the pluralism of *any* culture including the Southern one. To take the selling of the

Richard Gray

South first: in Lee Smith's 1983 novel *Oral History,* the old family home place still stands, but it has become an appropriately decaying part of a successful theme park called Ghostland. Again, during an interview for the British Broadcasting Corporation in 1993, the jazz musician Wynton Marsalis, who is from New Orleans, explained, "I wasn't into jazz as a kid. I thought it was just shakin' your butt for the white tourists in the French Quarter."[10] Both Smith and Marsalis are making the same point about a very particular kind of commodification that turns the South itself—or, to be more exact, the idea or image of the South—into a product, a function of the marketplace. "Music is integral to our marketing plan," the director of the New Orleans tourist board declared. The company that manufactures Jack Daniel's bourbon now acts as a sponsor to the Faulkner conferences in Oxford, Mississippi. Popular films, like *Driving Miss Daisy, Doc Hollywood, My Cousin Vinnie,* and *Fried Green Tomatoes,* for all their obvious differences, all play upon the idea of the South as a provincial, peripheral, backward but essentially "homey" place. And, of course, we are all familiar with advertisements—frequently for alcohol—that play upon the idea of the South as both exotic and authentic—exempt, somehow, from both the banality and the artificiality of the everyday urban world. The ironies of Southern history have always run deep, and surely one of the deepest in recent times is this curious case of change within continuity within change. Some aspects of the South retain their grip on the imagination despite the economic metamorphosis of the region, but then that drift towards the past, that undertow of resistance itself becomes a saleable asset. The legends of the South are not necessarily dying, nor being fiercely protected or even resurrected. In some cases they are merely being turned into cash.

The question that attaches itself to any debate of this nature concerning change, continuity, and commodification is, What *kind* of South we are talking about? Is it the South, for instance, of Lee Smith or the South of Wynton Marsalis that is in the process of being sold? A question like that has always lurked at the back of any attempt to chart Southern thinking: but the drawing of the mental maps of the region has become acutely challenging in the past few years with the growth of cultural pluralism. Makers of the South and things Southern whose achievements previously tended to be ignored or minimized for reasons of caste and/or gender now come much more into debate and play. They range from popular novelists like Margaret Mitchell, through blues singers and jazz musicians, to those numerous and frequently anonymous men and women who have resurrected and reshaped the traditions of African art in the region. Just as much to the point is our vastly expanded sense now of exactly what "making" a culture involves: the recognition that a culture expresses and in fact creates itself by a variety of means—that include the individual book or essay, but go far beyond this to incorporate the artefacts of everyday life and the endless products of mass culture, the voice perhaps heard in passing on the radio or images flickering on a screen. What emerges with particular power is the possibility that even the process of commodification, the turning of an image of the South or a regional icon into a marketable asset, may be regarded as playing an integral part in the making of a culture. After all, whether anyone likes it or not, Southerners are "known" to themselves and others through the mass media, among many other forms of communication. And what emerges with even more power is that our perception of the South must now, more even than before, acknowledge the various and often antagonistic influences and energies that go into it: we are faced with not so much Southern culture, as Southern *cultures*.

It is between those cultures that Southerners continue to live—and, not least among those Southerners, the writers. They are living between them, too, in a double sense. In the regional context they are caught between the conflicting interests and voices that constitute the region and the regional debate, all of them demanding recognition and power. Similarly, on the national and even international stage they betray intense uncertainty about whether to become assimilated or to resist: Southern books, in particular, very often become a site of struggle between, on the one hand, the culture(s) of the South and, on the other, the culture of the global marketplace. As a matter of general practice, this is perhaps not quite as extraordinary as it may sound. After all, as Fredric Jameson has argued, historical epochs are not monolithically integrated social formations, but, on the contrary, complex *overlays* of different methods of production that serve as the bases of different social groups and classes and consequently of their worldviews. It is because of this that, in *any* given epoch, a variety of kinds of antagonism can be discerned, conflict between different interest groups. One culture may well be dominant, but there will also be—to borrow Raymond Williams's useful terms—a residual culture, formed in the past but still active in the cultural process, and an emergent culture, prescribing new meanings and practices.

Writers, in effect, like any other members of any society, are not the victim of some totalizing structure, since—to quote Williams—"no dominant culture ever in reality includes or exhausts all human practice, human energy and human intention."[11] They are therefore able to insert themselves in the space between conflicting interests and practices and then dramatize the contradictions the conflict engenders. Through their work, by means of a mixture of voices, a free play of different languages and even genres, they can represent the reality of their culture, as multiple, complex, and internally antagonistic. They can achieve a realization of both synchrony and diachrony: a demonstration, on the one hand, of structural continuities between past and present and, on the other, of the processes by which those continuities are challenged, dissolved and reconstituted. So they have more of a chance than many other members of their society of realizing what Hayden White has called "the human capacity to endow lived contradictions with intimations of their possible transcendence."[12] They have the opportunity, in other words, of getting "into" history, to participate in its processes, and, in a perspectival sense at least, getting "out" of it too—and so enabling us to begin to understand just how those processes work.

All of this may sound a bit abstract. But it is only a way of making what, I believe, are two fairly basic, concrete, and specific points. First, the crisis in which the South finds itself now is not really that peculiar. Stability as a social condition is an illusion, the preserve of pastoral dream and utopian literature. At some moments, the pace of change may well accelerate—thanks to such factors as the information revolution of the past twenty years—but change is the one constant, guaranteeing the plural character of any culture. And second, if any group is likely to help us understand the exact forms that change has engendered in the contemporary South, the conflicting forces at work at present there, it is the writers, precisely because of the chance their writing gives them to live both "in" and "out" of history—and then communicate that understanding to us.

This is not the place to embark on a survey of recent Southern writers and their representation of conflicts that go to make up the South now. But perhaps some idea of just how much we can learn from the writers can be suggested by pointing towards three different kinds of writerly practice often found in contemporary Southern writing—which, for the sake of simplicity and economy, I will identify with three different characters or possible *personae*: the expatriate, the maverick, and the homekeeper. Needless to say this does not begin to exhaust the different strategies employed by or available to Southern writers. The best of contemporary Southern writing (of which there is a great deal) generally offers a plurality of approaches. There are many ways to dramatize the slippage between old and new, a variety of means for revealing the edgy, richly various nature of Southern culture now. Most good texts use several; these three *personae* merely suggest some of them.

The writing practice of the expatriate is implicit in his or her change of locality: Richard Ford has moved to the Northwest, James Wilcox has gone to New York, Alice Walker to the West Coast, and Cormac McCarthy to the Southwest and the Mexican border. With the change of locale has come an alteration in the fictional landscape and a shift in perspective—Wilcox, for instance, has started writing about Louisianians displaced in New York (in *Polite Sex*) or New Yorkers marooned in Louisiana (in *Sort of Rich*). The case of Cormac McCarthy is perhaps more complicated and more interesting.

McCarthy's early works are indelibly attached to the traditions of his region: serving to illustrate the point that, while Southerners did not invent Original Sin, they often appeared to have taken out the American patent. And his books have been admired by other writers for some time, particularly writers from the South like Larry Brown and Barry Hannah. But he began to receive more widespread recognition only after he moved into the Southwest and the Mexican border country and made that, rather than Tennessee, the site of his fiction. That shift in locality has also often been characterized as a shift in allegiances. The shadowy presence of Faulkner, it is said, or Flannery O'Connor in books like *Child of God,* has been supplanted by that of another literary father-figure entirely, Ernest Hemingway. Things are not as simple as that, however. Certainly, McCarthy has moved literally and figuratively from the claustrophobic landscapes that characterized his first few novels. But, as this passage from *All the Pretty Horses* surely illustrates, those landscapes still haunt him, he has taken something of the South and of Faulkner with him, where he has gone:

> In the evening he saddled his horse and rode out west from the house.... At the hour he'd always choose when the shadows were long and the ancient road was shaped before him in the rose and canted light like a dream of the past where the painted ponies and the riders of that lost nation came down out of the north with their faces chalked and their long hair plaited and each armed for war which was their life.... When the wind was in the north you could hear them, ... the young boys naked on wild horses jaunty as circus riders ... and the dogs trotting with their tongues aloll and foot-slaves following half naked and sorely burdened and above all the low chant of their traveling song which the riders sang as they rode, nation and ghost of a nation passing in a soft chorale across that mineral waste to darkness bearing lost to all history and all their remembrance like a grail the sum of their secular and transitory and violent lives.[13]

Prose like this moves to the old, ineradicable rhythms of Faulknerian speech and conjures up that sense of the immanence of the past in the present that is perhaps the signature, the characterizing mark of Southern writing. True, the landscape is different in some of its particulars; equally true, the prose elsewhere in the book offers a fresh, unfamiliar mix of anglicisms and the Hispanic that indicates a change of imaginative register and attention. *All the Pretty Horses* is not as embedded in the South as McCarthy's earlier work is; some of the relevant comparisons here may be to Hemingway, and, even more, to those postcolonial writers who have learned from Faulkner and then transplanted what they have learned—people like the Colombian novelist Gabriel Garcia Marquez or the Australian writer Tim Winton. All of that is simply to

Richard Gray

say that there is both change and continuity here. In its own way—which is, of course, unique to it—McCarthy's more recent work exposes the mixed, plural medium that the South and Southerners inhabit: that process of innovation and restitution, escape and recovery, that turns every day into a crossing of borders.

A different kind of relationship to Faulkner—the writer whom Flannery O'Connor famously referred to as "the Dixie Limited"—and, by extension, to the residual culture of the South, is suggested by the people I have called the mavericks. By this I mean writers like Barry Hannah, Blanche McCrary Boyd, and Harry Crews. Here, too, the sense of distancing, loosening the ties with the past of the region—and, in particular, its literary past—is unmistakable. In one of his novels, *Karate Is a Thing of the Spirit,* Harry Crews goes so far as to use the greatest of all Southern writers, William Faulkner, as a kind of running joke: a way of commenting, among other things, on professional Southerners, the institutionalization of Southern literature, and the welcoming of Southern writers into the literary pantheon of the good and the great. The central character, a drifter called John Kaimon always wears a jersey with Faulkner's face embroidered on it. And, when asked why he does so, he simply replies, "I come from Oxford, Mississippi, so I keep the face of Faulkner around." "If I was a Catholic," he goes on, "I'd wear a Saint Christopher medal. I knew a Hell's Angel that wouldn't get on his bike without a Saint Christopher. But he was a fucking Catholic. He could afford it. I'm not a Catholic. I'm from Oxford, Mississippi."[14] Of course, Kaimon has never read any of Faulkner's books. His girlfriend, though, vaguely remembers that she had "a whole month of Faulkner" at high school, on a book she never got around to looking at, called, she thinks, "the fury of sound." "They say Faulkner wrote over twenty books!" Kaimon tells his girlfriend in "a savage whisper." "That's *twenty*. Have you ever actually *looked* in a book?" he asks her, "I mean really looked? All them little words there. All them letters. Did you ever think what that might take out of a man? Have you ever thought about sitting down with a pencil and copying a book? Just word for word, writing it down on another piece of paper?"[15] Kaimon has, he reveals. "I copied the first twenty pages of a book called *The Sound and the Fury,*" he declares, "and saw that it was impossible. It was there in front of me so it was true, a fact, but impossible." Crews is clearly making a series of not so sly digs here at anyone who might want to continue the Southern tradition by simply "copying" Faulkner and turning him into an icon. In their very different ways, both character and author sense that to write in the way of the grand old man of Southern letters now is not really possible. The Dixie Limited would simply run over them, and crush them, if they tried.

Still, for all his jokes about professional Southerners, Crews turns out to be a maverick, a rebel of a peculiarly Southern kind. "I come from a people who believe the home place is as vital and necessary as the beating of your heart," Crews has admitted in a book called *A Childhood: The Biography of a Place*. "It is your anchor in the world," he goes on, "that memory of your kinsmen at the long supper table every night and the knowledge that it would always exist, if nowhere but in memory."[16] The undertow of memory is, in fact, constantly there in Crews's work. His very first novel, for instance, *The Gospel Singer,* opens with the sentence "Enigma, Georgia, was a dead end," and then introduces us to a brooding, melancholy, stealthily disturbing small town that seems to have been relocated from Yoknapatawpha, Mississippi—or, for that matter, from the imaginative territory of Southern writers from Mark Twain to Carson McCullers and Truman Capote. Certainly, Crews's later novels leave places like Enigma to follow the route taken by the South recently, from the small town to the city or suburb and a surfeit of commodities. But, moving to the city, Crews then casts the kind of cold eye over the world of commodification that reminds us of just how much he owes to his literary as well as to his blood "kin." Here, for instance, is how he describes the main character, called Hickum Looney, in his 1995 novel, *The Mulching of America*. It occurs towards the beginning of the action:

> It had been a good day, an unprecedented day, for Hickum Looney. As he eased his dirty yellow dented Dodge through bumper-to-bumper traffic, he whistled a gay little tune, his favorite. It had been a Coca-Cola kind of day and he was whistling a Coca-Cola commercial from a good while back. . . . And he loved it so much, he invariably saved it for those days when sickness, suffering, death, and the rankest kind of blasphemy . . . opened every door he knocked upon. . . . Without quite being able to help it, he suddenly pushed back in his seat, stretched his neck, and sang: "Co-o-oke is the *re-al* thing." He pounded the steering wheel . . . and sang at the top of his voice: "And so is Hickum Looney!"[17]

By the end of the novel, Hickum Looney is about to be mulched by the company that employed him for twenty-five years as a door-to-door salesman. The company no longer has any use for him and so is turning him literally into what, in a figurative sense, he has always been: a product, a commodity—no more "real" than a popular brand of soft drink and perhaps in an odd sense slightly less so, because he is so unimportant to the systems of exchange. The world Looney and his kind inhabit is, of course, one unknown to earlier Southern writers. But the terms in which Crews chooses to expose that world to us tap a vein of freakish humor—comedy that dissects social change with a coldly comic scalpel—that begins with the writers of the old Southwest in the nineteenth century, passes through the Faulkner of *As I Lay Dying* and *The Mansion* as well as Erskine Caldwell, to Flannery O'Connor, a more recent innovator in Southern Gothic. Crews has acknowledged a debt to some of these writers; even if he had not, however, it would have been clear enough. At the very least, writers like Harry Crews remind us that to be a maverick is itself a sly way of admitting a regional allegiance. In some times and places to be a rebel and to be Southern have been one and the same—and, presumably, they will still continue to be.

A similarly fluid exchange between the different dimensions of Southern culture is to be found in the writers I have labeled the homekeepers. This label is not meant to denote an allegiance to domesticity or nostalgic drift. What I am referring to here is that tendency to be found in many contemporary Southern writers to react to the pluralism of their found world by attempting a kind of recuperation. They offer a searching—sometimes skeptical, sometimes hopeful—examination of the degree to which moral continuity is possible in a materially changed world. This examination can take many forms. The provincial social comedy that was a particular skill of earlier novelists like Ellen Glasgow is sustained in the work of, say, T. R. Pearson and Clyde Edgerton. Sustained but also altered, as even the most provincial backwater in the South feels the assault of mass culture and its new moralities.

Alternatively, many contemporary Southern novelists seem to be commemorating the tradition of Thomas Wolfe: by writing about growing up and growing away from the small-town South. Writers like Ferrol Sams, Pat Conroy, Ernest Gaines, and Thulani Davis quietly acknowledge the fact that the homes their young protagonists are growing away from are radically changing, even as they are. Still, whatever the form of their examination, these writers usually end up issuing a mixed verdict. There is tension, instability as their work engages with the shifting, plural kaleidoscope of life below the Mason and Dixon line. In *Rich in Love,* for instance, by Josephine Humphreys, the seventeen-year-old narrator Lucille Odom ends her account of the time when the marriage of her parents broke up with this observation: "Our family is not what it was, but we are all gravitating back into family lives of one sort and another; it is a drift that people cannot seem to help, in spite of lessons learned the hard way. . . . I think often of the ancient times, long before Latin, when words were new and had no connotations. Pure words stood for single things: 'Family' meant people in a house together. But that was in a language so far back that all its words are gone, a language we can only imagine."[18] It would be too easy to say that a word is being redefined here, or that a fundamental fact of Southern life, the family, is being reconstituted to accommodate it to radically altered circumstances. Nevertheless, this is part of the process that a writer like Humphreys is observing and imagining. The old cultures of the South may have expressed themselves in "a language we can only imagine": but they and the words they formulated are still there, running like a hidden stream beneath the new regional cultures. Those words connect us inexorably to the past even while they acquire a new edge, different dimensions of meaning; in short, they are the coinage—which is to say, the active medium and expression—of both past and present, continuity and change.

Words are not, of course, the monopoly of the writer, least of all the writer from the South. "We need to talk," Faulkner declared of Southerners once, "to tell, since oratory is our heritage";[19] the need to create and confirm identity and community through language may be something that makes human beings distinctively human, but Southerners—as Faulkner was by no means the first or the last to observe—seem to feel that need more intensely than most. People know themselves through words—who we are, where we are, and what we belong to have to be spoken into life—and this general truth seems to apply with particular ferocity in the South. Writers may be in a privileged position here, because of the free play of different writing practices available to them, but they are by no means uniquely privileged. Language, telling, gives us all the chance to be "in" history and "out" of it: to participate in the different levels and constant changes of our culture and to articulate them, to tell them to others and ourselves. What this rather abstract statement means is that I would not like to place my final emphasis just on *writing*—since it is not the only tool Southerners have used to invent and understand their localities, even if it is the one I have been concerned with here. Talking has been just as important. If the South has emerged as one of the determining concepts of American history and culture—one of the crucial ways in which significant groups of Americans, past and present, have attempted to make sense of their lives and changes—it is as a concept active in the everyday speech of communities as well as in written and published texts. "I liked history," Lucille Odom recalls of her younger self early on in *Rich in Love*, "I also felt strongly that history was a category comprising not only famous men of bygone eras, but *me, yesterday*. Wasn't I as mysterious as John C. Calhoun, and my own history worth investigating?"[20]

The history of the way the South has been created through language is there in the written texts. Writers like those I have termed the expatriates, the mavericks, and the homekeepers tell us with intense energy about the particular terms in which that history is being altered and recovered. But—as the best books by the best Southern writers remind us, and as that remark given to Lucille Odom quietly discloses—it is also there in the lives that remain unrecorded, in the voices that do not always manage to get heard.

Notes

1. Fred Hobson, *Tell about the South: The Southern Rage to Explain* (Baton Rouge: Louisiana State University Press, 1983), p. 297; George Brown Tindall, *The Ethnic Southerners* (Baton Rouge: Louisiana State University Press, 1976), p. 224.

2. James C. Cobb, "The Sunbelt South: Industrialization in Regional, National, and International Perspective," in *Searching for the Sunbelt: Historical Perspectives on a Region*, ed. Raymond A. Mohl (Knoxville: University of Tennessee Press, 1990), p. 39; Leonard Reissman, "Urbanization in the South," in *The South in Continuity and Change*, ed. John C. McKinney and Edgar T. Thompson (Durham, N.C.: Duke University Press, 1965), p. 79. See also, Gavin Wright, *Old South, New South: Revolutions in the Southern Economy since the Civil War* (New York: Basic Books, 1986), p. 50; David R. Goldfield, "The City as Southern History: The Past and the Promise of Tomorrow," in *The Future South: A Historical Perspective for the Twenty-First Century*, ed. Joe P. Dunn and Howard L. Preston (Urbana: University of Illinois Press, 1991), pp. 29–40.

3. Numan V. Bartley, *The New South 1945–1980* (Baton Rouge: Louisiana State University Press, 1947–95), pp. 468–69.

4. Marshall Frady, *Southerners: A Journalist's Odyssey* (New York: New American Library, 1980), pp. 281–82.

5. Charles Lerche, *The Uncertain South: Its Changing Patterns of Politics in Foreign Policy* (Chicago: Quadrangle Books, 1964), p. 243; Sheldon Hackney, "Southern Violence," *American Historical Review* 74 (1969): 924.

6. John Shelton Reed, "Afterword, 1986: Still Enduring?" in *The Enduring South: Subcultural Persistence in Mass Society* (1972; Chapel Hill: University of North Carolina Press, 1986 edition), p. 100. See also p. 91.

7. "A Survey of the American South," *Economist*, December 10, 1994, p. 18.

8. Reed, "Afterword, 1986," p. 100.

9. Eugene D. Genovese, *The Southern Tradition: The Achievement and Limitations of an American Conservatism* (Cambridge, Mass.: Harvard University Press, 1994), p. 2.

10. Wynton Marsalis, BBC 3 interview, September 11, 1993, cited by Connie Zeanah Atkinson, "'Shakin' Your Butt for the Tourist': Music's Role in the Identification and Selling of New Orleans," in *Dixie Debates: Perspectives on Southern Cultures*, ed. Richard H. King and Helen Taylor (New York: New York University Press, 1996), p. 155. See also p. 154.

11. Raymond Williams, *Marxism and Literature* (Oxford: Oxford University Press, 1977), p. 126. See also Fredric Jameson, *The Political Unconscious: Narrative as a Socially Symbolic Act* (Ithaca, N.Y.: Cornell University Press, 1981).

12. Hayden White, "Getting Out of History," in *Tropics of Discourse: Essays in Cultural Criticism* (Baltimore, Md.: Johns Hopkins University Press, 1978), p. 17.

13. Cormac McCarthy, *All the Pretty Horses* (New York: Knopf, 1992), p. 5. James Wilcox, *Sort of Rich* (New York: Harper & Row, 1989), and *Polite Sex* (New York: Harper Collins, 1991).

14. Harry Crews, *Karate Is a Thing of the Spirit* (New York: Quill, 1971), p.80. See Flannery O'Connor, "Some Aspects of the Grotesque in Southern Fiction," in *Mystery*

and Manners, ed. Sally Fitzgerald and Robert Fitzgerald (New York: Farrar, Straus, Giroux, 1972), p. 45.

15. Crews, *Karate Is a Thing of the Spirit,* p.141. See also, p. 79.

16. Harry Crews, *A Childhood: The Biography of a Place* (New York: Quill, 1978), reprinted in *Classic Crews: A Harry Crews Reader* (New York: Poseidon Press, 1993), p. 31.

17. Harry Crews, *The Mulching of America* (New York: Simon and Schuster, 1995), p. 22. See also, *The Gospel Singer* (1968; New York: Perennial Library, 1995 edition), p. 7. *Car* was first published in 1972.

18. Josephine Humphreys, *Rich in Love* (1988; New York: Viking, 1992 edition), p. 260.

19. William Faulkner, "An Introduction to *The Sound and the Fury,*" *Mississippi Quarterly* 26 (1973): 412.

20. Humphreys, *Rich in Love,* pp. 46, 47.

The Southern Heritage and the Semiotics of Consumer Culture

Lothar Hönnighausen

In view of present-day tendencies towards regionalization in many areas of the world, manifesting themselves in the economic squabbles within the European Community and in the bloody ethnic strife in the Balkans and other former Eastern bloc countries, the question of the role of regions takes on a particular urgency. No less important is the impact of the conflicting pull of the tendencies toward "globalization" and "regionalization" on one hand, and toward "multiculturalism" and "ethnic identity" on the other. A region such as the South, which is not just a physiographic unit but a value-charged and symbolic space, remains relevant in our globalized world because it plays a major role in helping us define our identity.

This is the context in which I propose to deal with manifestations of Southern identity in recent Southern fiction. Among the several public images reflecting the clash between the collective experience of Southern tradition and a new all-American or globalist consumer culture, the Civil War is a particularly relevant one. As the Civil War, in memory and myth, has been one of the great unifying experiences shaping the Southern imagination, continuity and changes in people's attitude towards this key event deserve to be carefully registered. Although Southern identity reveals itself in many different and contradictory ways and in many layers and kinds of Southern culture, there is no doubt that contemporary regional fiction is a major indicator of the current state of Southern feelings. A brief comparison of the handling of the Civil War in past and present Southern literature illustrates this. The Civil War is the theme of the greatest twentieth-century American novel, William Faulkner's *Absalom, Absalom!* as well as the most popular, Margaret Mitchell's *Gone with the Wind,* both appeared in 1936, at the peak of Southern regionalism. These works, despite their great dissimilarity, have one trait in common: they give us the Civil War as an event of tragic dignity and undisputed relevance. Not only to Mitchell, the best-selling admirer of

The Southern Heritage and the Semiotics of Consumer Culture

the Southern past, but also to Faulkner, its critical explorer, it would have been unthinkable to make the Civil War the subject of irony, parody, and even farce. This is, however, the case in Bobbie Anne Mason's "Shiloh" (1982), in Clyde Edgerton's *Raney* (1985), in Barry Hannah's "Bats Out of Hell Division" (1993), and several other works that are characteristic of the literature being produced in the postmodernist South.

There is a question arising from this, which I intend to address: Does the change in attitude toward the cardinal event in Southern history imply a selling-out of regional values? Or is the implication merely a revisionist modification of traditional views? The appropriate way to deal with these questions and to assess the volatile Southern identity of our time is obviously a detailed analysis of the Civil War motif in contemporary texts. The analysis should pay particular attention to post–civil rights Southerners' impatience with the way they and their habitat are still rendered stereotypically. In his amusing essay "Upon Being Southernovelized," which opens Noel Polk's memoir *Outside the Southern Myth,* the author has presented a vivid picture of his feelings at seeing "his town, his department, his friends, and himself in a Carpetbagger novel."[1] The irony is that this characteristic attempt of a modern Mississippian to draw himself up by his own bootstraps, as it were, from Southern myth, only marks a new phase in Southern culture. Although he insists, "I do not come from a slaveholding family; nobody that I know of in my ancestry was a Confederate soldier and I still do not know all the names of the Confederate generals," the memoir places him well "inside the Southern myth."

For a European looking at the South from the outside, it is as revealing that non-Southerners should write novels about post-civil rights Southerners—or like John Berendt in *Midnight in the Garden of Good and Evil* (1994) rehash old clichés of the South in best-sellers—as it is that a modern Southerner should resent being "Southernovelized" by a Yankee. After Anne Moody in the sixties had shown us "that coming of age in Mississippi" was very different from what *Gone with the Wind* had led us believe, Polk in the nineties makes us wonder whether there are still Southerners left and whether the South is any different from the rest of the United States. As a consequence we rush back to John Shelton Reed for his sociological assurances that there is an "enduring South."[2] Nevertheless, the doubts about the South that found their first major expression in Walker Percy's *The Moviegoer* of 1960, remain. It was perhaps Polk's encounter, in Percy's first novel, with housewives from his own nondescript hometown Hattiesburg that initiated his parodic discourse on the ludicrous pains of being stereotyped as a Southerner. When we study in detail how the Civil War has been treated in contemporary Southern fiction, we shall meet with the same ironic and parodic spirit.

Lothar Hönnighausen

In Percy's *The Moviegoer,* it is above all the leitmotif of *moviegoing* that throws the theme of regionalism into relief. Wide in scope and complex in its reference, the film motif communicates the contemporary problem of authentic perception and, ultimately, of the reality crisis precipitated by our media-dominated world: "*Panic in the Streets* with Richard Widmark is playing on Tchoupitoulas Street. The movie was filmed in New Orleans. . . . Nowadays when a person lives somewhere, in a neighborhood, the place is not certified for him. More than likely he will live there sadly and the emptiness which is inside him will expand until it evacuates the entire neighborhood. But if he sees a movie which shows his very neighborhood, it becomes possible for him to live, for a time at least, as a person who is Somewhere and not Anywhere."[3] Percy's achievement lies in conveying this "evacuation" of reality not only through the movie metaphor but also, paradoxically, through a detailed but "problematized" rendering of New Orleans as a topographic as well as sociocultural ensemble.

In the following instance the withdrawal of hero and heroine from the Mardi Gras pageant and its ambivalent metaphors (crusaders, black eye sockets, strangely good-natured specters) suggests the problematic nature of Walker Percy's "regionalism": "Yet these specters are strangely good-natured, leaning forward and dropping whole bunches of necklaces and bracelets or sailing them over to the colored folk in the neutral ground. High school bands from North Louisiana and Texas follow the floats. Negro boys run along behind the crowd to keep up with the parade and catch the trinkets that sail too high. The krewe captain and a duke come toward us on horseback" (*Moviegoer,* p. 62). Does the reality crisis, expressing itself in Percy's novel chiefly through the motifs of moviegoing and role-playing, also mean the end of literary regionalism? Perhaps, the rendering of the regional experience and identity in Percy's novel may help us advance the debate on "The New Regional Image of the South" beyond the frustrating alternatives "whether the Americanization of the South proceeds more rapidly than the Southernization of the U.S."[4] and "whether the South has as much of a future as it has a past."

In the terms of *The Moviegoer,* it becomes possible for the main character to live, for a time at least, as a person who is somewhere on account of the fictional authority that the film momentarily lends his regional world. The specific quality of the new regionalism manifests itself in the "fact" that the characteristically Southern taste of okra[5] occurs only metaphorically and in the fictional world of the movie theater. "There is a danger of slipping clean out of space and time. It is possible to become a ghost and not know whether one is in downtown Loews in Denver or suburban Bijou in Jacksonville. So it was with me. Yet it was here in the Tivoli that I first discovered place and time,

The Southern Heritage and the Semiotics of Consumer Culture

tasted it like okra" (p. 75). Clearly, regionalism, the experience of cultural space, plays a major role in the symbolization processes related to identity as the final human reference point. That being the case, neither the multiplicity of present or past civil wars nor, in the cultural sphere, the variability[6] of literary regionalism is to be wondered at.

The choice of the texts discussed in the main part of this essay was suggested by my semiotic approach, which is focused on public images representative of Southern culture rather than on private metaphors reflecting the writer's individual experiences. Among the several public images reflecting the clash between the collective experience of Southern tradition and a new all-American or globalist consumer culture,[7] the Civil War is a particularly relevant one, whether we think of Confederate war memorials, the Confederate flag, or the souvenir and hobby industry. Moreover, it has enjoyed a privileged status in Southern literature, reflecting a fascination shared by the whole nation to this day. In John Esten Cooke's romance *Surry of Eagle's Nest* (1866), as in Walt Whitman's poems *Drum-Taps* (1865), William Faulkner's *Absalom, Absalom!* and Margaret Mitchell's *Gone with the Wind,* the Civil War appears as a "lofty theme." Even in cases where irony informs the narrative stance, as in Sam R. Watkins's memoir *Co. Aytch* (1882) and Stephen Crane's *The Red Badge of Courage* (1895), or where grotesque features mark the description, as in Ambrose Bierce's "Chickamauga," readers are not left in doubt that they are witnessing a tragedy.

This is also true of the treatment of the Civil War in several contemporary African American novels. Although Margaret Walker's *Jubilee* (1966), Ernest J. Gaines's *The Autobiography of Miss Jane Pittman* (1971), and Alex Haley's *Roots* (1976) present the Civil War from a black perspective and only as an episode in black fictional autobiography (Walker, Gaines) or family history (Haley),[8] they, as well as the above mentioned white authors, give us the Civil War straight and directly, not as parodically reflected by a later time. Parody is, however, the approach in the following works that are characteristic of the literature being produced in the postmodernist South.

The great event that had so profoundly moved the Southern imagination appears in Clyde Edgerton's *Raney* as the subject of a farcical episode. But the episode constitutes an integral part of the whole critical context of the novel in which Edgerton satirizes Baptist bigotry and its impact on Southern sexual mores, Southern family codes, the cult of Southern cooking, and, most important, Raney's display of continuing Southern racism[9] in comic counterpoint with Charles's ostentatious civil rights progressivism. Raney's and Charles's visit with the Golden Agers to Mr. Earls, a Civil War buff, is a parodic inversion of a major Southern ritual, the reenactment of Civil War battles: "Mr.

Earls had one of those little sheds out back and one side had a big hole in it which he'd covered with clear plastic. 'I don't know how in the world it happened,' he said. 'I had a box of powder and I guess a spark got to it some way. We'd been firing at a reenactment and maybe some spark got in there somewhere and smoldered. I been in the Civil War business over forty years and nothing's blowed up but twice'" (p. 101). Mr. Earls does not transmit the Civil War as part of a "usable past" but as a reactionary "survival." In terms of the semiotics of culture his comic incongruity as caricature of a Civil War hero[10] and enslaver of wife Birdie[11] are ironic signals to the reader of the major changes in the regional consciousness and in the regional value system since the sixties. Charles's progressivist disgust at Mr. Earls's flying the Confederate flag[12] and Mr. Earls's own grotesque reference to his forty years in the Civil War business with only two explosions further illustrate the new function of the Civil War as ironic metaphor. Moreover, the parodic purpose of the Civil War motif in *Raney* becomes evident from the fact that not the actual reenactment—a more than modest affair—is foregrounded but its preparation and its television coverage. Charles's and Mr. Earls's comic chat on what Civil War books to read[13] makes the reader wonder whether the Civil War continues to function as a metaphor of a living regional heritage or simply as an icon of the hobby industry.

Bobbie Ann Mason's short story "Shiloh" explores the Civil War theme in a more complex and profound manner. In this story, reflecting the postmodern spirit in which contemporary fiction writers deal with the Southern past, the "misleading" title and the associations of Shiloh as part of the mythicized history of the South produce an incongruous patriotic backcloth for the trivial tragedy of the truck driver Leroy Moffit and his body-building wife Norma Jean. Leroy, despite his name, to which he will later doubtfully refer, is not the active force in the story, but only its reflecting center. The historic title notwithstanding, Leroy and Norma Jean Moffit have little in common with the stereotypical heroic Southerner and the Southern Lady;[14] rather, they illustrate the extent of the change in regional culture and ideology that has taken place since the South has emerged as part of the Sun Belt. The very first sentence symbolizes the specific love- and power-relations between the partners of this failing marriage: "Leroy Moffit's wife, Norma Jean, is working on her pectorals. She lifts three-pound dumbbells to warm up, she progresses to a twenty-pound barbell. Standing with her legs apart, she reminds Leroy of Wonder Woman." Meanwhile, Leroy, in a reversal of traditional gender roles shows his mother-in-law his needlepoint pillow cover with motifs that characteristically are not from Southern folk art but from the popular culture of all-American media (i.e., *Star Trek*). In his reflections on his wife Leroy also draws

The Southern Heritage and the Semiotics of Consumer Culture

on the iconography of popular culture, in turning Norma Jean, who works at the Rexall drugstore, into the icon of Wonder Woman.

In fact, the whole semiosis of the tale is informed by the arsenal of televsion–mail-order–shopping-mall clichés that have been pushing the Confederate–Lost Cause stereotypes of a previous South, "the Civil War business"—as Mr. Earls says in Clyde Edgerton's *Raney*—into the background, or rather, they have intermingled in one nondescript semiotic cosmos. All themes of Mason's "Shiloh" are symbolically communicated through direct or indirect borrowings from or references to this artificial consumer-oriented world.[15] As Leroy is incapable of doing anything meaningful, he has turned to the world of empty "hobbyism" and makes things from craft kits. His failing love-relation is ironically conveyed in the scene where he smokes a joint and listens to Norma play on the electric organ he has given her as a Christmas present: "Can't Take My Eyes off You" and "I'll Be Back." The death of their baby—as in Albee's *Who's Afraid of Virginia Woolf,* it is the avatar of what went wrong in their marriage—occurs, while the parents were at the drive-in, watching a double feature, *Dr. Strangelove* and *Lover Come Back.* Ironically, the only reminder of Southern tradition is a "new white-columned brick house that looks like a funeral parlor" in one of the expensive subdivisions. It belongs to the prominent doctor from whose son Leroy, disturbed by these culture-changes, buys grass.

Bobbie Ann Mason explodes the inauthenticity of images of the Old and the New South by ironically juxtaposing them in what looks at first sight like straightforward description: "He will probably not be able to drive his rig again. It sits in the backyard, like a gigantic bird that has flown home to roost. Leroy has been home in Kentucky for three months, and his leg is almost healed, but the accident has frightened him. . . ." The grotesque image of Leroy's abandoned truck, which "sits in the backyard, like a gigantic bird," jumbled together with the connotations of the proverbial chicken that has come home to roost, invites the reader to parodically associate (Kentucky) fried chicken (it is also among the favorites that Norma Jean cooks for him) and the notoriously nostalgic song "My Old Kentucky Home." The theme of the song is also represented by the leitmotif of the miniature log cabin that Leroy builds from notched Popsicle sticks. "It reminds him of a rustic Nativity scene." While this miniature log cabin symbolically anticipates Leroy's abortive project of building a full-size log cabin home for Norma Jean, the Nativity scene insidiously introduces the motif of the absent child.

Mason, in her parodic modulating of Leroy's narrative voice, makes a particularly subtle use of the semiotics of all-American consumer culture, in this way displaying the kind of postmodernist consciousness that inspires much of the new

85

Lothar Hönnighausen

Southern regionalism. "After fifteen years on the road, he is finally settling down with the woman he loves. She is still pretty. Her skin is flawless. Her frosted curls resemble pencil trimmings" (p. 3). Through the narrator's comic repetition, in the following direct narrative statement, of the hit song title "'I'll Be Back.' He is back again. . . . he is finally," she signals that she is reporting Leroy's own, self-congratulatory assessment of his wife's well-preserved attractions. As a result of this sly rhetorical hint, the sensitive reader knows how to take the cliché phrasing of the popular culture ideals ("he is finally settling down with the woman he loves"), characterizing the naïveté of Leroy's voice.

In parodic contrast to what the title leads us to expect, the picnic trip to Shiloh occurs well into the story and at the instigation of Norma Jean's mother, Mabel, for whom her acceptance into the United Daughters of the Confederacy in 1975 continues to be gratifying.[16] Mason shows her ironic ingenuity in making the trip to the battlefield of Shiloh, planned by Mabel to heal the marriage of her children, the scene of Leroy's final defeat. Mason's vitriolic sense of satire manifests itself in the funny shift from the narrator's Corinth of the war to the Corinth of Mabel's point of view: "General Grant, drunk and furious, shoved the Southerners back to Corinth where Mabel and Jet Beasley were married years later, when Mabel was still thin and goodlooking" (pp. 15–16). Mabel's memories of her private "romance" trivialize the tragic event of Southern history and underline the misery of Leroy and Norma Jean's marriage.

Through Norma Jean's repetition of her mother's anecdotal distortion of the landmark of collective remembrance and above all through the masterful handling of poor Leroy's viewpoint, Mason conveys the "otherness" of history: "At Shiloh, she drives aimlessly through the park, past bluffs and trails and steep ravines. Shiloh is an immense place, and Leroy cannot see it as a battleground. It is not what he expected. He thought it would look like a golf course" (p. 13). The hero's inability to come to terms with the tragic reality of past human suffering is symptomatic of the synthetic sensibility of the New South and its new regionalism: "He tries to focus on the fact that thirty-five hundred soldiers died on the grounds around him. He can only think of that war as a board game with plastic soldiers" (p. 15). His attempt to cover his inability to cope with history by facetiously adopting a slangy jargon and a patronizing tone is as revealing as Norma Jean's association of Corinth and Mama, which reveals her mother complex. Mason has said, "I don't think the people I write about are obsessed with the past. I don't think they know anything about the Civil War, and I don't think they care. . . . But I think they reflect that tension that's in the culture between hanging onto the past and racing toward the future."[17] Mason uses Leroy's and Norma Jean's lack of historical understanding and sympathy as much to evoke a fitting stage for their own tragedy as to reflect the changing historical consciousness of the South: "Leroy says, 'So the boys in gray ended up in Corinth. The Union soldiers zapped 'em finally. April 7, 1862.' . . . 'Corinth is where Mama eloped to,' says Norma Jean. They sit in silence and stare at the cemetery for the Union dead and, beyond, at a tall cluster of trees. . . . Norma Jean wads up the cake wrapper and squeezes it tightly in her hand. Without looking at Leroy, she says, 'I want to leave you'" (p. 14).

Barry Hannah's short story "Bats Out of Hell Division" shares with Bobbie Ann Mason's "Shiloh" and Clyde Edgerton's *Raney* not only the Civil War content but also a central narrative device: the use of a mediator or interpreter. Naturally, in each of the stories, the device of the interpreter takes a different form: In *Raney,* Mr. Earls's reenactment of the Civil War rituals would seem to confirm the traditional regional code, but Raney's funny first-person comments, in conjunction with the narrator's ironic hints to the reader—and Mr. Earls's own comic lapses—serve to destabilize them. In "Shiloh," the ironically detached, third-person narration of Leroy's interpretation of his and Norma Jean's experience of Shiloh-battlefield park is a critical mechanism of cultural change. In "Bats Out of Hell Division," the interpretations of the scribe enforce the black humor of his seemingly naive eyewitness account. His grotesque descriptions of the heroic attack of the dead Confederate soldiers parody the tradition of the battlefield scenes in fiction, memoirs, and photos that have played such an important role in bolstering the Lost Cause myth to which the text satirically alludes at the beginning and the end: "Our cause is leaking."[18]

In all three stories, the narrative refraction through the interpreter serves the same purpose: It allows the authors to manipulate our reading of the Civil War as cultural metaphor and to capture the recoding of regional values. Obviously, the interpreter device introduces into these contemporary renderings of the great regional theme of the Civil War an additional dimension of postmodernist reflectiveness, which, absent from *Gone with the Wind,* is characteristic of the New South of our time. What seems important to note is that the internal interpreter operates in addition to and in collaboration with an external interpreter, the reader, who by the definition of semiotics is a constituent component of the sign as carrier of meaning.[19] It is in line with the heightened literary consciousness of postmodernism to have an internal interpreter reflecting the external one and thus to enforce the theme of *figuration* that makes the works of modern Southern fiction key documents of the semiotics of regional culture. In this respect, it is not surprising that in "Bats Out of Hell Division," as in the other stories, the theme is not so much the Civil War itself but the problem of historically and artistically coming to terms with it. That the roles of the historian and the writer are blending—the narrator refers to himself as "scribe"—is quite characteristic of a time that is as aware of the fictional dimension in history as of the documentary quality of literature.

On the surface, Barry Hannah's short story is a parody of the many biographies of Civil War generals and their memoirs that have substantially contributed to the Lost Cause: The general "is dead-set on having these battles writ down permanently in ink and will most certainly push me on afterward, whatever befalls, into working up his own biography" (p. 45). The soldiers, too, are ironically represented as fighting to get into the history books. The man who claims to have been shot through the heart "doesn't want to miss a minute of it," because he knows "it will set the tone for a century and will be in all the books. . . . Already he is practicing his posture. . . . They say he has a mirror, . . . at which he practices" (pp. 46–47). At a deeper level the text's theme is the modern Southerner's urge to explode the Lost Cause and other Southern myths, and from its satirical rewriting create a usable past. In this respect Hannah's scribe takes over where Quentin Compson left off.[20] But, in reworking the Southern saga, which Faulkner had already transformed into a relentless search of the Southern soul, Hannah turns it into a fantastic farce, the narrator claims: "I have license to exaggerate."

In comic anachronism the scribe turns the Revolutionary War hero Kosciuszko into Kosciusky and lets him fight in the wrong war; he has the band play a military arrangement of Tchaikovsky's concerto for violin in D, opus 35, of 1878, and distorts the famous "happy" repetitions of Keats's "Ode on a Grecian Urn" into "Oh, happy bayonets high, oh happy, happy, happy!"[21] Indeed, "there is mystery and miracle left in this hard century!" (p. 48). The "license to exaggeration" shows no less in the *dance macabre* of the soldiers, the narrator who has "become the scribe . . . because all limbs are gone except my writing arm" (p. 43), "Corporal Nigg . . . , frozen upright, long dead but continuing as the sentry," and the general—"you can hear the wind whistling through him" (p. 45). It reaches its peak in a kind of operatic finale in which Appomattox seems reversed into the imaginary Hastenburg, and the Confederate vision seems realized after all. Impressed by the sheer gallantry of the dead Confederate soldiers, the Union general admits defeat, and the scribe parodically slips into the lingo of historians to confirm the fantastic: "'Stop it! Stop it! I can't take it anymore. The lost cause! . . . By God, we surrender!' he shouted. . . . The music, The Tchaikovsky! . . . Our general, stunned, went over to take his sword. . . . Nothing in history led us to believe we had not simply crossed over to paradise itself and were dead just minutes ago" (p. 49).

In semiotic terms, Hannah and the other authors dealing in this ironic fashion with the mythicized Southern past engage "in a drama of interpretations that *is* the mechanism of cultural development."[22] The paralysis of Southern culture had first been diagnosed by Southern writers like Ellen Glasgow, William Faulkner, Tennessee Williams, Lillian Hellman, Flannery O'Connor, and Eudora Welty. Its special stasis is of the narcissistic type which the MacCannells find "best decribed by Lacan's 'stade du miroir.'"[23] It has been caused as much by political as by sociocultural causes that have only in part been removed through the civil rights legislation. The premodern culture of the South confronting Faulkner and his generation seems more adequately defined by the MacCannells' semiotic concept of a "culture that reproduces itself as a series of endless mirrorings,"[24] than by Mencken's catchy image of the "Sahara of the Bozarts."

The new Southern writers who have launched a parodic attack on the South of Civil War memorials and Lost Cause rituals, of veterans' parades and the activities of the United Daughters of the Confederacy, do so to overcome the cultural narcissism of their region. In fact, my analysis of their parodic strategies shows that they are engaged in what other writers in other cultures—Rousseau and Kant, Baudelaire and Nietzsche, Derrida and the postmodernist novelists—have done before them: they deconstruct dead structures, revaluate regional values, recode paralyzed cultural codes. The reason why they parody the glorified past of Southern hagiography is not that they are globalists without a sense of history and place. Rather, their situation seems encapsulated in an episode in Josephine Humphreys's *Rich in Love* where Lucille, the heroine, joins her disguised friend Rhody, a black writer, doing research for a book about their native Charleston. They ride a sightseeing bus to experience their native city from the new, if alienated, perspective of tourists: "I liked touring my own city. It was a new perspective."[25] Visiting one's own city as tourist is a form of role-play, offering the opportunity not only of a new perspective of one's place but also the distancing and transformation of one's identity through masks. Lucille and Rhody enjoy themselves revising their own previous views of the city as well as the tourist vision of it. In this they experience one of the pleasures of all cultural activity that entails a permanent recoding of the old cultural values in terms of the new political and social experience: "The essence of culture may reside in an interplay between its mnemonic function (memory, recording, writing) and resistance to such remembering."[26] Rhody's recoding of the history of Charleston takes the form of an aggressively burlesque supplement to the white account of the tourist guide. Her emancipatory black perspective is matched by Lucille's revisionary white view of regional history:

> She read from a brochure. "Historic downtown Charleston, where descendants of the original lowcountry planters preserve the traditions of their forefathers." The guide pointed out sights and lectured on their history. Rhody amended and corrected where necessary. "Bull *dog*," she said, when the guide said slaves jumped over a broom to get married.

> "Here is where they hung the pirates," Rhody said to the people in front of us. A little farther on she said, "Here is where they hung the Negroes." "Is that really true?" the lady in front of us said, ... "Twenty-two all at once, 1822," Rhody said. "But they were troublemakers." (p. 195)

Not only does Lucille speak of her historical interest several times, the whole metaphoric texture of the novel is imbued with a sense of history, characterizing the specific regional world that Humphreys has created. But history as Lucille experiences it is not dead and done; it is something currently taking place. Representative of this are the sinister nuclear submarines from the naval base, suggesting, in the regional context, the threat of global warfare and the leitmotif of tearing down an old and building a new South of quickly spreading subdivisions, of postmodernist hotel architecture,[27] and pseudohistorical inner city facades.

Above all, the historicity, fascinating Lucille and uncannily inherent in the postmodern present, reveals itself in disturbing personal encounters and epiphanies, as Lucille puts it in her inimitable seriocomic teenager jargon: "History should give you goose bumps" (p. 47). Memorable examples in *Rich in Love* of this are the imaginative and distortive "resurrections" of monuments, particularly that of John C. Calhoun (1782–1850), the *pater patriae* of the sectionalist South, and, as a kind of counterpoint, that of the Seminole chief Osceola (1804–38), the representative of the suppressed Southern history of exploitation and victimization. In the farcical linkage of the apocryphal story of Calhoun as the "true father of Abraham Lincoln," the idols of both the South and the North are pulled from their pedestals:

> In old cities there are always statues. Charleston had John C. Calhoun, Henry Timrod (Poet of the Confederacy), and a toga-clad woman who was meant to be Confederate Motherhood, sending her naked son into battle with the Yankees. But my favorite was Osceola, the Seminole chief. Down the road from our house was Fort Moultrie, where his statue rose from the top of a hill, looking seaward. . . . Bees lived in him. . . . A warrior, secretly filled with sweetness. In life Osceola had been betrayed in Florida, captured under a flag of truce, and sent here as a prisoner, where he died under what I consider suspicious circumstances. . . . When he died, the attending physician sawed off his head and took it home to Savannah, where he pickled it and hung it on his son's bedpost whenever the child misbehaved. I swear this is true. (pp. 70–71)

In erecting a ten-foot cypress representation of Osceola's head in profile at the entrance of the "bankrupt development on the bypass" (p. 71), built "in violation of seventeen sections of the building code" and in brutal disregard of environmental concerns, Humphreys satirically links several instances of exploitation. From a semiotic perspective, the cheaply built development, Osceola Pointe, which ironically evokes the victimized Seminole chieftain and where Rhody, the investigative black writer, lives, impacts on the reader as a cultural *chiffre* of Native American and African American victimization, of historical and current exploitation.

The historical vision in *Rich in Love* is very much Lucille Odom's, and her "personalizing" of history corresponds with her exploring her own past as history. Her parallel probings of regional and personal history result in her dismantling the Southern tradition with Calhoun as overfather[28] and in her recovering from her own father complex. The emphasis on a personal assessment of history is one of the several features that Humphreys's *Rich in Love* has in common with the three texts dealing with the Civil War. What is relevant from the viewpoint of a semiotics exploring *chiffres* of major cultural trends is the obvious fascination with history and attitudes towards it of Josephine Humphreys, Bobbie Ann Mason, Clyde Edgerton, Barry Hannah, and many other contemporary Southern authors. This is more important than the fact that Leroy only gropes unsuccessfully for the meaning of "Shiloh," while Lucille and Rhody display a sophisticated and critical view of Southern history, that Hannah, in the scribe's eyewitness account, presents the Civil War as burlesque *danse macabre,* whereas Edgerton deals with the subject in a harmless farce.

What matters is that all four authors treat the theme parodically, in varying forms of satiric inversion, often ironically drawing on the standardized interests and verbal clichés of very ordinary people, living in a media-prescribed world. "The place looks eligible for a feature article in *Southern Living*" (*Rich in Love*, p. 260), says Lucille of her transmogrified home, before she reports, in a parody of Victorian novel endings, on the final whereabouts of all characters. But the rendering of a battlefield as a theme park in "Shiloh" or the Civil War as object of black humor as in "Bats Out of Hell Division," the farcical playfulness, in *Rich in Love,* of the sightseeing scene or, in *Raney,* of Mr. Earls's "Civil War business" do not herald the end of any deeper interest in history. On the contrary the parody of history only implies the end of history as an ideological justification of the status quo.

History with these postmodernist writers has become an area of personal scrutiny and sociopolitical critique. This is a major deviation from the American tradition of reading American history as the fulfillment of a prophecy and a dream. Inevitably contemporary Southern fiction's revision of the Southern saga strikes a familiar cord in a German of my generation, for whom the approach to history has been that of *Trauerarbeit,* or "work of mourning." This kind of attitude is encapsulated, in *Rich in Love,* in a dialogue between Lucille and her mother that moves from the inextricability of "memory and

Lothar Hönnighausen

pain" in the heroine's personal history to her painful experience of Southern history.[29] Lucille's urge to "take the tourists on a different tour" is equally pertinent from the perspective of cultural semiotics. As a symbol of a cultural trend among progressive Southerners it embodies the effort of relating the dead facts of a selective white history to the multicultural forces shaping the present global mass culture and interracial regional inspiration.

The study of the Civil War in contemporary Southern fiction shows that there is no need to worry that a total globalization of Dixie might be imminent. Although the texts by Bobbie Ann Mason, Barry Hannah, Clyde Edgerton, and Josephine Humphreys leave no doubt that there are strong tendencies toward a globalization—which for that matter amounts to an Americanization—of the South, as of other regions, they also make it abundantly clear that there remains a strong regional consciousness. As we have asked these Southern writers "to tell us about the South," we have learned that there is still a specific awareness of history. This historical consciousness, tempered by revisionist intentions and parodic strategies, continues to inform the regional sensibility. In this respect the Southern identity of our time is distinct from that of other regions of the United States. Recent Southern fiction suggests that an intense awareness of "the transformation of the world" is the dominant motive of both the preoccupation with regional history and of its postmodernist expression.

Notes

1. Noel Polk, *Outside the Southern Myth: Life in a Parallel Universe* (Jackson: University Press of Mississippi, 1997), pp. 3–17. Subsequent references are cited in the text.

2. John Shelton Reed, *The Enduring South: Subcultural Persistence in Mass Society* (Lexington, Mass.: D. C. Heath, 1971), and *One South: An Ethnic Approach to Regional Culture* (Baton Rouge: Louisiana State University Press, 1982). See also Anne Moody, *Coming of Age in Mississippi* (New York: Dial Press, 1968); and Daniel Singal, *The War Within: From Victorian to Modernist Thought in the South, 1919–1945* (Chapel Hill: University of North Carolina Press, 1982).

3. Walker Percy, *The Moviegoer* (New York: Alfred A. Knopf, 1961), p. 55. Subsequent references are cited in the text.

4. John Egerton, *The Americanization of Dixie: The Southernization of America* (New York: Harper's Magazine Press, 1974).

5. For okra as an emblem of Southernness, see also Clyde Edgerton, *Raney* (New York: Ballantine, 1985). Subsequent references are cited in the text.

6. Compare, for instance, the critical and exploratory regionalism in Walker Percy's *The Moviegoer* in contrast to the sentimental and ideologically affirmative regionalism in Margaret Mitchell's *Gone with the Wind*, in Knut Hamsun's *Growth of the Soil* (1920), and in H. W. Seliger's *The Concept of Heimat in Contemporary German Literature* (Munich: Nidicum Press, 1987).

7. Egerton, *The Americanization of Dixie*.

8. Their ideology is thus diametrically opposed to that of John Esten Cooke's *Surry of Eagle's Nest* (1866), Thomas Dixon's *The Clansman* (1905), and Margaret Mitchell's *Gone with the Wind* (1936), which in their various historical approaches to the Civil War all affirm white supremacy. This reduction of the Civil War to an episode constitutes a major difference from fictional white "biographies" such as Ellen Glasgow's *The Battle-Ground* (1902) or William Faulkner's *The Unvanquished* (1938), where the fates of the heroine and the hero are presented as part of the white antebellum cosmos collapsing in 1865. In contrast to the white view of the Civil War as disaster for the region, the dominant sociocultural orientation in Margaret Walker's, Ernest Gaines's, and Alex Haley's treatment of the Civil War is neither regional nor national but ethnic, heralding an important and more positive phase in black history.

9. The originality of Edgerton's satiric mode consists in using Raney's naïveté to render in a pleasantly humorous way shocking political attitudes: "The army has been segregated since 1948, you said, but Listre still has the black laundromat and the white laundromat and nobody complaining—neither side" (p. 61).

10. "Abraham Lincoln, without a beard" (p. 106), "I model my life after Stonewall Jackson" (p 109).

11. "She's a slave if ever I saw one" (p. 110), and she is not a "Southern Lady" but "like one of those migrant worker women in Charles's photography book," (p. 109). In this regard, one is reminded of the photos from the depression era by Dorothea Lange, Walker Evans, and Arthur Rothstein. See, for instance, Dorothea Lange, "Migrant Mother, Nipomo, California" (1936), and her volume *An American Exodus: A Record of Human Erosion* (New York: Arno Press, [1939] 1975).

12. On the several confederate flags and their mythic implications, see Allen Cabaniss, "Flag Rebel," *Encyclopedia of Southern Culture,* ed. Charles Reagan Wilson and William Ferris (Chapel Hill: University of North Carolina Press, 1989), p. 685, and John Shelton Reed and Dale Volberg Reed, "Confederatalia," *1001 Things Everyone Should Know about the South* (New York: Doubleday, 1996), pp. 91–92.

13. "He went on to talk about all these books on the civil war, by Bruce Catton and by Shelby Foote."

14. On the conventions of Southern womanhood, see Anne Firor Scott, *The Southern Lady: From Pedestal to Politics 1830–1930* (Chicago: University of Chicago Press, 1970).

15. Bobbie Ann Mason, "Shiloh," *Shiloh and Other Stories* (New York: Harper and Row, 1982). Subsequent references are cited in the text.

16. *Encyclopedia of Southern Culture,* ed. Wilson and Ferris, and Angie Parrot, "'Love Makes Memory Eternal': The United Daughters of the Confederacy in Richmond, Virginia, 1897–1920," *The Edge of the South: Life in Nineteenth Century Virginia,* eds. Edward L. Ayers and John C. Willis (Charlottesville: University Press of Virginia, 1991), pp. 219–38.

17. Bobbie Ann Mason in Wendy Smith, "*Publisher's Weekly* Interviews Bobbie Ann Mason," *Publisher's Weekly,* August 30, 1985, p. 425.

18. Barry Hannah, "Bats Out of Hell Division," *Bats Out of Hell* (Boston: Houghton Mifflin/ Seymour Lawrence, 1993), pp. 43–50.

19. "Semiotics—indeed the very definition of the sign—includes the interpreter (perceiver, addressee) as a constitutive component of meaning," in Dean MacCannell and Juliet Flower MacCannell, *The Time of the Sign: A Semiotic Interpretation of Modern Culture* (Bloomington: Indiana University Press, 1982), p. 11.

20. William Faulkner, *Absalom, Absalom!* eds. Joseph Blotner and Noel Polk (New York: Library of America, 1990), p. 7: "So maybe you will enter the literary profession as so many southern gentlemen and gentlewomen . . . and write about it. . . . *Only she don't mean that,* he thought. *It's because she wants it told.*"

21. Stanza 3 of Keats's "Ode on a Grecian Urn" reads:

> Ah, happy, happy boughs! that cannot shed
> Your leaves, nor ever bid the Spring adieu;
> And, happy melodist, unwearied,
> For ever piping songs for ever new;
> More happy love! more happy, happy love!

22. MacCannell and MacCannell, *The Time of the Sign,* p. 26.

23. MacCannell and MacCannell, *The Time of the Sign,* p. 28.

24. MacCannell and MacCannell, *The Time of the Sign,* p. 28. The full text reads, "culture that reproduces itself as a series of endless mirrorings, yet adds nothing either to the original 'image' of it, [and] is literally the death of culture—[conserving] itself as is."

25. Josephine Humphreys, *Rich in Love* (New York: Viking, 1987), p. 196.

26. MacCannell and MacCannell, *The Time of the Sign,* p. 27.

27. ". . . the new look of the cities he loved: Columbia, Charlotte, Atlanta, Charleston. He had helped clear the way for all their downtown Mariotts and Sheratons" (p. 81).

28. In addition to Lucille's encounter with Calhoun (pp. 46, 70) see also Rhody's, the black woman's, association with the Calhoun statue (pp. 97, 190).

29. "Pain is inconsequential if it's not remembered." "What hurts is forgetting." "I also kept a diary" (p. 52). "The place was full of history. . . . The military history alone . . . Fort Moultrie from the Revolution and Fort Sumter from the Civil War . . . the highest concentration of nuclear warheads" (p. 53).

Beyond the Tumult and the Shouting

Black and White in South Carolina in the 1990s

Walter Edgar

South Carolina is a state of contrasts and contradictions. Since the 1960s one of the biggest contrasts has been between public and private action. During the civil rights era white public officials sometimes advocated resistance and damned "outside agitators." Some black leaders pressed stridently for change and condemned those who acted differently as Uncle Toms. Behind the scenes, in what historian John C. Sproat and others have termed a "conspiracy for peace," a strange alliance of black and white leaders negotiated South Carolina's retreat from segregation. While both black and white leaders paid some attention to those who advocated different, and usually violent, alternatives, they either neutralized or ignored them. And so did the majority of the state's population—black and white.[1]

The media, distracted by the violence elsewhere in the South, tended to ignore South Carolina's quiet dismantling of Jim Crow. Agreements reached in back rooms, sometimes literally in the dark of night, had far-reaching effects. Yes, the state's establishment opted for desegregation and the maintenance of law and order, but without the cooperation and grudging acquiescence of the general population, all the secret meetings would have come to naught.[2] There is very little written record of those 1960s meetings. Many of the key participants died before scholars began to investigate the reasons for South Carolina's relatively peaceful transition from a segregated society to a desegregated one. Also unrecorded are what Will Campbell has called "the thousand acts of human kindness" that occurred throughout the South in the 1960s. These were just as important as the clandestine meetings, but they usually occurred outside the glare of the public spotlight. They were personal. And personal relationships are a key component of the ethos of all Carolinians, regardless of race. Some of the most unexpected occurred in newly integrated high schools as young men and women reached across the racial divide.[3] A generation later, in the 1990s, South Carolina was the subject of a great deal of media scrutiny, not for landing a new BMW plant or for having 10 percent of its legislature arrested for bribery and corruption. No this time the news story was the Confederate battle flag's flying over the State House.[4] Governor David Beasley, a Republican elected on a platform to keep the flag flying, suddenly announced, after a series of racially tinged incidents, that he had decided that it should come down. The political aftershocks from that announcement are still being felt. In the months that followed, the Republican-dominated House of Representatives refused to go along with the governor, and a senior Republican state senator compared the governor to Neville Chamberlain at Munich. The Republican state superintendent of education received a threatening letter in which a Republican legislator recommended that she seek the federal witness protection program for supporting the governor. Despite the strong support of the state's business and religious leaders, the effort died.[5]

The public debate was shrill. There were demonstrations and counterdemonstrations. A number of individuals on both sides of the issue postured and posed for the cameras. It made me, as a historian of South Carolina, wonder if the clock had not been turned back a generation. Then I remembered the words of Charles Joyner, my soft-spoken friend from Myrtle Beach, who had been willing to challenge the status quo in the 1960s: "I know that we have come a long way since 1960. Some have dragged their feet all the way, but they have come. Some say there has been no progress, but they have forgotten where we started. Some would stop here, for they cannot see how far we still have to go."[6] Things had changed in South Carolina largely as a result of individuals dealing with one another—person to person—freely. This is not to say that there were no problems.

Despite the progress made, South Carolina still has a long way to go. The following is a sampling of incidents over the past decade. A restaurant in Aiken County, named, ironically, the Buffalo Room, refused to serve black patrons. An integrated youth group was turned away from a Saluda County pool operated by the local Jaycees. In Norway (Orangeburg County), a charity softball tournament rejected an integrated team from Fairfield County. Near Pelion (Lexington County), a drive-by shooting at a biracial nightspot injured three persons. The dock and trees on property purchased by a black couple in a predominantly white Charleston neighborhood were sprayed with racist graffiti. Between 1991 and 1996 thirty-five rural churches (twenty-three black, twelve white) burned under suspicious circumstances. One has been confirmed as a hate crime (the torching of an Hispanic church in Walhalla in Oconeee County), and two others, one each in Clarendon and Williamsburg Counties, were Klan-related.[7]

If one wanted to look at the glass half-empty, all one would have to do would be to point to these events and say, "See, South Carolina has not changed." And it would be easy to do that, but it would be a skewed story. As Edgar Wideman points out, whenever race is tossed into any situation, it becomes a "word hovering like a toxic cloud, obscuring discourse at all levels." In this instance, the rest of the story is forgotten. Each of these events triggered an immediate reaction. The state attorney general, Travis Medlock, succeeded in having the Buffalo Room's business license revoked, and the 1990 General Assembly passed a public accommodations law. Then Republican governor Carroll Campbell invited the Saluda County youths to a cookout and pool party at the Governor's Mansion. Almost before the first news reports went out, the mayor of Norway was issuing a public apology. In Charleston, students, faculty, and alumni of the College of Charleston (of which the couple were alumni) cleaned up the property within twenty-four hours of the event. These things never should have happened, but they did. Instead of their being simply déjà vu, they were déjà vu with a difference.[8]

There is racism in South Carolina. No doubt about it, but racism is a two-way street, an equal opportunity prejudice. In some small towns, it is palpable. For example in Scranton (Florence County), whites believe that the town's increased crime and drug problems are related to the number of blacks moving into town; the local manufacturing plant closed because blacks were not good workers; blacks were stupid and lazy; and children could not play outside because of crack deals going down. In Neeses (Orangeburg County), a black-majority town, the few white students are regularly harassed in school by teachers as well as students. The terms "honky," "white cracker," and "nigger" are still commonly used and accepted. In Lodge, a white university student is cussed out by uncle for using the term "black" for persons of color. In Allendale a young faculty member was asked by a colleague: "How can you be white and vote for Democrats?" Outside the main library at the University of South Carolina, a young black couple discusses something that has happened on campus, "We have suffered, we have suffered too long."[9]

Racism exists in South Carolina and nothing the president of the United States or anyone else can do will change it. As the young woman from Neeses wrote, "The hatred has been handed down for generations; it's almost like it's in the blood or the mother's milk." A recent national poll revealed that 55 percent of all Americans (54 percent whites and 58 percent blacks) thought that race would always be a problem, while 42 percent said that things would work out (38 percent blacks and 42 percent whites).[10] South Carolina of the 1990s *is not* the redeemed community that James McBride Dabbs and others hoped it would be. A thoughtful examination of Dabbs and his influence on the American South at the University of South Carolina in April 1996 pretty much reached the same conclusion. While those present knew how far we had come, they also knew that we still had a way to go. South Carolina has not become the promised land; nor, I might add, is it any longer the segregated world that William D. Workman, Jr., defended in *The Case for the South,* a world he thought should never change. The South Carolina of 1962 is as dead as the South Carolina of 1862.[11]

One of the best descriptions I have seen of contemporary race relations in South Carolina is by John Edgar Wideman, who is one of America's leading black writers. He lives and teaches in Amherst, Massachusetts. In 1992, he and his father, a retired laborer in Pittsburgh, traveled to South Carolina to visit the place whence their forebears had come. As a child, the author had refused to go South with his grandfather: "Going to South Carolina was about as appealing as going to Africa and living in the jungle. Only difference was the size and variety of the animals. And Africa won that battle. South Carolina had fewer trees and no celebrity like Tarzan swinging through them. In both places the colored people and monkeys were too close for comfort. Huh-uh. No thanks, Grandpa. I don't think I want to travel back to slavery days this summer." The adult Edgar Wideman's opinion really had not changed much, but the journey to South Carolina was a revelation to him.[12]

In October 1992, he and his father were headed to Greenwood County, South Carolina: birthplace of Benjamin Mays, whose first memories were of the Phoenix riots, site of one of the most violent racial incidents in the post-Reconstruction period and the location of Promised Land, a thriving all-black community. The Widemans, father and son, had a difficult time, at first, believing present-day Abbeville: "Pleasant manners, amiable sociability, folksy charm, public access everywhere for blacks and whites, a black sheriff on the courthouse steps in Abbeville, land for sale to anyone who has the dough." It took several days, but eventually the elder Wideman had "learned to relax around southern white people, gotten used to the atmosphere of casual acceptance." One evening, the two men stopped by the motel desk to ask where they could go in town for a drink. The clerks at the local Holiday Inn (a black male and a white female) replied, "There's black clubs and white clubs and mixed. No problem with youall going in just about any of them. Depends what youall looking for." In just a few days, a Northern black writer had made a telling observation on the state of black and white in contemporary South Carolina.[13]

As Melton McLaurin wrote in a recent essay, "Rituals of Initiation and Rebellion," young Southerners (black and white) were taught early in their childhoods the rules of segregation. Some, as a young black woman from Promised Land reported, were taught other things: "we weren't like the black kids in town. They don't like white people." Or, as James McBride Dabbs recalled: "I remember no feeling against Negroes; but that I had the usual sense of white privilege." What for Dabbs was "sense of white privilege" was for others racial superiority that sometimes bordered on negrophobia.[14] During the 1960s and 1970s, as legal barriers were removed, white and black Carolinians began working out their interpersonal relationships. There were separate worlds, as William H. Barnwell noted in *Richard's World*. Barnwell, a Charleston native, an old Charlestonian, came back home as an Episcopal seminary student. Assigned to work in a black mission, he wrote that during the day he was with "the Negroes at the mission" and at night with "my parents and old friends." From the squalid slums of the upper parts of the city to cocktails on a piazza south of Broad Street was about as marked a contrast as one could find. He moved in both worlds and, somehow, got a few childhood friends to understand that there was another Charleston. But there was no denying that there were still separate worlds of black and white.[15]

The separate worlds began to commingle in the late 1960s and have been doing so ever since. Despite the so-called Americanization of Dixie, relationships are still important to all Southerners. At first, both blacks and whites were tentative about social interaction. And there was some pulling back. However, across what had once been a barrier as real as the Berlin Wall, black and white Carolinians began, however hesitantly, to reach out, to entertain one another in their homes. This uncertainty was captured poignantly by Dori Sanders in her description of the silver tea that Mae Lee, the protagonist of *Her Own Place*, decides to host in her home and a tea, to which she has invited her longtime black friends and her new ones, the white volunteers from the local hospital. It was one thing for whites to entertain blacks in their homes (which is something so common today as to go almost unnoticed), but quite another for blacks to entertain whites in theirs (again, today, it is commonplace). Would whites come? How would they behave? Mae Lee and her children had the same trepidations that Septima Poinsette Clark had a generation earlier when she invited Mrs. Waites Waring to hers. "Every time I had gone to her house there had been two caterers and a cook . . . ," wrote Clark, "I was anxious to see if she could sip tea in a common, ordinary house. And when I found out that she could and would, I felt better."[16]

Just getting along with casual acceptance slowly became the order of the day. The Columbia Kiwanis Club, the civic club of the city's metropolitan elite, recruited black members in 1975 (and later was the first civic club in the city to admit women). It took a bit longer, but now Columbia and Greenville's civic and downtown business clubs have open membership policies. In most instances racial barriers were dropped without fanfare. When the Kosmos Club in Columbia, the city's oldest dinner-discussion club, invited its first black member, the Hon. Matthew Perry, two of those who spoke in his behalf were attorneys David W. Robinson and Robert Figg—men who had defended the state's Jim Crow laws against Perry's numerous lawsuits. After Judge Perry broke the barrier, Kosmos considered individuals regularly without regard to race or gender.[17] It took a generation for that to occur, but who in 1960 would have believed that it would have? Interracial socializing was one of the things that white Southerners supposedly feared the most, yet, in the 1990s, it occurs without much comment. The black and white characters of Josephine Humphreys's *Rich in Love* interact naturally without any awkwardness. Three of the racial incidents I mentioned earlier involved biracial groups, young men and women playing and socializing together. There are innumerable others. These are some that stand out: The 1997 Cub Scout day camp in Orangeburg with a black female director and white female assistant had a large enrollment of black and white scouts. At an end of summer camp party for a South Carolina army reserve unit, the white mayor of Darlington and a black woman led the group in line dancing the electric slide. A wedding party at Columbia's First Presbyterian Church (Associate Reformed Presbyterian) was biracial. The son of one of the lowcountry's most prominent families, a member of Kappa Alpha Order at Wofford College, married a black woman in a formal ceremony at Bethel AME Church in Columbia. All of the normal social entertaining associated with a large Southern wedding occurred, and every event was biracial—and the wedding write-up complete with two-column photograph appeared in the *Calhoun County Times*.[18]

In their own fashion, South Carolinians have gone about the business of dealing with people, not races. Individuals, not groups. In Orangeburg the largest real estate company in town is Middleton and Associates, a black-owned firm that has a biracial staff (male and female). At Airport High School in Cayce (Lexington County) a flier appeared on campus calling for white students to boycott Black History Month programs. Immediately, a biracial group of students organized a task force and the matter died. One young white female was quoted as saying, "It's time to take a stand and show that we do not accept racism of any kind." After attending a dinner in honor of Darlene Clark Hine at the University of South Carolina (at which about one-half of the guests were black), Charlestonian George C. Rogers, Jr., wrote, "If Orangeburg was a low point, last night was a high point. Darlene's remarks about Judge Perry and Governor McNair were on target for the occasion." The dinner was, he continued, "the sign of a new age in South Carolina. Everybody enjoyed being present. They all wanted to be together." White Methodists in the rural sections of Lexington and Orangeburg Counties greeted their black female district superintendent, Angeline Simmons, in their churches as they would have her white male predecessors. Herbert Milette, Jr., was a wealthy white businessman, born and reared in Clarendon County. Before he died, he selected a black friend, Albert Cooper, to be his head pallbearer. On his deathbed he remarked to his brother, "As far as we have come, most people won't even notice."[19]

One has only to drive around and look to see that at several levels South Carolina does have a biracial society. Not only do black and white children attend public school together, but they also attend the same parochial and independent schools. Columbia's Heathwood Hall Episcopal School has the largest minority enrollment (10 percent) of any independent school south of Washington, D.C. At the University of South Carolina black students comprise 18.7 percent of the undergraduate student body, the largest at any formerly all-white Southern flagship university. In classrooms and on playgrounds black and white children can be seen playing together. In bars and restaurants black and white patrons enjoy their drinks and meals, sometimes separately, sometimes together. Even in pool halls and adult entertainment clubs, one can find black and white staff and patrons. Clerks and servers use courtesy titles with all patrons. Almost every grocery store in South Carolina reflects the more than 300 years of the exchange of food ways across racial lines. A black newcomer from Connecticut was astounded when he went into a grocery store in an upscale Columbia neighborhood and found what he considered soul food ingredients. "Back home," he commented, "food items are segregated by race and class. Down here they aren't."[20]

Perhaps there is no better symbol of the casual acceptance of personal relationships across the racial divide than the Columbia band "Hootie and the Blowfish." Their album "Cracked Rear View," has sold more than fifteen million copies. When *Newsweek* did its 1995 annual year-end review, it described the group in this way: "An interracial band that made only passing mention of their racial identity, they became the most popular rock group in America, shaping the musical year in their image. In a year of intense racial polarization, highlighted by the Million Man March and the response to the O. J. verdict, their catchy, pedestrian songs and videos made just getting along feel downright commonplace." "Just getting along": that was what many South Carolinians, black and white have been trying to do. Unfortunately, the success of individual relationships have been overshadowed by public events, especially the rancorous debate over the Confederate battle flag.[21] The flag is a symbol of the partisanship that has evolved in South Carolina since 1965. Increasingly, the two major parties have become racially identified: the Republicans as the party of the white majority and the Democrats as the party of the black minority. Yet, Robert Ford, a black Democratic senator sponsored

Walter Edgar

legislation to protect Confederate monuments and street names, as well as those honoring civil rights leaders, from being removed or changed without a two-thirds vote of the General Assembly. When the General Assembly authorized the erection of an African American monument on the state house grounds, Republican senator Glen McConnell, one of the staunchest defenders of the battle flag, became one of the monument's strongest proponents and serves as cochair of the commission to oversee the project.[22]

An enduring symbol of the old order and of change is the state's senior senator, J. Strom Thurmond, one of the few living South Carolinians who actually heard Ben Tillman speak. In 1970 he became the first member of the state's delegation to hire a black staff member, and his legendary constituent service is color blind. Civil rights activist Victoria DeLee of Dorchester helped with his 1972 reelection campaign. When questioned as to why she did it, she replied: "What a man was yesterday doesn't matter. It's what he is today that counts." In May 1996, Thurmond called for the removal of the battle flag—six months before the governor did.[23]

Elsewhere in public life in South Carolina, blacks have been elected to office in increasing numbers. In 1990, there were 322 black elected officials; three years later, there were 450. In 1994, Ernest Finney of Sumter was elected Chief Justice of the state supreme court. In 1997, there were 34 black legislators (21 percent of total), 26 in the house and 8 in the senate. Hundreds of other black Carolinians hold appointed positions, among them the police chiefs of Columbia and Charleston and the county manager of Greenville.[24] Are the sound and the fury of public debate a valid reflection of what is going on in the hearts and minds of everyday South Carolinians? I think not. One of the bromides from the politicians opposed to desegregation was that you cannot legislate people's feelings. Well, that is just as true today. Not all of the rhetoric from politicians is going to change how black and white Carolinians get along with one another. Individuals have made and will make their choices. Some (white and black) will still hate, no matter what the situation, but others will choose to associate with whomever they please. White South Carolinians are, as Mae Lee told her children after the silver tea, "no better than colored people. And no worse."[25]

And there are some Carolinians, black and white, who choose to avoid individuals of another race if at all possible. As the clerks at the Abbeville Holiday Inn told the Widemans, "There's black clubs and white clubs and mixed. No problem with youall going in just about any of them. Depends what youall looking for." For individuals to have the freedom to choose their own companions, regardless of race, is something that is relatively new in South Carolina and the American South. The South Carolina of 1997 is far removed from the separate worlds of William Barnwell. It is not the redeemed community of James McBride Dabbs or Harry Ashmore, nor is it the Jim Crow world of William D. Workman, Jr. It was a new South Carolina about which John Edgar Wideman wrote: "Could the changes I observe really be as drastic, as swift and final as they seem? . . . Were human beings capable of undoing hundreds of years of history virtually overnight? Maybe. If they weren't, but were trying damned hard and succeeding pretty well, maybe, if I could believe the evidence of my eyes and ears in Greenwood, South Carolina . . . in October 1992, then more power. Wasn't that good enough? Why knock it? Go with the progressive flow. Be grateful. Encourage what seems to be the good intentions of the good-hearted." Although Wideman was in Greenwood seeking his family's roots in Promised Land, I will be the first to say that while things are better, South Carolina is not the New Zion and probably never will be. But it is a different place as Joyner noted: We "have come a long way since 1960. Some have dragged their feet all the way, but they have come."[26]

If that be so, why has there not been more notice of it? One answer might be that good news does not increase newspaper circulation or television ratings.[27] But there is, I believe, another reason, a very South Carolina one. It has to do with manners and style. The South Carolina style is understated, low-key, laid-back. Actually, it is very Caribbean in that respect. We tend to do things quietly, not as flamboyantly as others do. In that respect, we are very much like Maggie and Brick in the movie version of *Cat on a Hot Tin Roof*. I am sure that you know the scene well. Maggie has announced that she is carrying Brick's child and Brick confirms it. Mae, the frumpy, frustrated wife of Brick's brother, Gooper, calls both liars. Then, as Brick begins to climb the stairs, Mae follows him into the hallway and screams: "We hear the nightly pleadin' and the nightly refusal." To which Brick retorts: "Sister Woman, not everybody makes as much noise about love as you do."[28]

Notes

1. John G. Sproat, "'Firm Flexibility': Perspectives on Desegregation in South Carolina," in *New Perspectives on Race and Slavery in America: Essays in Honor of Kenneth M. Stampp*, eds. Robert H. Abzug and Stephen E. Maizlish (Lexington: University Press of Kentucky, 1986), pp. 164–84; Sproat, "'A Conspiracy for Peace': Pragmatic Conservatism and Desegregation in South Carolina," unpub. ms.

2. Sproat, "Firm Flexibility,'" passim. Sproat, "'A Conspiracy for Peace,'" passim.

3. Campbell used the term in replying to questions after a lecture at the University of South Carolina in 1982. Although the term is not used, he described two such actions that happened during a sit-in demonstration in Nashville: Will D. Campbell,

Walter Edgar

Forty Acres and a Goat (Atlanta: Peachtree Publishers, 1986), pp 71–79. Sproat, "'A Conspiracy for Peace,'" pp. 17–18. For examples of black and white teenagers reaching across the racial divide, see Henry H. Lesesne, "'With Common Courtesy and Effort from Everyone': Desegregation at Spartanburg High School" (seminar paper, University of South Carolina, 1996), passim.

4. See *Der Spiegel,* November 4–11, 1996, and "Klan Rides out to Save Last Flag of South," *London Sunday Times,* December 8, 1996. "Is God's First Name Bob!" *Point* (Columbia), February 1997, p. 11.

5. Lee Bandy, "Beasley 'Not Discouraged' by Backlash to Flag Proposal," *State* (Columbia), November 19, 1996, sec. A, p. 1. "Debating the Flag: 3 Views" and "Who's for Moving Flag? Our State's True Leaders," *State* (Columbia), December 1, 1996, sec. D, pp. 2, 4. Robert Adams, "Confederate Flag's Future Is in the Hands of Legislature's Leaders," *State* (Columbia), February 4, 1997, sec. A, p. 4. Allison Askins, "'Let All Old Wars Die Out,'" *State* (Columbia), December 13, 1996, sec. A, p. 1. Cindi Ross Scoppe and Michael Sponhour, "Banner Divides House," *State* (Columbia), December 4, 1996, sec. A, pp. 1, 6. Cindi Ross Scoppe, "House Unravels on Flag," *State* (Columbia), April 4, 1997, sec. A, pp. 1, 10.

6. Charles Joyner, "The South as Folk Culture" (paper presented at the University of South Carolina, June 24, 1994), p. 6.

7. Walter B. Edgar, *South Carolina in the Modern Age* (Columbia: University of South Carolina Press, 1992), pp. 135–36. John Allard and Leroy Chapman, Jr., "Drive-by Shooting Injures 3," *State* (Columbia), October 28, 1996, sec. A, p. 1. "Recent S.C. Church Fires," *State* (Columbia), December 15, 1996, sec. D, p. 5. "A Triumph from the Ashes," *State* (Columbia), June 7, 1997, sec. A, pp. 1, 7. "Responding to Racism," *State* (Columbia), May 5, 1996, sec. A, p. 8. Across the rest of the South, the burning of churches (black and white) was attributed to random acts of violence or viciousness. There was no Klan-backed conspiracy and "many of the arsons had nothing to do with race at all." Peter Applebome, *Dixie Rising: How the South Is Shaping American Values, Politics, and Culture* (New York: Times Books, 1996), p. 139.

8. Edgar, *South Carolina in the Modern Age,* 135–36. Allard and Chapman, "Drive-by Shooting Injures 3." "Responding to Racism." John Edgar Wideman, *Fatheralong: A Meditation on Fathers and Sons, Race and Society* (New York: Random House, 1995), p. xii. For a brief overview of racial accommodation, see Willis C. Hamm, "Human Affairs Agency Has Battled Racial Division for 25 Years," *State* (Columbia), July 16, 1997, sec. A, p. 9. Wim Roefs, a Dutch journalist now based in Columbia, believes that there are a number of people who look at the glass as either full to overflowing or totally empty—because they lack historical perspective. He sees the progress that has been made, but like Joyner sees that there is still room for improvement. Wim Roefs, interview, Columbia, S.C., July 14, 1997.

9. Suzanne Burgess, interview, Columbia, S.C., March 29, 1995. Aimee Berry, "An Essay" (honors seminar paper, University of South Carolina, 1996), pp. 1–4, 7–9. Philip Carter, interview, Columbia, S.C., March 14, 1994. Myron Cox, interview, Columbia, S.C., April 19, 1995. Bryant Sapp, interview, Columbia, S.C., April 19, 1995.

10. Berry, "An Essay," pp. 7–8. "Race Colors Our View of Racism, Poll Says," *State*

(Columbia), June 11, 1997, sec. A, pp. 1, 10.

11. William D. Workman, Jr., *The Case for the South* (New York: Devin-Adair Company, 1960).

12. Wideman, *Fatheralong*, p. 17.

13. Wideman, *Fatheralong*, pp. 109–18.

14. Melton McLaurin, "Rituals of Initiation and Rebellion: Adolescent Responses to Segregation in Southern Autobiography," *Southern Cultures* 3, no. 2 (1997): 5–24. Elizabeth Rauh Bethel, *Promiseland* (Philadelphia: Temple University Press, 1981), p. 261. James McBride Dabbs, *The Southern Heritage* (New York: Alfred A. Knopf, 1958), p. 12. Workman, *The Case for the South*, pp. 141–247.

15. William H. Barnwell, *In Richard's World: The Battle of Charleston, 1966* (Boston: Houghton Mifflin, 1968), pp. 19–57 (quotation, p. 23), 177–78.

16. Jack Bass, *Porgy Comes Home: South Carolina after Three Hundred Years* (Columbia, S.C.: R. L. Bryan, 1972), p. 143. Jack Bass and Walter DeVries, *The Transformation of Southern Politics: Social Change and Political Consequence Since 1945* (New York: Basic Books, 1976), pp. 275, 283. Septima Poinsette Clark with LeGette Blythe, *Echo in My Soul* (New York: E. P. Dutton, 1962), pp. 100–107. Dori Sanders, *Her Own Place* (Chapel Hill, N.C.: Algonquin Books, 1993), pp. 151–64.

17. Columbia Kiwanis Club of Columbia, S.C., *Officers, Directors, Committees, Roster* (1984), 20. Kosmos Club,"Minutes," Columbia, S.C., January 19, 1988, South Caroliniana Library, University of South Carolina, Columbia.

18. Workman, *The Case for the South*, pp. 211–26. "Cannon-Lemon," *State* (Columbia), May 8, 1994, sec. E, p. 7. "Cannon, Lemon," *Calhoun County Times* (St. Matthew's), May 17, 1994. Deborah U. Roland, interview, St. Matthew's, July 2, 1997. Wedding at First Presbyterian Church, Columbia, S.C., April 27, 1996. Annual Training, 3287th United States Armed Forces School, Hattiesburg, Miss., June 1990. WIS-TV report, June 20, 1997. Josephine Humphreys, *Rich in Love,* (1987; New York: Penguin Books, 1992 edition).

19. George Calvin Rogers, Jr., to the author, February 6, 1996. Elizabeth R. Giles, interview, Columbia, S.C., April 16, 1997. "Orangeburg Business Has Cut across Racial Lines," *State* (Columbia), May 3, 1992, sec. G, p. 1. "Funeral Told the Story of Changes in a Lifetime," *State* (Columbia), April 30, 1996, sec. A, p. 9. Lezlie Patterson, "'Racist' Flier Crashes at Airport High," *State* (Columbia), February 8, 1996, sec. A, p. 1. While individual relationships across the racial divide are many and meaningful, once an issue becomes one of black and white, a group issue, then the old feelings surface. Lorena D. Land, interview, Columbia, S.C., July 15, 1997.

20. Walter B. Edgar, *South Carolina in the Modern Age* (Columbia: University of South Carolina Press, 1992), pp. 128–29. J. Robert Shirley, interview, Columbia, S.C., July 11, 1997. James Miller, interview, Columbia, S.C., January 23, 1997. *University of South Carolina Statistics 1996–1997 Fact Book* (Columbia: Office of Institutional Planning and Analysis, University of South Carolina, 1997), p. 21. For a discussion of the desegregation of independent schools in the South, see Zebulon Vance Wilson, *They Took Their Stand: The Integration of Southern Private Schools* (Atlanta: Mid-South Association of Independent Schools, 1983). In 1996, the minority enrollment at previously all-white

Walter Edgar

Southern flagship universities was Virginia (11 percent), North Carolina (10 percent), Tennessee (5 percent), Georgia (7 percent), Florida (6 percent), Alabama (12 percent), Mississippi (9 percent), LSU (9 percent), Texas (4 percent), Arkansas (6 percent). *Peterson's Guide to Four Year Colleges, 1997,* 27th ed. (Princeton, N.J.: Peterson's, 1997).

21. John Leland, "Crossover Culture: Goodbye Gangstas, Hello Hootie," *Newsweek,* December 25, 1995–January 1, 1996, pp. 126, 128.

22. "A Bill to Amend Chapter 1, Title 10, Code of Laws of South Carolina," May 27, 1997. "An Act to Establish an African-American Monument to Be Erected on the State House Grounds," July 3, 1996. African-American History Monument Commission Meeting, "Minutes," January 15, 1997.

23. Nadine Cohodas, *Strom Thurmond & the Politics of Southern Change* (Macon, Ga.: Mercer University Press, 1993), pp. 410–13, 427. "Thurmond Shows the Way," *State* (Columbia), May 31, 1996, sec. A, p. 10. Bass, *Porgy Comes Home,* p. 143. Bass and DeVries, *Transformation of Southern Politics,* pp. 271–72. "The Legend of Strom Thurmond," *Economist,* October 12–18, 1996, p. 34.

24. *Black Elected Officials: A National Roster,* 21st ed. (Washington, D.C.: Joint Center for Political and Economic Studies, 1994), pp. 377–96 (this is the latest compilation available). Sandra K. McKinney, ed., *1997 Legislative Manual,* 78th ed. (1997), passim. Alan Richard, "Leadership Choice Wasn't Black and White: Batesburg-Leesville Vote Breaks Stereotypes," *State* (Columbia), November 10, 1997, sec. B, p. 1. Chief Justice Finney is one of four black chief justices of state supreme courts. The others are in Georgia, Maryland, and Michigan.

25. Aimee Berry, "Extended Essay" (honors seminar paper, University of South Carolina, 1996), pp. 2–4. Sanders, *Her Own Place,* p. 164.

26. Wideman, *Fatheralong,* pp. 111–12. Joyner, "The South as a Folk Culture," p. 6. Archie Vernon Huff, Jr., interview, Greenville, S.C., July 17, 1997. Rhett Jackson, interview, Columbia, S.C., July 21, 1997.

27. In 1981, the *Los Angeles Times* sent a reporter to Columbia to investigate private schools and race relations. Although the reporter spent about a half day with the headmaster of Heathwood Hall where the story was one of welcoming black students, the story, when it was printed, focused only on what was then James Henry Hammond and its segregationist policies. J. Robert Shirley interview, Columbia, S.C., July 12, 1997. In *Dixie Rising,* the chapter devoted to the rise of neo-Confederates zeroes in on Columbia (where the *Southern Partisan* is published), while that on folks just trying to get along is on Charlotte, a city the author "loves" as a symbol of the New South. Applebome, *Dixie Rising,* pp. 115–81.

28. The original script is worded differently. Tennessee Williams, *Cat on a Hot Tin Roof* (New York: New Directions, 1975), p. 165. Richard Brooks and James Poe, screenwriters, *Cat on a Hot Tin Roof,* Loew's Incorporated, Avon Productions, 1958.

Refighting Old Wars

Race Relations and
Masculine Conventions in Fiction
by Larry Brown and
Madison Smartt Bell

Suzanne Jones

Since the Civil War white male writers of the American South have created fond fictions about childhood friendships that crossed the color line. For example, much of the poignancy of Faulkner's *The Unvanquished* (1938) comes from Bayard Sartoris's description of the close relationship he had with a black servant boy Ringo in the Mississippi small town that will separate them as they grow older and that from the beginning marked them as different, based on race. After their boyhood games and real Civil War adventures together, Bayard and Ringo grow up to be, not close friends, but master and faithful servant when Bayard departs for Ole Miss. Representations of true friendships between blacks and whites beyond the period of childhood innocence have only recently begun to emerge. Contemporary Southern novelists like Larry Brown and Madison Smartt Bell begin their interracial buddy novels where earlier fiction about male friendships ended—when innocent boys become racially self-conscious men.

In 1989 both Larry Brown and Madison Smartt Bell published novels that explore the physical and psychological consequences of the Vietnam War. That both novelists also select two protagonists of different races suggests that the representation of interracial Southern male friendships concerns them as well. Their novels examine the possibilities and limits of such friendships formed because of shared experiences in Vietnam, but Bell's novel *Soldier's Joy* disrupts masculine conventions of bonding in ways that Brown's *Dirty Work* does not. In *The Warriors*, J. Glenn Gray argues that while combat settings are "unequaled in forging links among people of unlike desire and temperament,"[1] these links can be fragile. Although such relationships are based on loyalty to a group, dependence on group members for survival, and even knowledge of individuals in the group, they are not based on reciprocal relationships of mutual intimacy between individuals, and so they may mean little outside the combat setting.[2] Both Brown and Bell test the significance of the similar experiences their black and white protagonists have in Vietnam against their different histories of segregation and their different experiences of racial prejudice in the American South.

Brown's protagonists, who occupy adjoining beds in a veterans' hospital in Mississippi, are comrades; their male bonding is based on their war experiences, but more immediately on coping with their debilitating injuries and their frustrated desires for more normal lives. Braiden Chaney, who is black, has no arms; Walter James, who is white, has no face. For the first half of the novel each man silently reminisces about parallel subjects, which are designed to show readers that, despite their racial differences, they have significant similarities: growing up poor in rural Mississippi, coming of age with loving mothers and absent fathers, Marine combat in Vietnam, and the devastating consequences of their war wounds. But Brown reveals more to the reader than Braiden and Walter disclose to each other. The alternating first-person narratives are related in distinctively individual voices. Their conversational styles seem to have given some readers the mistaken impression that the two men are talking to each other more than they really are, because several reviewers single out for praise the "conversation" these men of different races have and the "dialogue" they engage in.[3]

Even when Braiden and Walter begin to share their stories, they have very little dialogue. One, then the other, tells his story, sometimes on different topics altogether—an adult example of what sociologists call parallel play in children,[4] or to put it in a Southern context, what Allen Tate termed the "traditional Southern mode of discourse," or "rhetorical" mode, which "presupposes somebody at the other end silently listening."[5] In "A Southern Mode of the Imagination" Tate contrasted this nineteenth-century "rhetorical" mode of discourse with the more modern "dialectical" mode, which involves the give and take of two different minds. Although Walter frequently apologizes to Braiden for going "off like that,"[6] he does not change his rhetorical mode of communication, and Braiden does more listening than talking.[7] Brown's narrative technique, alternating first-person monologues in separate chapters, replicates the nature of the emerging comradeship between Braiden Chaney and Walter James, which in all respects except one remains on a superficial level.

The only frank exchanges that occur in the novel concern the morality of suicide and assisted suicide in situations such as the one Braiden finds himself in—twenty-two years of living in a hospital bed with no legs and arms, totally dependent on others. While the heart-wrenching storytelling of both protagonists portrays the staggering toll of war on the survivors, Braiden's story-telling convinces Walter that assisted suicide, in Braiden's case, is not only a valid choice but a moral imperative. Before Walter is discharged from the hospital, he fulfills Braiden's wish and helps him die. Braiden's storytelling enables Walter to imagine himself in Braiden's situation, but the relationship that develops only passes for an intimate friendship. Before Walter finally decides to assist in Braiden's suicide, he promises himself, in order to ease his guilt, that he will come back and visit Braiden, "knowing all the time it was a damn lie" (p. 148). Their emerging relationship is not rooted in a concern for the particularity of the individual other, which might create the basis of a friendship, but instead is based on a respect for and loyalty to a person of similar type, a comrade—in this case, a disabled Vietnam veteran living a death in life with no future. Both men respond to each other's stories of woe as problem solvers, the role Deborah Tannen argues men have been socialized to play in conversation.[8] Although Walter solves Braiden's problem, Braiden decides that he is unable to help Walter and as a result thinks it "surely didn't do me no good to hear all that," i.e., Walter's long involved stories of relationships with his family and his new girlfriend.

The way Larry Brown handles Walter's responses to Braiden, when Walter is initially resisting Braiden's request for suicide assistance, suggests Brown's sensitivity to interracial dynamics, but also his reluctance to directly confront topics of race that might deepen his characters' encounter. It is not clear from the text whether Braiden actually tells Walter how he thinks "all kinds of bad shit about white people" whenever a white person does not act as he expects (p. 102), or simply thinks this for readers to overhear. What is clear is that Walter behaves as if he is aware of this dynamic. The two times that Walter refuses to assist Braiden in committing suicide, Walter immediately tells him stories that he hopes will show Braiden he is not refusing him because he is black. He relates poignant memories of his father's relationship with a black man, his family defending a black family when both families were picking cotton for a corrupt white landowner, and his own comradeship with a black soldier in Vietnam. Walter does not directly respond to any of Braiden's comments about what it means to be black in America or how growing up poor in Mississippi may have been different for a black boy despite the class similarities across racial lines. Because Brown gives Walter a disfigurement that causes people to render him invisible or to avoid him, Brown has created a potential opportunity to allow a white character to better understand the discrimination black people experience, but Brown does not make use of this situation either directly or indirectly.

Although Brown assigns different races to his protagonists, he does not handle this difference as complexly as he might. While Brown has successfully given voice to individuals of both races, a narrative choice not always made in writing about race relations, he shies away from a real dialogue between them about racial issues, which he acknowledges when he has Braiden bring up prejudice and discrimination in his spoken and unspoken monologues and when he has Walter reminisce about his family's good relationships with blacks. But, the contrast between their disagreements and dialogues about the touchy subject of assisted suicide and their anecdotes and monologues about the equally touchy subject of race relations in America is striking. Throughout the novel there are times when each man has questions he does not ask the other, costly hesitations that invariably result in misunderstandings. For example, Braiden becomes emotional when talking about the waste of human lives caused by the war, and when Walter does not respond, Braiden assumes that his silence means he is "thinking about his woman." Indeed Walter is reflecting not only on war's horror but on the injustice in the conscription for the Vietnam War that made its soldiers "young and black and poor" (p. 187). Such reluctance to speak the unspoken not only limits the nature of the understanding between the two men but their self-understanding as well. Walter and Braiden remain comrades; they do not become friends.

In contrast, Madison Smartt Bell's black and white protagonists, Rodney Redmon and Thomas Laidlaw, move beyond comradeship to a friendship of genuine intimacy. They have known each other as boys, but unlike an older generation of white writers, Bell suggests that they have not been close because of their personal history, which is typically and complexly Southern. Redmon's father took care of Laidlaw when he was a boy, and Redmon has always suspected that Laidlaw stole his father's love. While the two never had much of a relationship as boys, the Vietnam War makes them comrades. But the way Laidlaw contrasts his relationship with Redmon in Vietnam with the one back home matches J. Glenn Gray's belief that the strong bonds formed in combat can be fragile when the war is over: "He'd already been over there a good while when we happened to meet up. And we were both just so glad to see somebody from home. . . . So that's when we really got tight. And we made sure to take care of each other ever after that, but I don't know. . . . It don't seem to work out the same back here, quite. I don't see why it shouldn't myself, but it seems like he's got some things eating on him."[9] Although Laidlaw and Redmon have depended on each other for their very lives in Vietnam, when the two men return to the Tennessee hills they both call home, they do nothing to seek each other out, until their paths cross by chance in the middle of the novel. With the representation of their relationship Bell may be questioning the depth of the interracial relationships forged by the institution the United States likes to think of as a model for race relations.

The five books into which Bell divides *Soldier's Joy* mirror the evolution of Laidlaw's and Redmon's friendship. In the first two books the narration is filtered through alternating limited third-person viewpoints. Thus readers get a sense in Book I of Laidlaw's and then in Book II of Redmon's thoughts and feelings as each tries to make a place for himself in the post–Vietnam War South. Laidlaw's task is easier because he is white and because his father has owned property: his father has left him land, a small tenant house, and outbuildings even though fire has destroyed the family home. In contrast Redmon, whose family owned no property, has gotten a job as a real estate agent, and has been betrayed by his white colleagues in a land-development scheme. Redmon ends up taking the rap for all of them and serving time in jail, though not in the jail customarily reserved for white white-collar criminals.

In Books III and IV, where Laidlaw and Redmon become reacquainted, readers experience their tentative friendship first on Laidlaw's territory—at the bar where Laidlaw plays music and at Laidlaw's house—then on Redmon's territory, at his father's house and at a Black Muslim friend's vegetarian restaurant. Their emerging friendship is threatened from the beginning by prejudice on both sides of the racial divide. On Laidlaw's territory Redmon runs afoul of white racism, a mild form when white bigots vacate the bar as soon as he enters to hear Laidlaw's band and a more dangerous form in his job at the warehouse, where a racist coworker not only operates machinery irresponsibly but finally starts a fight. On Redmon's territory Laidlaw encounters Redmon's Black Muslim friend's belief that whites are "blue-eyed devils." While Raschid verbally tries to undermine Laidlaw and Redmon's emerging relationship, the Ku Klux Klan plots to burn Laidlaw out of his home when they discover that he is socializing with a black man.

The relationship between Laidlaw and Redmon is superficial at first. They catch up over a six-pack, exchanging news of housing, work, women, and the aftereffects of the Vietnam War—the kind of conversation that Larry Brown's characters engage in throughout *Dirty Work*. With their first two conversations, Bell suggests that although they know the facts of each other's lives, they do not fully understand one another. On the one hand, Laidlaw, who has no family, naïvely wants to think of Redmon as family because of their acquaintance as boys. He desperately desires intimacy with Redmon without the hard work and time required to produce it. On the other hand Redmon is too quick to suspect Laidlaw of being sympathetic to the racist Giles boys simply because their father has helped Laidlaw plant his garden. Laidlaw's naïveté about white racism, such as why the Ku Klux Klan targeted him, particularly infuriates Redmon who does not have the luxury to be unaware of racial issues. Their second encounter ends acrimoniously with

Redmon declaring that the cost of their relationship is too high. But Laidlaw persists and it pays off for both men.

Their relationship does not become an intimate friendship until Book IV when they begin to speak thoughts and feelings that traditionally have not been expressed across the color line. Laidlaw and Redmon have the conversations Larry Brown's Braiden and Walter never have. Because Laidlaw makes Redmon welcome in his home—sharing drinks, a bed, and a table of food, and thus breaking all the old Southern codes for black/white interaction—Redmon comes to believe in Laidlaw's professed liberal ideology about race relations. Finally Redmon trusts Laidlaw enough to disclose information about his betrayal by his white partners and his resulting incarceration, facts he does not divulge to white acquaintances. Similarly Laidlaw confesses that on one of his insomnia-induced midnight prowls around his property he has impulsively knifed a deer poacher. He trusts Redmon to understand such behavior because of their guerrilla-warfare experiences together in the Vietnam jungle, experiences Redmon is still reliving in his dreams. This self-disclosure of vulnerabilities strengthens and deepens their relationship because it helps them to trust and to better understand each other:[10] Laidlaw to understand Redmon's racial sensitivity and Redmon to understand Laidlaw's tendency to overreact in stressful situations. Bell mirrors their evolving intimacy with his mode of narration, mixing narrative perspectives within Books III and IV so that discreet chapters are filtered from alternating viewpoints,[11] first Laidlaw's, then Redmon's, even though most chapters are devoted to Laidlaw. As their lives open up to each other and include each other, so the separate books of Bell's novel include both perspectives.

The narration of the fifth and last book is at first limited to Laidlaw's perspective but becomes omniscient, which suggests the lowering of the psychic boundaries that enclose each individual male self. Western social and cultural patterns that have made comradeship, not intimacy, the predominant model for male friendships, also have made some men reluctant to reveal their vulnerabilities. Susan Pollak and Carol Gilligan contend that the western male social conventions of hiding and denying one's feelings have made it difficult for some men not only to share their feelings with others but even to be aware of them.[12] Philosophers Strikwerda and May argue that "in order to have strongly positive emotional feelings for another person, as well as sustained mutual self-disclosure, it is important to be able both to have such feelings and to express them."[13] In Book V Laidlaw and Redmon finally confront the particular history of their own relationship and articulate feelings they have been reluctant to voice. In one very painful interchange Bell reminds readers of an important but neglected person in the black servant/white child relationship so prevalent in Southern social and literary history—the black servant's child.[14] Laidlaw is hurt that Redmon has not told him of his father's death or invited him to his funeral because Laidlaw has finally realized that Redmon's father, Wat, was more of a father and mother to him than his own parents. Laidlaw's mother deserted him when he was a baby, and his father left him in Wat's care because he was frequently away shoeing horses on the race circuit. Readers of Southern literature are familiar with this old story, but for a change they also hear from the adult black child, who desperately needed some of the love and attention that his father showered on the white boy he was paid to care for. Redmon thinks his father loved Thomas Laidlaw not just because he was a smart little boy but mainly because he is white. As the two men talk, Laidlaw almost says the word "father" to explain to Redmon how close he felt to Wat, but Redmon angrily cuts him off, "*Don't you say it. . . .* Don't you never. He was *my* father. *Mine*" (p. 377). Finally these two grown men are revealing the truth of both their present and past feelings to each other, but Bell emphasizes that they must work to get at the more complex truth of Wat's feelings for them.

In *The Dialogic Imagination* Mikhail Bakhtin argues that we must know the other's language because understanding occurs "on the boundary between one's own and someone else's consciousness."[15] Laidlaw and Redmon, unlike Brown's Braiden and Walter, behave as Bakhtin says they must in order to improve understanding: they "transmit, recall, weigh, and pass judgment on other people's words, opinions, assertions, information"; they "agree with them, contest them, refer to them."[16] Laidlaw insists that Redmon's belief that Wat preferred him because of his race is "not the truth," and Redmon qualifies his statement saying, "not the whole truth, anyway" (p. 378). Bell uses several long dialogues in Book V between the two men to work through the history of their tangled relationship, not only to better understand what each other is saying and to correct misunderstandings, but to better understand themselves.

Besides Wat Redmon, the other issue that has made a friendship back in the States more difficult than their comradeship in Vietnam is the economic difference in their families' relationship to the same piece of land. Because Laidlaw's father owned this small farm in the Tennessee hills, Laidlaw can fall back on subsistence farming if his music does not earn him a living, unlike Redmon who feels "stuck" "in a corner" in his dead-end warehouse job (p. 390). Redmon reminds Laidlaw that his father Wat lived and worked on this land before Laidlaw's father bought it, "You all didn't do anything but buy it. And then you put him off it in the end" (p. 378)—a perspective on land ownership that is similar to the one Ernest Gaines advances in *A Gathering of Old Men*. For the first time, Laidlaw understands the power and privilege of his whiteness. Laidlaw immediately agrees with Redmon's point and generously, if impulsively, offers him half of the property, saying, "I'd do it for justice" (p. 379).

The nature of coowning this property, however, becomes a bone of contention that the two men chew on intermittently for the rest of the novel. Laidlaw wants a joint ownership that would follow the agrarian philosophy of his father, and of Madison Smartt Bell for that matter, who grew up with the Nashville agrarians as guests in his parents' home.[17] Redmon pronounces such a deal in which Laidlaw calls the shots just as paternalistic as the one his father was engaged in with Laidlaw's father. But Bell is clearly on the side of Laidlaw as far as appropriate use of the land is concerned.[18] The half-built tract homes of the failed development scheme that landed Redmon in jail are depicted as a blight on the landscape. Bell even has Redmon, who admits he was "all for it at the time" (p. 306), wish the land "back the way it was before" (p. 154). Book IV of the novel ends with an unexpected chapter from Wat's perspective, which Bell uses to elevate Wat's kinship with the land. This dreamlike sequence is printed in italics and written in the beautifully lyrical style that Bell takes up throughout the novel whenever he is describing the Southern landscape, but especially when he is describing the reciprocal relationship of a man who is in tune with the earth's rhythms. In an interview with Mary Louise Weaks, Bell indirectly reveals his own approach to writing in a Southern tradition when he distinguishes contemporary writers of "small-town life," like Jill McCorkle, Mary Hood, and Lee Smith, from the earlier agrarian tradition of writers, like Andrew Lytle and Allen Tate, who wrote about "a culture of small farms" and who were concerned "about the destruction of the natural rhythms of life in connection to the land."[19] In *Soldier's Joy* some of Bell's most sympathetic characters have retained a traditional connection to the land: Laidlaw, Wat, Mr. Giles. To use Walker Percy's terms, one of Bell's favorite novelists, these characters feel "at home" on the earth.[20] Bell's least sympathetic characters, Vietnam veteran Earl Giles and real estate developer Goodbuddy, are neither in tune with nature nor in harmony with those around them. They are depicted as ill at ease with their lives.

In *Soldier's Joy* Bell harks back to his own Southern agrarian roots, both emotionally and intellectually, but he goes beyond his agrarian predecessors' preoccupation with the machine invading the Southern garden by acknowledging the evil of prejudice and discrimination that made that garden grow. At the same time that Bell would like to get back to agrarian relationships to the land, he knows they can never be the same as they were in his parents' day. Like Laidlaw he "wanted to make up something new" (p. 310) in *Soldier's Joy*, and indeed he almost succeeds, except for the ending. In the middle of the novel when Redmon and Laidlaw spend their first companionable night together in Laidlaw's mountain cabin, the house Redmon has grown up in, readers experience great expectations that the two men will succeed in creating "something new." As the sunlight streams down from "a deep untrammeled blue sky" the next morning, Bell writes that Redmon looks "well at home there in the daylight" (p. 304). The day they spend together close to nature and each other is Edenic.

Soldier's Joy is long and slow-moving, an attempt I think to represent the process of becoming aware of one's feelings and the difficulties involved in sharing them with a male friend of a different race, especially in the South. Interestingly a number of reviewers, who are obviously used to the urban eccentrics and fast-paced plots of Bell's New York novels, have faulted *Soldier's Joy* for its "somnolent pace"[21] and found his rural Southern setting and introspective narrative technique boring, or as Winston Groom put it, "The story's at its best when the action becomes fast paced, not when the writer lapses into his 'descriptive' mode: giving us the weather report or gaggles of complicated interior thoughts."[22] Such readers seem to resist Bell's disruption of masculine social conventions, a disruption that depends on "gaggles of complicated interior thoughts." Other reviewers, such as David Bradley and David Nicholson find fresh and appealing just the characteristics that Johnson and Groom criticize.[23] And while Johnson and Groom find the concluding violent confrontation between the Klan and Redmon and Laidlaw the most engaging part of the novel, it is perhaps not surprising that Bradley and Nicholson judge the ending contrived and cliched or as Bradley says, "degenerating into a gun-and-chase sequence à la 'Miami Vice.'"[24]

I think the ending works symbolically as a continuation of both the Vietnam War and the Civil War and an end to neither. For Bell, offended by the tactics of contemporary Southern Klansmen, who he felt were trying to speak for him as a white Southerner, he told an *Atlanta Journal-Constitution* reporter that the novel was a chance to speak for himself and advocate integration.[25] Bell suggests through his representation of Vietnam vets that neither the Civil War nor the Vietnam War has made the South safe for cross-racial friendships, despite the strong desires of some individuals of both races. The Klan targets Laidlaw as soon as he initiates a friendship with Redmon, and it tracks the activities of Brother Jacob who, in the style of an evangelical preacher, advocates interracial friendships in open meetings throughout the South. From the subject matter of Bell's other novels,[26] it is clear that he is fascinated by the causes of violence. He creates a plot in *Soldier's Joy* that allows him to speculate that the license to kill that was granted soldiers by the Vietnam War has become something close to instinctual in Vietnam veterans and not just those who are racially prejudiced.

Bell prepares readers for his explosive ending because throughout *Soldier's Joy*, violence is not far below the surface. Long before the novel's concluding bloody confrontation over improved race relations, racist Earl Giles draws his gun instinctively when his brother and some friends play a practical joke on him, Rodney Redmon tortures Goodbuddy in Laidlaw's barn, and Laidlaw in the style of a guerrilla fighter stalks and knifes a deer poacher. All three of these characters are Vietnam veterans. Bell's explanation of the cause of the poaching incident is disturbing, "That taste in [Laidlaw's] mouth was certainly of blood, and vaguely he heard a familiar voice telling him that once acquired it was extremely hard to cure" (p. 106). Bell uses Laidlaw's lover's first experience with a gun to solidify this position. Although Adrienne at first refuses to participate in the race war that ends the novel, she grows afraid she may have to defend Laidlaw's life so she has a change of heart and decides to learn how to shoot. When her first bullet hits the sign she is using for target practice, Bell writes that "she felt her face creasing into a weird smile" (p. 457), a sign that she now is also under the spell of a gun's power. Until this point Adrienne's perspective has called the reader back from the precipice of viewing Laidlaw's and Redmon's violent instincts as somehow normal. In the middle of the novel Bell briefly filters the action through her consciousness, a technique that causes readers to distance themselves from Redmon's and Laidlaw's tendencies to escape into alcohol and violence and to endanger their own lives.

In contrast to the critical reception of the novel's conclusion in 1989, readers in 1997 could view the violent ending of *Soldier's Joy* as prophetic given the proliferation of antigovernment militia groups since the novel was written. Rather than "a contrived, unconvincing climactic explosion of melodrama,"[27] the ending could be seen as the inevitable lethal outcome of situations in the United States that combine rage and hatred with readily available guns. Although the western part of the United States takes a slight lead over the South in numbers of paramilitary groups, the South still leads the country in hate groups.[28] In *Warrior Dreams: Paramilitary Culture in Post-Vietnam America,* James William Gibson delineates the personality profile of men engaged in such activities:

> First, they were deeply affected by the Vietnam War: their participation or their failure to make a personal appearance on the battlefield was a crucial event in their lives. Second, whether they fought in the war or not, these men drew the same conclusion from the defeat of the United States in Vietnam as did a certain part of the mass media: the white man's world was gone; dark forces of chaos had been unleashed and dangerous times made it not only permissible but morally imperative for them to take their personal battles far beyond the law. Paramilitary mythology offered men the fantastic possibility of escaping their present lives, being reborn as warriors, and then remaking the world.[29]

Certainly the weapons necessary are easily obtained. In a recent study the South still emerges as the region where people are "more likely to own guns" and "more likely to view their guns as instruments of protection."[30] As soon as Laidlaw hears that he has been targeted by the Klan, he thinks first, not of the local sheriff, but of the guns hidden beneath his house. Laidlaw and Redmon succeed in thwarting the attempt on Brother Jacob's life and in saving each other's lives, but men are killed on both sides, and the novel ends with the possibility that Laidlaw may die in Redmon's arms.

But the ending hints at another outcome and reminds readers of an ending that Bell abandoned, an ending that could perhaps have represented "something new" (p. 310) with blacks and whites living integrated lives together in the South. Hit with submachine gun fire in the chest during the shootout with the Ku Klux Klan, Laidlaw is certain he is going to die, but Redmon refuses to give into his pessimism, willing him to live with a reminder of the offer Laidlaw has made to split the land, "Hey, we still got a house to build. Are you taking back all you said?" (p. 465). In a way this remark comes as a bit of a surprise to the reader because the two men have never resolved their differences about joint land ownership; indeed the last time the subject comes up, it does not seem as if Redmon is interested in Laidlaw's gift unless Laidlaw will give him full rights to half of the property (p. 391). Bell has tantalized the reader with the possibility of a happy ending, Southern agrarian style—but racially integrated as befits the later part of the twentieth century. In many ways Bell's narrative technique with its lyrical descriptions of the land, its dialogic working through of racial misunderstandings, its several filter characters providing readers with both black and white perspectives, and its psychological realism of the first four books does not seem to prepare us for the shootout with the Klan over Brother Jacob's promotion of a fully integrated South. Opting for violence Bell chooses the more familiar Southern masculine ending when race relations are involved, only selecting late twentieth-century fire power—submachine guns instead of shotguns. The ending can certainly be seen as a chilling reminder that not all white Southerners are reconstructed. But the ending can also be seen as a capitulation to today's reading public, which eschews a "somnolent pace" and "gaggles of complicated interior thoughts." In the article "Literature and Pleasure: Bridging the Gap," Bell makes the case that the conventions of genre fiction should be "recovered for serious literature," arguing that "a little dabbling in genre does not necessarily corrupt the serious literary writer" and concluding that "as we take back some of that territory abandoned to genre fiction, we may get back some of the audience too."[31]

Once Vietnam veteran Ratman enters the novel to aid Laidlaw and Redmon with his military-style bunker and his arsenal of vintage Vietnam weapons, Bell's style changes from psychological realism to pulp fiction, and his subject changes from the struggle to forge adult male friendships across racial lines to the comradeship of warriors. Perhaps interracial agrarianism is to be seen as an "escapist fantasy" equal to the "New Age menu of magical solutions" Bell disparages in his 1991 article "An Essay Introducing His Work in Rather a Lunatic Fashion,"[32] and yet its presence in the novel can not be dismissed so easily. For in the same article Bell argues that for the novelist "what the unconscious labors to discover is never a fact, but a vision"; he goes on to say, "what maybe all my characters have always been after in all my books, is a visionary solution to the fatal problem which our collective consciousness is virtually unable to acknowledge."[33] Perhaps then the violence in *Soldier's Joy* is meant to be seductive to late twentieth-century readers, particularly young male readers, brought up on *Lethal Weapon* and *Die Hard* movies. Perhaps Bell hopes with enough violence "to soften the mind and render it receptive to all the more sophisticated pleasures that the finest literature can produce" as he says in "Literature and Pleasure." As a reader I feel, like David Bradley, that this "little dabbling in genre" in *Soldier's Joy* does "corrupt" the integrity of the novel. With his choice of conclusions, Bell abandons his "visionary solution" to the South's chronic racial problem—a problem that he, unlike Larry Brown, presents in its complexity. Bell's violent ending harks back to literary conventions that a previous generation of writers used "to solve" relationships that crossed the color line.

With both *Dirty Work* and *Soldier's Joy* readers dwell momentarily in the tantalizing possibility of friendships between black and white men. Although the relationships they represent are different in degrees of intimacy, they are similar in that they work only in cloistered settings: a veterans' hospital and a mountain cabin. Larry Brown does not test the relationship he creates in the larger context of Southern society. Madison Smartt Bell does, but he cannot quite imagine how such a friendship will sustain itself in a society where hate still lurks in the shadows.[34]

Notes

1. J. Glenn Gray, *The Warriors* (New York: Harper Torchbooks, 1959), p. 27.

2. Recently some philosophers and psychologists have asserted that the western paradigm of friendship between men is comradeship, which is characterized by loyalty, fellow feeling, and a concern for each other's interests. In "Male Friendship and Intimacy" (*Hypatia* 7, no. 3 [Summer 1992]: 110–25) Robert A. Strikwerda and Larry May summarize these arguments and assert that the characteristics of comradeship "have been stressed much more heavily than intimacy in male friendships" (p. 110).

3. See Chris Goodrich's review of *Dirty Work* in *Publisher's Weekly,* June 23, 1989, p. 32, and Susan Wood's review in the *Houston Post,* August 27, 1989, sec. C, p. 6. See also Greg Johnson's review in the *Atlanta Journal-Constitution,* September 3, 1989, sec. L, p. 10.

4. Strikwerda and May, "Male Friendship and Intimacy," p. 112.

5. Allen Tate, "A Southern Mode of the Imagination," in *Essays of Four Decades* (Chicago: University of Chicago Press, 1968), p. 583.

6. Larry Brown, *Dirty Work* [1989] (New York: Vintage Books, 1990), p. 120. Subsequent references are cited in the text.

7. Braiden listens to Walter, except when he talks about having sex with his new girlfriend Beth, a topic Braiden does not want to hear because it reminds him of his own unfulfilled desires.

8. Deborah Tannen, *You Just Don't Understand: Women and Men in Conversation* (New York: Ballantine Books, 1991), pp. 49–53.

9. Madison Smartt Bell, *Soldier's Joy* [1989] (New York: Penguin Books, 1990), p. 339. Subsequent references are cited in the text.

10. Strikwerda and May, "Male Friendship and Intimacy," p. 115.

11. There is one exception. In chapter 35 Redmon comes to pick up Laidlaw to visit Wat, Redmon's father. When Redmon is at Laidlaw's house, the narration is filtered through Redmon's perspective; when Laidlaw arrives at Wat's house, the narration is filtered through Laidlaw's perspective.

12. Susan Pollak and Carol Gilligan, "Images of Violence in Thematic Apperception Test Stories," *Journal of Personality and Social Psychology* 42 (1982): 159–67.

13. Strikwerda and May "Male Friendship and Intimacy," p. 118.

14. Toni Morrison first presented this black adult/white child character configuration from a more complex perspective when she focused on the black child whose mother was a servant in a white home in *The Bluest Eye* (New York: Holt, Rinehart and Winston, 1970).

15. See Mikhail M. Bakhtin, *The Dialogic Imagination: Four Essays,* ed. Michael Holquist, trans. Michael Holquist and Caryl Emerson (Houston: University of Texas Press, 1981), p. 353, and Bakhtin, *Problems of Doestoevsky's Poetics,* ed. and trans. Caryl Emerson (Minneapolis: University of Minnesota Press, 1984), p. 287.

16. Bakhtin, *The Dialogic Imagination,* p. 338.

17. Madison Smartt Bell, "An Essay Introducing His Work in Rather a Lunatic Fashion," *Chattahoochee Review* 12, no. 1 (Fall 1991): 1–3.

18. Mary Louise Weaks, "An Interview with Madison Smartt Bell," *Southern Review* 30, no. 1 (January 1994): 5–10.

19. Weaks, "An Interview with Madison Smartt Bell," pp. 5, 8.

20. Weaks, "An Interview with Madison Smartt Bell," p. 11.

21. Grey Johnson, "Two Numbed Vietnam Vets Turn to the Soil," *Chicago Tribune,* June 4, 1989, pp. 14, 5.

22. Winston Groom, "Fighting the Enemy from Tonkin to Tennessee," *Los Angeles Times,* July 2, 1989, sec. B, p. 2.

23. David Bradley, "The Battles Didn't End with the War," *New York Times Book Review,* July 2, 1989, pp. 3, 23, and David Nicholson, "Tennessee Mountain Nervous Breakdown," *Washington Post Book World,* June 25, 1989, p. 5.

24. Bradley, "The Battles Didn't End with the War," p. 23.

25. Don O'Briant, "Anger at Klan Fuels New Novel," *Atlanta Constitution,* June 12, 1988, sec. B p. 1.

26. See R. Reed Sanderlin, "Madison Smartt Bell," in *Contemporary Fiction Writers of the South,* ed. Joseph M. Flora and Robert Bain (Westport, Conn.: Greenwood Press, 1993), pp. 46–53. Bell writes of a revolutionary plot to blow up New York in *Waiting for the End of the World* (1985), of the Haitian slave revolt in *All Souls' Rising* (1995), and of Baltimore's gangs in *Ten Indians* (1996).

27. Bruce Allen, "'Joy' and Pain in the Backwoods," *USA Today,* July 28, 1989, sec. D, p. 5.

28. See "Active Patriot Groups in the U.S. in 1996," *Intelligence Report: Klan Watch and Militia Task Force* 86 (Spring 1997), pp. 18–19, and "Hate Groups in the United States in 1996" *Intelligence Report: Klan Watch and Militia Task Force* 86 (Winter 1997), pp. 20–21, Montgomery, Ala.: Southern Poverty Law Center, Internet.

29. James William Gibson, *Warrior Dreams: Paramilitary Culture in Post-Vietnam America* (New York: Hill and Wang, 1994), p. 196.

30. Dov Cohen and Richard E. Nisbett, "Self-Protection and the Culture of Honor: Explaining Southern Violence," *Personality and Social Psychology Bulletin* 20, no. 5 (October 1994): 562. This study determined that "although southerners were more likely to endorse violence to protect and restore order, they were not more likely to endorse violence to bring about change" (p. 554), which might explain why there has been more paramilitary activity in the West than in the South.

31. Madison Smartt Bell, "Literature and Pleasure: Bridging the Gap," *Antaeus* 59 (Autumn 1987): 134.

32. Bell, "An Essay Introducing His Work in Rather a Lunatic Fashion," p. 8.

33. Bell, "An Essay Introducing His Work in Rather a Lunatic Fashion," p. 13.

34. I wish to thank the National Endowment for the Humanities for a 1997 summer research grant, which allowed me to complete this essay.

"After Freedom"—Blacks and Whites in the 1990s

The Facts and the Fiction

Dori Sanders

I will address the South in the 1990s—but I will first address the past. I am a Southerner. It is a given—we cannot tell someone where we are, or where we are going, unless we tell where we have been. It is just a Southern thing.

Around 1915 a young, single black man made his first acquisition of eighty-one acres of farmland in a small rural community in South Carolina. He moved along with his share-cropping father, a former slave, and his mother to their own homestead, where there would be freedom to do what they wanted, whenever they wanted. That man was my father. Consequently this has been the basis of my entire life experience, for in order for me to even begin to address the present, I have to take a close look at the past—in the personal as well as the public arena. To have the freedom to walk on and cultivate his own land was a giant step forward for my grandfather, a man who could neither read nor write. When he learned about the life of Booker T. Washington, he compared his childhood to that of Washington, who wrote about his early childhood in his autobiography *Up from Slavery:* "From the time that I can remember anything, almost every day of my life has been occupied in some kind of labour. . . . During the period that I spent in slavery I was not large enough to be of much service, still I was occupied most of the time in cleaning the yards, carrying water to the men in the fields, or going to the mill, to which I used to take the corn, once a week, to be ground."[1] For my father, the words of Fredrick Douglass were singled out and often repeated: "If there is no struggle, there is no progress. Those who profess to favor freedom, and yet depreciate agitation, are men who want rain without thunder and lightning. They want the ocean without its many waters, they want crops without plowing the soil."

It would be the strengths of close-knit families that would enable determined people to survive the struggles that would lead to progress. The family unit offered that sense of belonging identified by Eudora Welty—"a sense of belonging somewhere, to a part of the country" as an especially strong characteristic in Southern people. Welty observes that if you understand where you live and the people around you, you can better understand other people.[2] Most households consisted of an extended family with grandparents, who passed down oral histories, a strong cultural heritage, and binding traditions. They were singing "sorrow songs," the lamentations of an oppressed people—songs that eventually influenced the blues. For the enslaved people, their hard labor produced a body of work songs that sustained them through backbreaking days and expressed the despair they must have felt. Music historian James Haskins writes: "the blues represented the cries of people who had nothing no matter how hard they tried, and whose lives seemed hopeless. . . . Such songs were often sung in lively rhythms like laughing to keep from crying."[3]

If pressed to define the culture of the South, one could surely produce a few factual statements that would cover a whole range of subjects, but the primary theme of all Southern culture has been biracial. It is scarred by unfair racial segregation, discrimination and their consequences. It was Southern culture that rose fully on the backs of slaves who produced the menial labor necessary for the prosperity that aggrandized it. If it had been done during the epoch of the World Wars, as in the Jew's sorrowful plight, torture, and exploitation at the hands of the Nazis, it would have similarly raised ethical barriers to the acceptance of the products of their enforced labor, and the glory of civilization would therefore have reduced human values because it valued human life with discrimination.[4]

No plantation owner during the early history of the United States could have afforded to hire blacks at minimum wage, or agricultural workers from a migratory pool, as they can today. Besides, agricultural workers today are savvy and are beginning to be unionized with demands of their own, before any contract is signed or hand is shaken in agreement. What the South produced early on was a white privileged world—a leisure world of refinement, culture, etiquette, and taste—all undergirded by the spilling of black blood, sweat, and tears. But even today this is very seldom acknowledged by whites, Southern or otherwise, as regards the consequences of this evil hegemony. The misery of a people cried out for equality as promised by the Bill of Rights, the Constitution and the Amendments. Long sermons on Christian virtues were useless to reform the country, and so was the slow moan of torment in black musical expression, which America so dearly loves. Black ethnic expression is considered quaint at best. But although it is part and parcel of the American heritage to demonstrate to others the glory of America's past, this does little to explain the evils which were further pared from the human skin of individuals with cruel whips and flails. Yet these were the new Israelites, without a Moses to champion them. The release from bondage was slow in coming and came only after President Lincoln freed the slaves formally at the time of the Civil War, the terms of their release would never be fully implemented, not even to this very day!

Blacks were not considered "humans" to whom the equality clause applied; they were considered a type of "hybrid," a meld of animal and human, perhaps with "good ape genes" included, and little talent for "intellectual reasoning" let alone the ability to define the distinction between "cultural imperialism" and "imperial cultism"! Even today the debate is renewed with fervor, as a number of spurious intellectual sophists demonstrate the idea in print and on television to a sensation-seeking, greedy, and gullible public—promoting the same old idea that blacks are incapable of achieving higher IQ rates than whites.[5] It is suggested that perhaps college courses are "wasted" on them because they lack "intellectual capacity." Yet what educated blacks have done for their race is to demonstrate clearly the falsity of these claims. Lacking university training in the bush, as many early blacks did, it could be expected that any aboriginal would need time to surpass the masters. We are confronted with the psychological scarring here of an invading culture that works adverse stimulus upon the conquered. Being without assenting will and intelligence, they were mere "property"[6] to be disposed of, at the whim of the owners, who bought them at auction with the proceeds from plantation earnings, thus compounding the sins of the forefathers.

What was this culture that flourished in the South? It was the binding of two races of people together in a type of fatal grip that will perhaps never be severed but will be constantly changing through redefinition, exacerbation, and even open conflict. It is a transplant of the English imperialistic system of agribusiness whose profits accrued to the Crown and its aristocrats. Those who were not indentured servants, fugitives from debtors' prison, were English "wannabee" aristocrats who envied people with wealth, position, and power. Slaves therefore were an accepted part of life in the original colonies. Imported from Africa to work the fields, they were the survivors of the great and terrible slave ships which carried live black wood instead of firewood to be burnt in the kilns and under the promising sun of America. They had been captured alive in the jungles, exported to holding bins and corrals on the coast awaiting the ships from America, whose captains would see that they were shackled sometimes hundreds deep, without a mouthful of fresh water or a crust of bread, lying in vomit and excrement, dying before they could breathe the "free air" of the American colonies.[7] They were treated as "cargo" to buy and sell, as uncomplaining ballast to mistreat or treasure as living symbols of gold and wealth. This attitude became ingrained in the foundations of Southern plantations. The wealth of the South was cane and cotton. Labor was King not Cotton—who could buy labor cheap and make fortunes on the agricultural products if it were not for this mighty black engine? Granted, some slave owners were kind and considerate according to basic ingrained Christian values, but others were vile and inhumane, exacting death as the cost of disobedience and believing only in the god of power and money.

Educable slaves, or those who had an observable IQ higher than the average, were found who could be transformed into house laborers or the more refined "personal" servant, maid, or butler. Even after the advent of freedom blacks were forced to take menial positions that other Americans shunned. Kitchen help or cleaning woman or handyman were the names for these. Whites never stooped to the same depth, even the most impoverished of them. The field hand was less well off than the average house laborer. Even the jobs open to the house servant could be in such limited employments as meal preparation, housekeeping, food preservation, serving at table, and in the important position of nursemaid or nanny to the heirs and heiresses of family plantation fortunes. Nursemaids held a very high place and even had a love-hate relationship with their charges, but they could seldom dictate to their charges. Having been suckled by a black woman, these children often demonstrated a type of emotional bonding that was different from the bonding with their biological mothers, but nonetheless just as binding emotionally and psychologically as natural blood bonding.

As a slave there was no way to rebuff sexual advances of the plantation owner either; therefore a great many children resulted from these unholy unions. They were different and set apart by color from the average African slave. Since the lactation response could only be produced by pregnancy, as was true with plantation livestock, it was necessary to cause nursing blacks to become pregnant in order to lactate for the suckling of infants. Although a good many Southerners would have you believe that the choice of nurses was made only with natural black pregnancy candidates, there is no way to confirm the methods because any child born was divorced from its family and either consigned to the fields or sold to another plantation. Good slave owners generally kept the family intact because happiness produced good workers. Many of the offspring ranged anywhere from coal black, medium brown, coffee, coffee cream, to tan or white. Blacks often talked about "high yalla," which was a lighter skin tone with a resulting snobbishness as to origins. Instead of bringing the black people together, it served to separate them by shade distinction. But this is no different a phenomenon than what can be observed in Latin cultures of the Caribbean or the Americas, where the infusion of black slaves produced the same ranges of color through interracial

"After Freedom"—Blacks and Whites in the 1990s

unions. There is still a color sophistry that adheres to the culture, even though it is denied for the sake of egalitarianism.

The reaction against freedom for blacks in the South took the form of Klansmen rallies, raids, threats, and hangings. Vigilantism flourished along with home-dispensed justice. A great many hangings, burnings, and maimings resulted, which instilled a fear underlying all Southern racial tensions. If it is not fear of repercussion, it is fear of sexual inadequacy, inequality, contagion, etc. Hypertension consequently among blacks is inordinately higher than in the white population because of a double-tiered structure of discrimination in American society. What bodes ill for the South today is the increasing reverse migration of black populations from the North to the South whereas the migration in the first century after the Civil War was northwards. What is causing this today is better economic conditions in the South and the worsening job situation in the industrial North.

Blacks in the past were often perceived as "dirty" not only because of their biological coloring but because of the conditions of their forced existence. It was a thought related to observations—for instance, the color of the African American palm or the sole of the foot is lighter in color than the surrounding skin. This natural biological trait was taken as proof that the rest of the person was dirty. Such "dirtiness" produced a biracial response. Whites were accorded their own services, functions, and venues, while blacks were given theirs in another location and were denied equality of environment. Segregation became well established after the Civil War when carpetbaggers swept the South telling blacks that they had full equality, that they could vote, that they would be given forty acres and a mule[8] as terms for their freedom, and that they could do the very same things white people did without a problem. The Klan saw to it that this would never be so. Granted virtual immunity by the concepts of freedom of thought in the Constitution and the Amendments, they fostered their own philosophy of hatred. They continue to exist in the South today openly and without social reproach, selling hoods, Klan garments, books of their philosophy, and flags of their movement. This made the national news promoting Laurens, South Carolina, as their town and causing a public outcry by blacks, the NAACP, and whites alike. There is never any mention of this as being similar to the Skokie March, which affected the primarily Jewish suburb in Illinois when it was invaded intentionally by a Nazi group because their freedom by Constitution and Amendments assured them the right to do so.

When it wishes to conceal certain improprieties from outsiders, the South takes the attitude of social nicety, refusing to discuss in public the conditions of unsolvable issues or basic Southern racial problems. Real confrontation therefore is impossible, because any improper subject is often kept sequestered within white society, or swept under the rug as unimportant frivolous talk. Certain parts of the South, however, are less visibly affected by racial tensions than others in the Southern tier. But discrimination and racial hatred are still evident there today. Segregation in the past was widely observed in Southern schools, on Southern transport such as buses and trains, in restaurants, neighborhoods, and even in the most unlikely place of Southern churches. One would think that where Christian values of the same denomination were evident, they would share one venue, but this was not so. Father Malcolm Boyd, the Episcopal priest, mentions in his book a case where there existed a white parish on one side of the street and a black parish on the other, and there was no intermingling not even for worship or for common denominational fundraising.[9] When he suggested that they cooperate he was rudely reined in by the parish trustees, and removed subsequently by the diocesan bishop to another less problematic parish.

Even in courthouses, where one would think that the scales of justice would be proudly held up as an example of blind equality, seating for blacks was high in the balconies and drinking fountains and restrooms were segregated into "Whites Only" and "Colored Only." Coloreds were not allowed in certain restaurants *at all*. Even in the five-and-dime or at the drugstore eating counter, they were not allowed to sit, eat, or drink with whites, but were allowed in the store only to buy what they needed and to leave. Loitering was forbidden as any loitering was perceived, because of a siege mentality, as time spent plotting the downfall of white Southern society. Where mixed transport was available, blacks throughout the South were forced to sit at the rear of buses. When Rosa Parks sat down in the front of the bus, it caused a great stir in the South, because she was thought to be inflicting her "impertinence" upon Southern society, flaunting good prudence and Southern values, instead of just being too tired to go to the back of the bus, where she was ordered to go.[10] Change of any sort is not without pain and suffering.

Although a climate of change was ushered in during the 1950s, the fight for equal rights was not solved by President Kennedy's administration. Although he was mildly and quietly in favor of civil rights legislation, his statement of support for President Eisenhower's "intervention" with troops in order to enforce the integration of Little Rock schools was less than vocal. But by the end of 1962 enforced segregation in interstate transportation, which was theoretically outlawed by the Supreme Court in the 1950s, finally ceased to exist. The signs for coloreds and whites were removed quietly and unobtrusively and life continued apace. Civil rights leader Dr. Martin Luther King, Jr., supported by the NAACP officials, pushed even further for change in the South in particular and nationwide in general. They knew that they had a president willing to listen to their

"After Freedom"—Blacks and Whites in the 1990s

pleas for assistance. Many weighed hope against the reality of the moment, but reality had become a fiction and was found lacking in the fundamental principles of human existence. It had become like a film script, filled with trite expressions of emotional support, false utopian ideologies, and a view of the biracial problem as real as white perceptions of Charlie Chan as the ultimate Chinese example of sophisticated crime detection. Although palpable, it was not a realistic paradigm for society to build upon. It was fiction not fact.

The South has never taken kindly to the fervent and difficult struggle for equal rights. Across the country there is nothing homogeneous about regional consciousness. What is observable in the North is not true for the South, nor is the West the model for Southern consciousness perception. Forcing school integration resulted in whites' boycotting the schools so that they became black educational bastions of victory, but without increasing educational levels of African Americans by a biracial or cultural competition. We know today that levels increase if both sides are allowed to vie for supremacy and through dialogue encounter the basic principles of liberty that are treasured in American society and open debate as a whole. The struggle for equality has not been just a political battle of wits, people have died as a result of the violence. Men, women, and children have suffered violence and death at the hands of emotional individuals or crowds of individuals who felt threatened. Children, although they should be the least affected by the violence, tend to be the most victimized. At a young age they accept individualism as the basis for their social expression. We see equality among all children of all races when they are exposed to others of a different race. Hatred is learned behavior, and we see how, as children grow, they take on the coloring of the perceptions of parents, peers, teachers, and mentors. So it is not surprising that they become the victims of discrimination and violence, and they emulate the perpetrators of the discrimination and violence.

The segregationists, fearing that their own existence would be changed by the racial situation, warned of impending dangers and the perils of inattention to racial issues. Mixed marriages having been forbidden for at least a century or two by misogyny laws, were found to be obvious overcompensation, for the fact obvious to all was that the races were already well mixed. And the issue of race had become a crisis. If one considers the fiction of the 1990s, it would seem that the problem of race is near the point of being resolved, but this perhaps is not the truth.

I hesitate to attempt to erase the past—to allow it to fade from my memory. One should not forget the past—but should instead face that dark page in history and move with tolerance into the future. Today, in the 1990s, it has been well over a hundred years after slavery was officially abolished in the

Dori Sanders

United States in 1865, when the Thirteenth Amendment to the Constitution went into effect—but racial tension is still with us, even though the 1990s represent an integrated South, very different from the South less than fifty years ago. Today, in the 1990s, from all appearances, the cultures have blended, it is an integrated South. Yet the private lives of black and white South Carolinians still tend to be separate. Most beauty and barber shops, funeral homes, and even churches are still separate, either black or white. However, it is usually a separateness dictated through choice. Many are divided and somewhat pessimistic about race relations today. John Hope Franklin, professor emeritus at Duke University, North Carolina, best known for his classic book, *From Slavery to Freedom,* and considered one of the preeminent historians of the 20th Century, observed in *The Charlotte Observer* on July 7, 1996, that "race relations are not good in the country at this time."

In my novel *Clover* (1990) the New South is explored in fiction through the eyes of a ten-year-old black girl who has to face life with a new white stepmother after her father was killed in a tragic car accident.[11] There are differences in backgrounds. Varied tastes in food emphasize the cultural differences that threaten to keep the newcomer, a white woman, an outsider. A review by Laura M. Zaidman, professor of English at the University of South Carolina at Sumter, notes that Clover grudgingly accepts her new stepmother. That is not to say Clover feels comfortable with the clash of black and white cultures. Clover describes how Sara Kate is squeezed in between her and Jim Ed on the crowded bench for her father's funeral "like vanilla cream between dark chocolate cookies" (p. 22). Then the child considers the irony, her daddy is dead and all she can think of is an Oreo cookie. At this point, however, she sees Sara Kate, not as an individual, but only as the striking differences between vanilla and chocolate.

Not only is Sara Kate a stranger to this region, but also being white, well educated, and well dressed make her even more the outsider in the black farming community. Racial prejudice also creates disharmony. Clover hears the women talk about Sara Kate: "Can't you just die from all that beige and taupe she's wearing?" "Girl, them some Gloria Vanderbilt's pants." "Aw shucks now, go on, girl." "Wonder what's wrong with her?" "I don't know, but there is something that's caused her to be rejected by her own men." "Well, something's wrong with her. Why would she take up with a black dude?" (p. 42). Prejudice on the part of family members makes it difficult for Clover. She is told by her Aunt Everleen to never repeat things discussed between them, that is family talk. Then in the very next breath she will tell Clover: "Now, remember Sara Kate is family, so be nice to her and tell her her cooking tastes real, real good. You know how white women are. They want you to brag on 'em all the time. To tell them you love 'em. They don't care whether it's the truth or not" (p. 59). Next

"After Freedom"—Blacks and Whites in the 1990s

Everleen tells Clover not to hurt Sara Kate's feelings. Thus having been told that most white women have been sheltered and petted all their lives and that the least little thing just tears them up, Clover lies about her stepmother's watery grits and chicken swimming in tomatoes and green peppers: "This chicken is some kind of good, Sara Kate" (p. 64). In the end it is Clover who makes her own decisions about her new stepmother and the kind of person she really is.

A wealthy white landowner starts showing interest in Clover's stepmother. He starts calling on her, and Sara Kate seems most pleased with his visits. Clover says, "In a way, I guess it's good he comes. At least, all that sadness that balls up in Sara Kate's eyes sometimes will go away. I tell you, a person would have to be blind not to see she likes Chase." In Clover's presence, the wealthy landowner, in conversation, mentioned that one of his cousins once had to work as hard "as a damn nigger woman" just to pay her rent:

> Sara Kate winced when he said that right before me, and sucked in her breath. The corners of her mouth tightened. What Chase said brought on a strange quiet. . . . Poor old dumb Chase. Now that it had sunk in what he'd said, he was so ashamed. He couldn't even hold his head up. Just kept his eyes fastened on his fancy boots. When he did look up, Sara Kate's face showed she'd heard him all right. Yet her face didn't show anger, just her disappointment in him. Her face just sort of closed down. She didn't choose to make something out of it. She didn't say anything and neither did Chase. . . . Sometimes when Sara Kate thinks that Chase Porter might be calling for her, she will let that telephone almost ring off the hook. She'll be just sitting right there looking at it and she won't even pick it up. But you know, it serves Chase right. Looks like with all the stuff you see on TV, Chase should know that you can't even say something unkind about black folks today and get away with it. Much less use the word nigger.
> . . . . I'm beginning to see I have to speak out for Sara Kate. My Aunt and Uncle simply can't go on always putting her down. . . . Yes, I'm taking her side right now. But that doesn't mean I'm turning against them. Why can't they understand—why can't people know, why can't they see that when you live with someone and they aren't mean or nothing they kind of grow on you?[12]

Alice Walker confessed recently on television of her childhood perceptions that the only good white person she ever knew as a child was Santa Claus. He came to visit them at Christmas and brought presents, not wanting anything from them. From this she deduced the value of other good white people, but it has not been without pain or suffering, or trial and error. I assure you the racial problem in America is far from resolved—especially in the South. Outward appearances are deceiving particularly because Southerners refuse to air their laundry in public and refuse any interference in their internal affairs.

Dori Sanders

The budding of Clover's consciousness regarding the natural progression of her development in a fictional treatment does not reflect the realities of the South as it materialized. It was more an adolescent child's perception, not reflective of an adult consciousness yet. Children of that age require an accommodation to life in order to survive the vicissitudes of the reality that confronts their consciousness, and they are forced upon almost all individuals with a longer curriculum vitae than theirs. Clover begins to see how just one white person has affected all her perceptions, and her world seems invaded by white divergent goals and avenues without their leaving a very deep impression on her. Her stepmother's goals are not Clover's own, nor will they be, but she accepts them on an individual basis as valid for her, true for her stepmother but not true for herself.

Southern society on the whole is not like this at all. In over forty years of the civil rights struggle, even with progressive legislation enacted by Congress, the separateness of the races is self-evident for the least observant. It remains impervious to change, because the South is distinctive, and it still inflicts its will in subtle as well as not so subtle ways. The controversy over the flying of the Confederate flag over the state house in Columbia, South Carolina, still rages. Whites see it as a proud heritage to be supported—that of being against Yankee imperialism, against antislavery, against crimes, against ownership (often meaning of slaves). To a black person that flag means something more cruel and more insidious than the innocent trappings of honor and self-determinism. It symbolizes blood, murder, rape, imprisonment, inequality, and shame. It means the same thing to black men and women as the swastika does to the Jew: it is emblematic of defeat and the blackest period of their history.

Economically, genocide was never an option for the South. Southerners needed labor to run their economy and support the lifestyles to which Southern families had become accustomed. The flag therefore is a minority issue rather than one of economics. Blacks are perceived as awkward, unintelligent, ignorant, and uneducable; therefore, they are paid less or have fewer benefits than whites would in comparable positions. This is a fact of Southern life. Although any inequal treatment of the individual is forbidden by U.S. law, there are many ways in which the law is circumvented. Due to economics, the administrative fields of power are still kept out of the reach of the average African American. There is a glass ceiling that cannot be penetrated. And just as certain as political positions are withheld from gays, ethnics, or women,—such as the presidency—blacks are also kept from entering these positions. When the Anita Hill case became newsworthy, we found that she was doubly damned by being both black and a woman.[13] What further destroyed her credibility, as she herself admits, was that she did not accord the male chauvinist legislators she was encountering the respect they demanded according to the traditions of Congress. She was required to be sponsored by someone before she could appear before the Congressional Committee, and she waived it much to her own detriment. Here was a brilliant professor of law being treated as a black prostitute would have been treated in the South!

When a black family moves into an all-white neighborhood, white families begin moving out. This was treated in Lorraine Hansberry's play *A Raisin in the Sun* from 1959, but it is still quite true today.[11] A white person can travel anywhere in America without much difficulty. But a similar black person is arrested, questioned, or told to be gone from many all-white sections of America. The premise for such behavior is that a black individual has "no business" in white residential sections of the country without a "slave" permit. Anita Hill describes this as a piece of paper which slaves were forced to carry on their person stating their name, their owner's name, and the business the slave was on, so that any illegal or runaway slaves or no-good freeds could be found, imprisoned or physically punished. Ms. Hill told her avid listeners at many of her lectures that she was a black without a slave pass when she journeyed to Washington to confront the congressional committee.

She was also butting her head against the wall of enforced perceptions of black women as sexual playthings. As a black woman she could be "used" by men any way they chose. This is an idea that descends from the rights of Southern slave owners, who could have their sexual way with any slave woman they chose. Since she was not considered human, but property, she had no say in what was demanded of her. And any accusation against a male likewise was inadmissible because it was not considered evidence of criminal activity. Thomas Jefferson also demanded sexual favors of his own female slave upon whom he sired several children without benefit of marriage or inheritance. He took his black woman to Paris with him and kept her as his own personal slave. There was offered to her for favors granted, however, freedom of person. But the relationship surfaced only recently in the context of a play. It seems that perhaps the truth can be told only within a literary context, but not within the scope of fact, even though corroborating evidence is there.

Notes

1. Booker T. Washington, *Up from Slavery* (New York: Viking Penguin, 1986), pp. 5–6.
2. Eudora Welty, *Atlanta Journal-Constitution,* June 24, 1978, "Magazine," pp. 7–8.
3. Michael Lasser, *Uniquely American: Singing the Blues* (San Diego: Geico Direct, Spring 1996).

Dori Sanders

    4. Thomas Keneally, *Schindler's List* (New York: Simon and Schuster, 1982).

    5. Michael Levin, *Why Race Matters: Race Differences and What They Mean* (Westport, Conn.: Praeger, 1997).

    6. Joshua R. Giddings, *Amistad Claim, History of the Case: Speech of Mr. Giddings of Ohio in the House of Representatives December 21, 1853* (Washington, D.C.: s.n., 1853).

    7. Alex Haley, *Roots* (Garden City, N.Y.: Doubleday, 1976).

    8. Claude F. Oubre, *Forty Acres and a Mule: The Freedman's Bureau and Black Land Ownership* (Baton Rouge: Louisiana State University Press, 1978).

    9. Malcolm Boyd, *As I Live and Breathe: Stages of an Autobiography* (New York: Random House, 1970).

    10. David Scott Brown, *Don't Ride the Bus on Monday: The Rosa Parks Story* (Englewood Cliffs, N. J.: Prentice-Hall, 1973).

    11. Dori Sanders, *Clover* (Chapel Hill, N.C.: Algonquin Books, 1990). Subsequent references are cited in the text.

    12. In these quotations, Cf. *Clover,* pp. 108–10 and Cf. *Clover,* pp. 139–40, Dori Sanders's wording differs markedly from the parallel passages in the published novel. Dori Sanders has confirmed that for her essay in this collection she prefers the present wording, which reflects her original manuscript.

    13. Emma Coleman Jordan, *Race Gender and Power in America: The Legacy of the Hill-Thomas Hearings,* ed. Anita Faye Hill (New York: Oxford University Press, 1995).

    14. Lorraine Hansberry, *A Raisin in the Sun* (1994 reprint, New York: Vintage Books, 1959).

Part III

Reconstructing Southern Identity

"We Ain't White Trash No More"

Southern Whites and the Reconstruction of Southern Identity

James C. Cobb

Surely Larry L. King spoke for many white Southerners when he responded to Jimmy Carter's acceptance speech at the 1976 Democratic National Convention by serving notice on multiple generations of sneering "damnyankee peckerwoods" that "We Ain't Trash No More!" The note of triumph sounded by King faded quickly, however, as the prospect of assimilation into the American mainstream quickly raised the specter of cultural anonymity. By 1983, John Shelton Reed was already observing that the well-educated, relatively affluent and upwardly mobile white Southerners who were leading the region's march toward the mainstream of American life were also those most likely to find the issue of regional identity "salient." In other words, the white Southerners least likely to be identified as "white trash" were those most likely to "categorize themselves and others as 'Southerners' and 'non-Southerners,' and to believe that they know what that means."[1]

This trend only accelerated throughout the 1980s and 1990s as, plunged into an identity crisis of major proportions, Southern whites began a desperate search for some tangible and demonstrable, hold-it-in-your-hand, see-it-with-your-eyes reaffirmation of their Southernness. For many of them that search seemed to begin with *Southern Living* magazine. In the February 1966 inaugural issue of *Southern Living,* president and editor in chief Eugene Butler explained that his magazine aimed at helping "urban and suburban families" to "live a more enjoyable life in the South by making better use of your growing incomes, your leisure and your mental and physical assets." Describing the South as a place "where emphasis is given to social, cultural, and recreational life," Butler promised that "month after month our new magazine will portray good Southern living ideas and qualities." As if to underscore this pledge, an advertisement next to Butler's piece offered a recipe for a "Frito Chili Pie," featuring Fritos corn chips, canned chili, onions, and American cheese.[2]

James C. Cobb

In 1985 *Southern Living* fell into the clutches of the Yankees at New York–based Time Warner, but its spokesman promised to continue "to give people in the South a sense of pride in being southern." By the 1990s the magazine's circulation stood at nearly 2.5 million, and recipes for Frito chili pies were no more likely to be found on its pages than stories about lynchings or pellagra. Nicholas Lemann observed recently that "for affluent southern whites today, 'the southern way of life' no longer means 'white supremacy' but includes a list of essentials such as the 'totally planned community' around a golf course, cheese grits and honey-baked ham at the pre-game brunch," and, of course, "a five-year subscription to *Southern Living*."[3]

Despite—or perhaps because of—growing statistical evidence of the white South's assimilation into the American mainstream, interest in the Southern cultural identity soared in the 1990s. As one journalist noted, "Institutes, centers and programs for the study of the South are becoming as ubiquitous on Southern campuses as Wal-Marts are in Southern suburbia." The University of North Carolina at Chapel Hill had its Center for the Study of the American South and its ambitious new journal *Southern Cultures*. At the University of Alabama, there was the Center for Southern History and Culture, while the University of South Carolina boasted the Institute for Southern Studies. Fittingly enough, however, the leader among Southern universities in this area was the University of Mississippi. By the 1990s Ole Miss's Center for the Study of Southern Culture offered both undergraduate and graduate degrees in Southern studies.[4]

The Southern studies boom on Dixie campuses reflected the growing involvement of Southern academics in the marketing of Southern culture to popular audiences throughout the South. On the one hand, it was encouraging to see those who scrutinized the South gaining not just acceptance but celebrity and status in a region where scholars, especially those who studied the South, were once regarded with both suspicion and contempt. Yet, there was nonetheless a concern among some observers that the "selling of Southern culture" to a popular audience might be getting a bit out of hand. The Center for the Study of Southern Culture, for example, organized cruises down the Mississippi on the Delta Queen, interspersing scholarly lectures with musical performances and other activities showcasing Southern culture in a generally airy and upbeat fashion. Critics of such activities feared that blunt truth-telling and hard-nosed analysis of the South's past and present is giving way to a sort of "Hollywood" effect that leaves racial, sexual, and class exploitation on the cutting room floor while popular audiences are left to gorge themselves, as one journalist put it, on "big houses, Brunswick stew and banjo pickers."[5]

Also concerned about "fetishization of a false past" was Eric Bates of *Southern Exposure,* a publication traditionally given not to celebrating the

Southern good life but to telling the unpleasant truth about the problems of the Southerners whose lives were not so good. In recent years, however, even the tone of *Southern Exposure*'s offerings has lightened considerably. These days instead of the familiar, unbroken litany of long-faced leftist critiques, *Southern Exposure* offers a section called "Still the South" that focuses on some of the more amusing and exotic aspects of Southern life. As this feature has shown, the South is a land of coon dog cemeteries and collard greens ("From age to age the South has hollered / The praises of the toothsome collard"). It is also saturated with mobile homes (half of the national total sits on cement blocks in the South) and miniature golf courses. In the latter case, at least, the authors could not resist pointing out that the reason that half of the official Putt-Putt golf franchises are in the South is that "land is less expensive, laws are less stringent, and labor unions are less difficult to deal with."[6]

Developments at *Southern Exposure* notwithstanding, however, when it came to showcasing Southernness, the University of Mississippi's Center for the Study of Southern Culture was, as Peter Applebome put it, "Bubba Central." In August 1995, two days after the conclusion of its twenty-second annual conference on William Faulkner, Ole Miss hosted the first "International Conference on Elvis Presley," whom Center for the Study of Southern Culture director William Ferris hailed as "the most important pop-culture figure of the twentieth century" and "a true modernist who eluded definitions like white or black, male or female." The other moving force behind the conference, English professor Vernon Chadwick, actually taught a course comparing some of the works of Melville to some of the films of Elvis, a course that students quickly dubbed "Melvis." The conference itself offered numerous surprises and innovations, including a performance by "El Vez," the "Mexican Elvis" (accompanied by his Memphis Mariachis and the Beautiful Elvettes), and a revelation by clergyman and folk artist Rev. Howard Finster (whose creations often featured a representation of Elvis) that he had once had a posthumous encounter with the duly departed "King." Finster maintained that "Elvis Presley came to visit me in my garden. . . . I said, 'Elvis can you stay?' He said, 'Howard, I'm on a tight schedule,' and then he was gone."[7]

Of the estimated two hundred or so in attendance at the Elvis Extravaganza, more than one hundred were journalists who at times gave the proceedings the air of a "media circus." Undeterred by the criticism heaped on them for the nontraditional nature of their endeavors, conference organizers announced that the theme for the 1996 conference would be "Then Sings My Soul: Elvis and the Sacred South." This gathering included an all-night gospel singing, an appearance by a man claiming to be Elvis Presley, Jr., and a concert by "Elvis Herselvis," a self-described "atomic-powered lesbian," who, with "the Straight White Males," was billed as "one of the hottest new acts on the West Coast club scene."[8] The negative publicity attracted by the first Elvis Conference and the controversial, nontraditional nature of the second one shocked even those ultimate arbiters of good taste, the officials at Graceland, the Presley estate in Memphis. Explaining why Graceland could no longer support the conference, a spokesman noted the inclusion of "quirky elements designed to get publicity" and explained that "it looks like a freak show down there.... We're not comfortable being associated with it." Even before Ole Miss had been "dissed" by Graceland, Provost Gerald Walton issued a memo announcing that the university would no longer host the controversial gathering, leading the *Oxford Eagle* to announce grimly but succinctly: "Ole Miss Kills Elvis."[9]

Quite naturally, the 1996 Summer Olympic Games in Atlanta afforded the opportunity for further "merchandising" of Southern culture to popular audiences. Following up on the success of the *Encyclopedia of Southern Culture,* the University of North Carolina Press produced the *Encyclopedia of Southern Culture Quiz Book,* which queried readers on topics ranging from the etymology of "Bubba" to the origins of the banjo and the Moon Pie. Like the ironic acquisition of *Southern Living* magazine by Time Warner, the publication of this and similar books simply confirmed the growing perception that, having at last secured the resources for full-scale participation in the national consumer culture, upwardly mobile Southern whites stood not just ready but anxious to consume their own regional culture as rapidly as commercial and academic marketers could commodify it.[10]

The process I am attempting to describe and analyze is one in which I am often a shameless participant. I am nonetheless inclined to share some of the concerns of Edwin M. Yoder, who complains that this obsession with idiom and idiosyncrasy threatens to turn the South of popular perception into little more than a homegrown caricature of itself. This trend is readily observable in musical circles where youthful Southern white urbanites and collegians flock to hear dozens of so-called "redneck chic" groups such as the Austin Lounge Lizards, whose offerings include the gospel favorite "Jesus Loves Me (But He Can't Stand You)." In Atlanta, young fans of both bohemian and preppy persuasion are drawn to Slim Chance and the Convicts, Redneck Greece and the Stump Broke Steers (whose "Don't Let Another Penis Come Between Us" is a real crowd pleaser), and numerous other similarly trendy aggregations who specialize in raunchy rockabilly interspersed with parodied renditions of country classics and bawdy uptown takeoffs on down-home humor. The Atlanta scene even features a hyperactive all-female honky tonker support group known as the "Dixie Hickies." The hottest such redneck chic group at present seems to be the (of all places) Chapel Hill–based Southern Culture on the Skids, a phenomenally popular college band whose name suggests both its repertoire and, quite likely, its social significance as well.[11]

Ironically, even as identity-challenged white Southerners embraced a caricatured and stereotypical vision of themselves and their region, they found that many of these caricatures and stereotypes were themselves being absorbed into mainstream culture. For more than a century, the term "redneck" had been the nation's most acceptable ethnic slur, suggesting the kind of white males who lynched blacks, slept with their sisters and married their cousins, and generally ripped around in their jacked-up, gun-racked pickups, dipping snuff, flinging their empties out the windows, and playing Hank, Jr., loud enough to wake Hank, Sr. By the 1990s, however, "redneck" had become something approaching a term of endearment, connoting above anything else a fierce independence in the face of the suffocating conformist pressures that permeated American mass society. Historian Jack Temple Kirby explained that the appeal of the redneck lifestyle was strikingly "countercultural," and sociologist Richard Peterson pointed out that "to call oneself a redneck is not so much to *be* a redneck by birth or occupational fate, but rather to identify with an anti-bourgeois attitude and lifestyle."[12]

Peterson's observation is borne out in Clemson, South Carolina, which countered Charleston's refined and somewhat precious Spoleto Arts Festival with its own "Spittoono Festival," emphasizing "Redneck Pride" and offering tobacco spitting and beer chugging contests as well. Elsewhere, a popular sweatshirt not only identified its wearer as "Absolutely Proud to Be a Redneck" but explained (somewhat expansively for a sweatshirt) that "This extremely proud group of Americans takes great pride in their laid back rural lifestyle. Dressed up in their baseball caps, flannels and bibs they cruise the dirt roads in their pickup trucks searching for a hoot'n and holler'n good time down at the local water'n hole!" At the local watering hole, one might well opt to sip on "Redneck," a beer that promised "the Taste of America" and defined rednecks (somewhat expansively for a beer bottle) as "Good ol' boys n' gals who love cold beer, hot romance, fast cars, slow dancin', Bar-B-Q, long kisses, country music, pick-up trucks, good fishin', America, mom, apple pie and are proud to defend any of 'em." If the foregoing evidence of the newfound and widespread respectability of rednecks was not overpowering enough, there was the phenomenal success of comedian Jeff Foxworthy, who turned a long list of one-liners ("You may be a redneck if . . . you've ever been too drunk to fish . . . you've ever worn camouflage pants to church or your family tree doesn't have any branches. . . .") into a series of hot-selling comedy albums and television shows on both the ABC and NBC networks.[13]

James C. Cobb

If middle- and upper-class white Southerners once described themselves as poor whites or rednecks as an almost obligatory act of self-deprecation, by the 1990s this act seemed less one of patronization than outright envy. When asked by an astonishingly clueless V. S. Naipaul if rednecks were actually descendants of pioneers, a successful Mississippi businessman eagerly responded, "There's no question about it. They're descendants of pioneers. They're satisfied to live in those mobile homes. . . . They don't want to go to the damn country club and play golf. They ain't got fifteen damn cents, and they're just tickled to death. They don't like being told what to do. It's the independent spirit." Confessing the obvious, he added, "you know, I like those rednecks. They're so laid back. They don't give a shit."[14]

Although those white Southerners most accurately described by the term "redneck" could take some heart in the radical overhaul of their image, it was obvious that those who were most enthusiastically buying (both figuratively and literally) into the redneck craze were the solidly middle-class folks who manicured the lawns and mangled the fairways of Southern suburbia. Redneck beer, for example, was the brainchild of Benson J. Fischer, a Washington, D.C., real estate broker, who was also a cofounder of the "Yummy Yogurt" chain. Although touted as a moderately priced beer, Redneck was most readily found among the imports and microbrews at stores catering to those whose taste buds craved something a bit more upscale than the bargain brews typically consumed by lower-income, working-class whites.[15]

The foregoing suggests that, as in other cases where mass society appeared to adopt certain aspects of the counterculture, eager marketers quickly took charge of the process, exploiting the appeal of an alternative, nonconformist, countercultural lifestyle so successfully that it soon ceased to be any of the above. Thus, the paradox: spurred by the appeal of being different, of exhibiting a distinctive identity, the aggressive marketing of redneckery soon threatened to render the redneck label virtually meaningless. Southern whites seemed largely astonished and amused to see their fellow Americans embrace a stereotypical version of their identity to which they had once objected so vehemently, but they were somewhat more frustrated by their slackening grip on the Confederate flag—a symbol whose honor they had long defended. By the 1990s, however, the Confederate banner had been coopted by a host of organizations advancing agendas ranging from unabashed white supremacy to militant antigovernmentalism. Southern whites who denied the flag's racist implications could hardly deny that it had been adopted for symbolic purposes by a host of racist hate groups such as the Ku Klux Klan, whom Shelby Foote condemned as "the scum who have degraded the Confederate flag, converted it from a symbol of honor into a banner of shame, covered it with obscenities like a roadhouse men's room wall. . . ."[16]

"We Ain't White Trash No More"

The taint of racism rendered the flag so controversial that it even made waves in the once ideologically inert world of bass fishing. The cover of the April 1997 *Sports Afield* magazine featured a Confederate flag on which largemouth bass with their large mouths opened wide replaced the stars, and an article in the magazine explained that the popularity of bass fishing made the South the "confederacy of bass." Those who held the flag in reverence seemed to view the cover as a desecration of their cherished symbol, while admirers of the bass who held the flag in low esteem objected to what they saw as a desecration of their favorite game fish.[17]

Though the flag's defenders remained numerous and vocal, there were indications that the banner's undeniable association with racist hate groups and the omnipresent reality of its disruptive potential were beginning to make even some of its most ardent proponents question whether the costs of defending it had grown too high. In South Carolina—the cradle of secession and the last state to fly the Confederate battle flag over the state capitol—Republican governor David Beasley reversed his position and suggested removing the flag from the capitol dome and placing it in a Confederate memorial on the state house grounds. Beasley's flip-flop on the flag came after a rash of church burnings and other ugly racial incidents had marred his state's image, threatening to derail the highly effective industrial development effort that recently brought, among others, a huge BMW assembly plant to the Palmetto State. Beasley faced a veritable firestorm of denunciation, but he also drew support from a number of prominent conservative South Carolinians, most notably the venerable Senator J. Strom Thurmond, who, contrary to legend, did not actually follow Pickett up the hill at Gettysburg behind the Confederate banner, but did in fact campaign for the White House under it as the Dixiecrat presidential nominee in 1948. In words that had the ring of Appomattox about them, Thurmond conceded that the presence of the battle flag over the capitol "has moved past its intended purpose of paying tribute to those who served South Carolina during the Civil War."[18]

Both the Confederate flag's racial connotations and its broader significance as a symbol of cultural and ideological conflict were revealed in all too tragic fashion in Todd County, Kentucky, the birthplace of Jefferson Davis (and, ironically, Robert Penn Warren as well). In January 1995 Michael Westerman, a young white man from Todd County, was shot and killed by a black youth after Westerman drove around the county flying a large Confederate flag from his pickup during the Martin Luther King, Jr., holiday weekend.[19] Although Westerman's reasons for flying the flag were unclear, the Sons of Confederate Veterans provided a Confederate veteran's iron cross marker for his grave and hailed him as a "martyr" who was joining "the Confederate dead under the same honorable circumstances" as those who died in combat. Westerman's death quickly took on multiple symbolic meanings, however, as his anointment as a neo-Confederate hero was soon overshadowed by the involvement not only of the Ku Klux Klan, but various other reactionary and militantly antigovernment groups. One speaker at Westerman's memorial service scattered blame for his death among the NAACP, Queer Nation, and "the goose-stepping storm troopers of the political-correctness movement." As Tony Horwitz observed, "This was a long way from the Confederacy, but, then, the speeches weren't really about the South and Westerman had metamorphosed again, from a Confederate martyr into a front-line soldier in the contemporary culture war."[20]

Meanwhile, more evidence that rather than a symbol of the Confederacy, the flag itself had become, as Horwitz described it, "a sort of talisman against mainstream culture" came in May 1996 when an Alabama state senator seeking a law requiring that the Confederate flag fly over the state's capitol insisted that the flag symbolized not white supremacy but "less government, less taxes, and the right of a people to govern themselves." In February 1997 a conservative spokesman even described the flag dispute in South Carolina in terms of a conflict over "Eurocentric" principles. With "the heritage of European people . . . under siege worldwide," he explained, "the South is the last semblance of resistance to one world order." This mingling of Confederate symbolism with widespread complaints about unwarranted interference by meddlesome "big government" could produce some intriguing associations. At a recent rally in Birmingham in support of an Alabama judge who insisted on defying a federal edict against displaying the Ten Commandments in his courtroom, the flag of the Confederacy waved alongside the flag of Israel.[21]

The antigovernment theme also permeated the propaganda of the Southern League, formed in Tuscaloosa, Alabama, in 1994. Denying his group had any ties to white supremacist and other hate groups, Southern League president Michael Hill nonetheless insisted that Southerners were the quintessential victims of governmental and mass society tyranny and repeatedly likened his efforts to defend "the unique social, cultural, and religious traditions of the southern people" to those of cultural nationalists elsewhere in the world. To some observers, it seemed that the Southern League's spokesmen were more comfortable emphasizing its similarities to ethnic or cultural separatist movements elsewhere in the world than explaining its specific relevance to residents of the contemporary South. Southern League materials even linked the group's advocacy of secession to events in Eastern Europe. A paper explaining "The Southern League Position on Secession" bore on its masthead a Confederate flag beside the inscription: "Independence: If it sounds good in Lithuania, it'll play great in DIXIE!"[22]

"We Ain't White Trash No More"

When the *Atlanta Journal-Constitution* ran a lengthy article on the Southern League in April 1996, some of the letters to the editor elicited by the story suggested that the league's antigovernment message merely echoed a chord already resonating throughout American society. One transplanted Northerner emphasized the "important values we Yankees share with our Rebel brethren that transcend petty regional differences." Consequently, he urged that "instead of alienating Yankees, [Southern League president Michael] Hill should work hard at cultivating us as allies of Southerners against our common enemy, the federal government."[23] Ironically, the difficulties many experienced in determining what exactly was "Southern" about the Southern League seemed to stem in some measure from the apparent national embrace of conservative values often referred to as the "southernization of America." In reality, however, the group's efforts to portray itself as the defender of Southern cultural traditions rang hollow not only because so many non-Southerners could relate to their efforts but because so many Southerners, black Southerners, in particular, could not.

By the 1990s Southern blacks had long been every bit as eager as their white counterparts to identify themselves as Southerners, but as their crusades against the Confederate flag and in behalf of numerous civil rights memorials indicated, they were altogether unwilling to have their Southernness defined for them by the yuppies at *Southern Living* or the polemicists of the Southern League. The behavior of both black and white Southerners underscores Eric Hobsbawm's observation that "myth and invention are essential to the politics of identity by which groups of people today . . . try to find some certainty in an uncertain and shaken world." Hobsbawm and others have argued, however, that the way a people perceive their past is the real key to this process. Well-intentioned Southerners of both races often refer to the shared history and heritage of Southern blacks and whites, but as the current conflicts over the Confederate flag suggest, black and white Southerners remain a people divided by their common past.[24]

Meanwhile, the desperate resort of white Southerners to what Freud called the "narcissism of small differences" and the exaggeration of those differences through striking displays of self-caricature calls to mind Edwin M. Yoder's description in 1964 of an "increasingly homogenized" Dixie that, in the act of "dying" both "gropes for and fondles its fading distinctions." As vivid as his imagery seemed at the time, Yoder's diagnosis of cultural masturbation as a symptom of impending death proved a bit premature. But by 1990 Hodding Carter was ready to proclaim the "End of the South" and explain that the region had been reduced to "at most an artifact lovingly preserved in the museums of culture and tourist commerce," because "the South as South, a

143

living, ever regenerating mythic land of distinctive personality" is "so hard to find in the vital centers of the region's daily life."[25]

Both Yoder and Carter were offering their observations from the Southern white perspective. More than one contemporary observer has been struck by the irony in the fact that black Southerners seem at this point considerably more confident and purposeful in their Southernness than do their white counterparts. There are signs, however, that fed by the region's economic progress and a swelling stream of black migration to the South, the generally improving socioeconomic circumstances of black Southerners may ultimately plunge them into an identity crisis of their own. The romanticization of the "redneck" that captivated so many Southern whites seems now to have a counterpoint among Southern blacks who flaunt their Southern lifestyles, dialects, and dietary preferences. Many even proudly identify themselves as "bamas," formerly a stereotypical term of derision directed by Northern blacks at Southern blacks who seemed "backward" and "country."[26]

The growing popularity of drawling, "Southern cool" rap artists like "Goodie Mob" and comedians like television's Steve Harvey clearly have strong parallels among white Southerners hooked on "redneck chic" music and the one-liners of Jeff Foxworthy. The same is true of the concerns expressed by Elizabeth Fortson Arroyo. Educated at Harvard and Columbia, Arroyo insisted, "I feel Southern the same way an Irish American feels Irish. My roots are in the South, and Southern words and ways are a part of me." Arroyo nonetheless termed herself an "asterisk Southerner," because although she takes "great pride in being a Southerner," she is just not sure if she is one. Her parents were indisputably Southern, but because of her birth in Washington and her lack of a pronounced accent, Arroyo could not help but worry, much like her upwardly mobile white contemporaries, "Is it enough to feel Southern, or must others around you (with shinier credentials) also take you to be so?" Although she was "concerned . . . that the very act of my self-analysis on this topic betrays me," Arroyo also noted Drew Faust's observation that "attempts at self-interpretation have become one of the region's most characteristic cultural products," and she posed a question appropriate for many contemporary Southerners, white and black, when she asked, "What could be more Southern than to obsess about being Southern?"[27]

What indeed? As the twentieth century comes to a close, the obsession of Southerners with their Southernness is a distinguishing cultural characteristic and the basis of a genuine growth industry as well. If, however, to borrow a phrase from George B. Tindall, black and white Southerners alike are to save themselves and each other from "drowning in the mainstream" of modern American life, they will have to move past stereotype and caricature and face up to the monumental challenge of transforming the divisive burden of Southern history into the common bedrock of a new regional identity on which all Southerners, regardless of race, are free to build.

Notes

1. Larry L. King, *Esquire,* November 1976, p. 88; John Shelton Reed, *Southerners: The Social Psychology of Sectionalism* (Chapel Hill: University of North Carolina Press, 1983), pp. 111, 114.

2. "Southern Living: In Tune with Today's South," *Southern Living,* February 1966, p. 4.

3. Diane Roberts, "Living Southern in *Southern Living,*" in *Dixie Debates: Perspectives on Southern Culture,* eds. Richard H. King and Helen Taylor (London: Pluto Press, 1996), p. 87; Lemann is quoted in John Shelton Reed and Dale Volberg Reed, *1001 Things Everyone Should Know about the South* (New York and London: Doubleday, 1996), p. 294.

4. *Atlanta Journal-Constitution,* September 5, 1993; *Southern Register,* Spring 1994, p. 3.

5. *Atlanta Journal-Constitution,* September 5, 1993.

6. *Atlanta Journal-Constitution,* September 5, 1993; *Southern Exposure* 1 (Spring 1973): n.p.; Jim Salem, "Coon Dog Graveyard," *Southern Exposure* 21 (Spring/Summer 1973): 38–39; Mary Lee Kerr, "Collard Greens," *Southern Exposure* 20 (Spring 1992): 64; Leila Finn and Mary Lee Kerr, "Mobile Homes," *Southern Exposure* 19 (Winter, 1991): 64; Harrell Chotas and Mary Lee Kerr, "Miniature Golf," *Southern Exposure* 20 (Summer 1992): 64.

7. Peter Applebome, *Dixie Rising: How the South Is Shaping American Values, Politics, and Culture* (New York: Random House, 1996), pp. 286–88; *New Orleans Times-Picayune,* August 13, 1995.

8. *New York Times,* August 5, 1995; *New Orleans Times-Picayune,* August 13, 1995; *Oxford Eagle,* July 30, 1996; *Atlanta Journal-Constitution,* July 31, 1996.

9. *Jackson Clarion-Ledger,* August 2, 1996; *Oxford Eagle,* July 30, 1996; *Jackson Clarion-Ledger,* July 21, 1997.

10. *Atlanta Journal-Constitution,* July 7, 1996.

11. Edwin M. Yoder, "Thoughts on Dixiefication of Dixie," in *Dixie Dateline: A Journalistic Portrait of the Contemporary South,* ed. John B. Boles (Houston: Rice University Studies, 1983), p. 161; Robert Kelly, "Redneck Chic: A New Honky-Tonk Craze Sweeps the City," *Highpoint* 1 (December 4–7, 1992), pp. 1, 8; James C. Cobb, "Community and Identity: Redefining Southern Culture," *Georgia Review* 50 (Spring 1996): 20–21.

12. Jack Temple Kirby, *The Counter Cultural South* (Athens: University of Georgia Press, 1995), p. 73.

13. *Atlanta Journal-Constitution,* September 17, 1995.

14. V. S. Naipaul, *A Turn in the South* (New York: Alfred A. Knopf, 1989), pp. 207–8.

15. *Washington Post,* August 22, 1995.

16. Shelby Foote to Walker Percy, June 15, 1970, in *The Correspondence of Shelby Foote and Walker Percy,* ed. Jay Tolson (New York, W. W. Norton, 1997), p. 144.

17. *Atlanta Journal-Constitution,* March 23, 1997.

18. *New York Times,* November 28, 1996.

19. Tony Horwitz, "A Death for Dixie," *New Yorker,* March 18, 1996, p. 63.

20. Horwitz, "A Death for Dixie," p. 73.

21. Horwitz, "A Death for Dixie," p. 73. *Charlotte Observer,* May 18, 1996; *Atlanta Journal-Constitution,* February 27, 1997, and April 13, 1997.

22. Horwitz, "A Death for Dixie," p. 72; "The Southern League Position on Secession," copy of manuscript in possession of the author.

23. *Atlanta Journal-Constitution,* April 28, 1996.

24. Cobb, "Redefining Southern Culture," pp. 21, 24; Eric Hobsbawm, "The New Threat to History," *New York Review of Books,* December 16, 1993, pp. 63–64; C. Vann Woodward, "The Narcissistic South," *New York Review of Books,* October 26, 1989, p. 13; Edwin M. Yoder, "A Dixieland Reverie," *Saturday Review,* May 30, 1964, p. 40.

25. C. Vann Woodward, "The Narcissistic South," pp. 13, 25; Edwin M. Yoder, "A Dixieland Reverie," p. 40; Hodding Carter III, "The End of the South," *Time,* August 6, 1990, p. 82.

26. *Washington Post,* January 5, 1997.

27. Ibid.; Elizabeth Fortson Arroyo, "The Asterisk Southerner," *Oxford American* (August/September 1996), pp. 26, 28.

A Native Son Led the Way

Jimmy Carter and the Modern New South

Russell Duncan

Standing in the Imperial City and seeing the man behind the curtain manipulating the Land of Oz, Dorothy scolded him: "I think you are a very bad man." The small man, embarrassed and slightly befuddled, turned to her and replied, "'Oh no, my dear; I'm really a very good man; but I'm a very bad wizard." This man/wizard had reinvented himself for public consumption, only to be found out for what he was. While Jimmy Carter would never admit to such a parallel characterization, many critics—and the American people generally—believe him to be a "good man, bad wizard." Strangely, he is more respected now than when he was the great and powerful wizard of Washington.[1]

Some know a different Carter. In 1994, after being asked about the American president he most admired, Walter Cronkite said, "I think that as far as intellect goes, sheer intellect . . . [Carter's] brain power was extraordinary." *Washington Post* publisher Katherine Graham agreed that Carter was "by far the most intelligent president in my lifetime." Longtime Speaker of the House, Tip O'Neill wrote that "when it came to understanding the issues of the day, Jimmy Carter was the smartest public official I've ever known."[2] Carter got smart by being a reader of books. "I have always read three or four books each week," he said. His favorite authors include James Agee, Søren Kierkegaard, Dylan Thomas, and Reinhold Niebuhr. James Agee spoke eloquently to the lives of dirt farmers during the Depression. Danish philosopher Søren Kierkegaard advanced the idea of the "existential dialectic"—by which he put man's relationship with God as "a leap of faith." The Welsh poet Dylan Thomas used humor to celebrate resurgent Christianity. The neo-Puritan Reinhold Niebuhr advocated social reform, active service, and Christian politics, arguing, "The sad job of politics is to bring justice to a sinful world." It is easy, without comment, to see the influences of their writings on the man from Plains.[3]

Carter is also a writer of books. Not since Theodore Roosevelt has a president reinvented himself or his times as often as Carter does. With thirteen books—six since 1992—and nearly 3,000 printed pages in different fields of history, philosophy, travel, autobiography, poetry, and children's stories, Carter is certainly America's most productive and literary president. He writes in a humble language that contrasts with the grandiose autobiographies by Theodore Roosevelt, John Kennedy, or Richard Nixon. His life is cast in the words of the common man and the American Dream as he insists, "My great strength is that I am an ordinary man, just like all of you." More often, Carter simply says, "I am a farmer." Actually, he is not like most of us and not that many farmers ordinarily get to sit in the most powerful office in the United States.[4] Taken together his books tell the story of a South coming of age to throw off racial segregation and of a boy determined to improve himself and his world. Numan Bartley, Dewey Grantham, Orville Burton, and other historians of the New South have told us that to reconcile the South into the nation, two things were necessary: (1) an overthrowing of the system based on white supremacy, segregation, and disfranchisement; and (2) an implementation of the 1962 *Baker v. Carr* decision of "one man, one vote." Carter's books explain how these things were done in Georgia from the viewpoint of a participant.[5]

Still, Carter is not a good wizard even if he is a bit closer to the sophisticated David Copperfield than to Oz's "man behind the curtain." He certainly lacks the escape power of a Houdini or the omniscience of a Merlin. Wizards deal in sleight of hand, deception, swamp gas, and mirrors. Carter relies on honesty and sincerity. He is the native son who made the difference in raising the South past the burden of Southern history, up from being down by the riverside, out from the baptism in blood of the Lost Cause, away from the "New South Creed," past Scottsboro, around Lester Maddox and George Wallace, and into a crusade selling the South to industry. He helped the Southern states overcome yesterday's labels of "Old South," "Sahara of the Bozart," "Benighted South," "Savage South," or "Way-of-Life South," and into the reconciled, industrialized, "Modern New South," "Sunbelt South," and "Southern Lifestyle South." Undoubtedly he could not have made the changes he did or become the symbol he has without the New Deal, World War II, the Warren Court, LBJ, Big Business interests, "the Second Reconstruction," Martin Luther King, Jr., Andrew Young, and others; but James Earl Carter III more than any other person or thing—except maybe air-conditioning—has come to symbolize the rise of the New South and New Southerner.[6]

Carter is a man of extremes, but not of contradictions. Instead of rugged contours and annoying nuances, he is straightforward and sincere. He is prideful and sure of himself while he is a dreamer of great dreams. Things are right or wrong according to the Golden Rule—which Carter calls "not a rule, but THE rule." He emulates an activist Christ by professing evangelical, born-again, never-give-up optimism, stressing virtues not failures, and believing that through individual effort each person has the capacity of a "savior." While he trusts in God, praying up to twenty-five times a day and reading the Bible every night, Carter is not a fundamentalist. In fact he berates Jerry Falwell's "Moral Majority" and Pat Robertson's "Christian Coalition" as being intolerant judges who exclude the poor to service the rich, the black to service the white.[7] His newest books *The Virtues of Aging* (1999), *Sources of Strength* (1997), *Living Faith* (1996), and *The Little Baby Snoogle-Fleeger* (1995) are pleas to old and young readers that uphold a "rags to riches" success story, individually and morally speaking. *Sources* is a collection of Carter's own Sunday school lessons, which, when combined with the memoir *Living Faith,* constitute a spiritual autobiography trying to promote community service through the question: "If you were arrested for being a Christian, would there be enough evidence to convict you?" In *Snoogle-Fleeger,* Carter continues his theme of individual accountability by concluding the story of a how a poor and physically crippled boy overcame all the odds: "It's all unbelievable. Jeremy is really strong and brave. All by himself he has tamed a ferocious sea monster."[8]

Carter's tenacious faith and moralizing have led critics to accuse him of self-righteousness or indecisiveness. He has been ridiculed as "the president who failed," has been largely ignored, or worse. But perceptions are changing. In a 1995 poll Americans gave Carter an approval rating of 74 percent—the highest ever for a living ex-president. The Discovery Channel ran a biography of him, appropriately called "Citizen Carter." His postpresidential activism with Habitat for Humanity, the Carter Center, Friendship Force, Global 2000, and the Atlanta Project combine with his continuing negotiation skills as a "trusted mediator" in settling disputes and monitoring elections worldwide. In the newest biography of Carter, Peter Bourne concludes that "Jimmy Carter is the best ex-president in American history." Carter himself recently joked that he would take the "ex" out of any such interpretation. To borrow from Andrew Lloyd Webber—and recalling the dramatic opening musical score for the televised 1976 Democratic National Convention—he has been born again by public opinion, biographers, and especially through his own memoirs, as "Jimmy Carter, Superstar."[9]

In his first book, the campaign autobiography *Why Not the Best?* Carter described his populist roots in the small-town rural America of mythology: "We lived in a wooden clapboard house alongside the dirt road . . . an outdoor privy in the back yard . . . a hand pump for water." Carter was born on October 1, 1924, south of the gnat line in isolated Plains, Georgia, a community closer to Selma than to Atlanta, closer to violence than to libraries. And while it may not have been the most Southern place on earth, it was very close to that. His slaveholding forebears had settled the land in 1849 after the deaths or eviction of the Creek Indian owners. His great-grandfather and his grandfather were murdered in fights. At different times, his father, Earl, worked nearly 250 sharecroppers in his fields and held them on the land by building a plantation store where the workers shopped and signed liens.[10] Earl was truthful, brutal, judgmental, and paternal. Carter described his father's "meticulous honesty" and wrote of a man who had "little patience with anyone who fell short of his own standards." Carter's mother, Lillian, said that Earl "hated a liar. He'd whip [with a flexible peach switch] for lying faster than anything else." Jimmy recalled being "punished severely" when he misbehaved, being whipped six times, while learning to walk around his father. Earl was a Southern patriarch in a culture where stoicism, control, and authority defined manhood. He was a small-town rich man who made money, voted for Eugene Talmadge, and got elected to the state legislature with the help of a stuffed ballot box. Jimmy learned that there was "always a reckoning" and that the bottom line in decision making was profit. Carter watched his "serious, driven, highly self-disciplined" father—and the son became the father even if Jimmy escaped the savage "gentleman" to be a gentler man.[11]

Carter's writings are full of definitions and understandings of Southern manhood. Besides the need to be obeyed, identity in the world of the Georgia male was partly shaped by hunting and fishing. In *An Outdoor Journal* (1988), Carter wrote of "the intimate feeling I had walking alongside my daddy behind a bird dog, or my pride when he included me in a grown man's world on trips to the Okefenokee Swamp." He reflected on the "feeling of exclusive masculinity within the group when men talked about hunting and laughed a lot at jokes and ribald accounts of sex adventures."[12] Carter enjoys the predator role, linking outdoor sport with the idea of civilized man over a primitive, natural world. Moreover, the open air tests him, just as did his experience in submarines where he "headed for open water" to navigate by the stars, learning about currents and sea floor topography "crucial," he says, "to our survival." Once, back on dry land, walking in the woods with Rosalynn, Carter proved his manhood. Describing how a rattlesnake had cornered her against a huge blackberry thicket, his writing becomes breathless but manly: "I had to resort to the rifle. My first shot broke its back, and the vicious snake began to thrash around at her feet, apparently still lunging toward her. . . . My second shot blew its head off. Rosalynn collapsed in my arms."[13]

Carter writes a lot about the patriarchy. In *Living Faith* (1996) he admits, "I inherited a male-dominant role. . . . I considered Rosalynn's household and family responsibilities relatively insignificant compared with mine." He also criticizes his own "impatience," "strict discipline," and having a "standard of absolute precision" and punctuality. Carter seems most able to criticize masculinity in his book of poetry, *Always a Reckoning* (1995), where eleven of the final twelve poems focus on the outdoors, dogs, death, the military, and a father too strong as a disciplinarian who passed on this intolerance to his son. He writes of "a pain I mostly hide, but ties of blood, or seed, endure" and so does the need for "just a word of praise." Carter "despised the discipline" but acknowledges his father's "own pain when he punished me." In an earlier poem, Carter writes of observing men from the vantage point of a boy. He saw cheating merchants and married men who "laid half-a-dollar whores, not always white; the same ones touting racial purity. And Klansmen's sheeted bravery at night."[14] Beyond the world of male privilege, Jimmy also learned about service to others and ministering to the poor through the local Baptist church, his mother, and a sharecropper's wife, Rachel. While his books have very few women in them and he doesn't examine femininity, Carter loves the women in his life. His mother worked as a nurse in the local hospital, invited black neighbors in through the front door, and spent a lot of time away from home as a volunteer worker. While she was away Jimmy often stayed with one of the farm families, the Clarks.[15]

Rachel Clark was an African American who served as "mother" and was closer to Jimmy, in his youthful years, than the colder, distant Lillian, who became warmer, closer after Earl's death. Carter does not write anything about that. He does describe Rachel in several of his books, but none so lovingly as in *Always a Reckoning,* where the first poem is about "the gentle touch of Rachel Clark" shaping "my young life." Carter remembered her admonitions "that blessings bring on debts to pay" and, in a rebuke of patriarchal definitions of manhood, "the brave and strongest need not fight." Carter's Rachel is worthy and strong for sure and perhaps symbolizes a black Madonna to Carter's Jesus.[16] Carter empathized with the downtrodden, but "queenly," Rachel and with the black boys he played with freely until age fourteen, when his playmates deferred to his white skin as boys became men in a culture as marked by conventions of color as they were by gender, class, and age. Carter grew up in Archery, Georgia, where two white families lived among twenty-five to thirty black families. He writes of a childhood which would sound too idyllic in its "easy interracial play" if it did not ring so true for most rural white children of that era. Carter passed through puberty and took to his learned role of white patrician manhood, Southern-style with its rural tradition of "noblesse oblige." Carter recalled the transition: "Growing up, I was like everyone else. I didn't believe in segregation—I believed in slavery.... It was part of the way of life."[17]

Carter enrolled in college at Georgia Southwestern before transferring to Georgia Tech, then Annapolis, where he majored in engineering and received a commission in the Navy in 1945. He married his sister's friend, Rosalynn Smith, age nineteen, after falling in love with her on their first date. Ambitious and driven, Carter scored high enough to obtain a choice assignment in the prototype atomic submarine *USS Sea Wolf*. Later, in 1952, when a new nuclear reactor at Chalk River, Canada, suffered a meltdown, Carter descended into the nuclear reactor core and helped prevent a tragedy. This is practical magic that a wizard can conjure.[18]

After his father's death in 1949, Carter returned to Plains. With little money—even if he did inherit 5,000 acres of land—Carter moved Rosalynn and their three children into a public housing project. He worked overtime farming and gaining customers for the peanut warehousing business. By 1964, Carter was both cash and land rich.[19] He also began to notice the plight of black Georgians. With Earl dead, his mother Lillian spoke more openly and more often. Her influence as well as his work in an integrated navy, his love of Rachel Clark, and the changing times helped him see clearer. He no longer believed in slavery. Carter ran for and won election to the school board the year after the second *Brown* decision had declared "all deliberate speed" and the rise of massive resistance threatened law and order. He confesses that he was "not directly involved in the early struggles to end racial discrimination." He certainly should have spoken out, at least when King and SNCC were only forty miles away in Albany.[20] Still, as chairman of the school board in 1961, Carter supported consolidation of the schools. That bravery went down to defeat at the hands of the voters and some group tacked up signs saying, "Coons and Carters Go Together." Furthermore, Carter was the only white man in Plains to oppose joining the White Citizens' Council, even when they boycotted his business. Carter admits that he weathered the storm because his family was among the pioneers in Plains and they were buried in the cemeteries. His father had been a community leader, his uncle had been mayor for twenty-eight years, he was a veteran, his mother was known to be "eccentric" on the race issue, and Rosalynn was "personally rooted in Plains." Biographer Peter Bourne concluded that Carter was a "conciliator" who had learned to be silent, itself "a measure of courage" when community leaders were supposed to declare their loyalty to their race.[21]

In 1962 Carter entered politics by running for the state senate. His autobiographical *Turning Point: A Candidate, a State, and a Nation Come of Age* (1992) details the corruption of the old county unit system that allowed small populations in rural Georgia counties to control the outcome of elections. Carter initially lost his bid after a massive stuffing of the ballot box for his opponent. When it became clear that 117 of the 733 total ballots had been cast for his opponent by *dead* Georgians who somehow had "lined up and cast their ballots in alphabetical order, even down to the second and third letter of the last name," Carter contested the election. Slugging his way through delays and

Democratic political "bosses," Carter was able to engineer, in his own words, "the first real defeat for the old system on its own turf." It is noteworthy that a tongue-in-cheek remedy to this afterlife voting was a proposed constitutional amendment that "no person may vote . . . in the State of Georgia who has been deceased more than three years." It failed to pass.[22]

Carter would steadily increase his activism in favor of civil rights. His first speech in the Georgia Senate aimed at eliminating the so-called "30 Questions"—"questions that nobody could answer . . . but which were applied to every black citizen that came . . . and said, 'I want to vote.'" In 1966 he ran for governor and lost to segregationist champion Lester Maddox. In 1970 he ran again and won, with the help of Andrew Young and Martin Luther King, Sr. While running a less than liberal campaign which emphasized governmental efficiency and industrial growth, Carter's inaugural speech marked the rise of moderate Southern governors and the elevation of the New South.[23] On January 12, 1971, standing on a platform placed appropriately next to the statue of Tom Watson, the last Georgia politician to appeal to the African American vote, Carter became the white native son that made the difference: "This is a time for truth and frankness. . . . The time for racial discrimination is over. . . . No poor, rural, weak, or black person should ever have to bear the additional burden of being deprived of the opportunity of an education, a job, or simple justice. . . . The test of a government is not how popular it is with the powerful and privileged few, but how honestly and fairly it deals with the many who must depend upon it."[24]

Numan Bartley has marked the rise of the New South with the election of Carter and other liberal governors who for the "first time in the twentieth century . . . endorsed equality before the law." *Time* magazine ran an issue about "New South Governors" and chose a picture of the Georgia governor for the cover. Carter became the first Georgia executive to appoint African Americans (53) to the state board of regents, board of education, human resources, and highway patrol—making sure to have one black trooper on his security detail. His administration hired an additional 1,834 African American employees statewide. Later, when he decided to hang the portraits of three black Georgians—Martin Luther King, Jr., Henry M. Turner, and Lucy Laney—in the state capitol, where none had ever been before, the Ku Klux Klan held a rally during the ceremony. Provoking the racists while assuring his New South image, Carter joined hands with Andrew Young and sang "We Shall Overcome." He would later recall "how far we had come . . . how far we had to go." Back home in Plains, his church voted to bar "Negroes and other agitators" from attending services; the vote was fifty-four to six, with five Carters in the losing column. While certainly an "agitator," no one told the town's most prominent citizen that he could not come to Sunday school next week. That is the difference between being an inside agitator and being an outside agitator.[25]

Beginning in 1972, he campaigned for the presidency. Four years later when he won the New Hampshire primary, Carter was the New South politician who did not hide his roots and was not ashamed of them. Americans were ready for his "I'll never lie to you" message and his outsider status. Andrew Young and Daddy King brought in 90 percent of the black vote nationwide. When he beat his biggest rival, George Wallace, for the Florida vote in a contest between New South and Old, he was assured the nomination. At the national convention, in the bicentennial year of the Declaration of Independence, in the Northern cultural capital of Madison Square Garden, New York City, Carter claimed the nomination for all Southerners. He appealed to the common man with his folksy opening: "My name is Jimmy Carter, and I'm running for president." Then Daddy King gave the benediction saying, "Surely the Lord sent Jimmy Carter to come on out and bring America back where she belongs." Few missed the reminder that the Lord had also sent two other sons, Jesus and Martin, Jr., on a similar mission in an earlier day. Jimmy Carter. Superstar. Skillful campaign advertising told the resurrection story to Southern voters: "On November 2 the South is being readmitted to the Union. If that sounds strange, maybe a southerner can understand. Only a southerner can understand years of coarse, antisouthern jokes and unfair comparisons."[26]

Carter beat Gerald Ford in 1976 and the New South had placed its brightest star in the Oval Office. The image of the "Sunbelt South" was here to stay. It was a cultural and political miracle as Carter became the first Deep South/Dixie president to be elected in 140 years. Dewey Grantham has noted that after the riots in Northern cities, military defeat in Vietnam, and Watergate, Northerners were no longer ready to "refashion the South in the likeness of the North [and] Southerners . . . were no longer acutely conscious of living under a powerful external threat." Novelist James Dickey was happy to have "a southernization of America" finally happening "after all these years." *New York Times* columnist Tom Wicker wrote: "whatever else he may do, Jimmy Carter has removed the last great cause of Southern isolation; and even in the remote little farm towns that dot the Southern countryside, it is already possible to sense that Southerners are coming to believe that they finally belong to something larger than the South."[27] Suddenly the South was "New World" and the North "Old World." In his recent book on presidential politics, political scientist Kenneth O'Reilly called Carter "an accidental" who won because of Watergate. But O'Reilly admits that Carter was "a racial radical by Washington standards" even if he did not do all he might have done for black Americans. Some have said that Carter scored "100 percent on talk" if nothing else. Bartley said that to speak out in itself was much more than nothing, an act of courage and a help to racial harmony.[28]

Carter's books *Blood of Abraham, Turning Point,* and *Keeping Faith* are detailed works by the chief player in the Middle East peace talks, in the destruction of the county unit system, and tell us about the White House years. Carter is best when detailing what happened and where; he is more secretive about his personal relationships. Strangely, for this very sensitive man, his works lack passion and are strangely non-Southern in that aspect, even if he does tell us repeatedly that he loves Rosalynn, his dogs, the South, and Jesus. His writing is so sterile in its lack of emotion that one might suspect it to have been written by Michael Dukakis instead of Carter—although that may be unfair. And where is his heralded historical consciousness? Carter almost never mentioned the Civil War even while it is still a defining experience for most Southerners and while books and movies about the war proliferate. That void is strange in light of the fact that Andersonville Prison Camp is just around the corner from Plains. His choice to exclude the war is a departure for Southern writers who have never been reluctant to redefine that conflict. When Carter does mention the war, significantly he chooses to call it "The War between the States" in the old, sectional, divisive way that seems at odds with his New South style. It is not that he does not know about the military or is not Southern in military tradition as men in his family fought in the Revolutionary War, Civil War, World War I, and Vietnam War with Carter himself being eleven years in the Navy. Perhaps it is New South not to remember the Old South?[29]

Carter does not mention the popular culture influences on his life such as television, movies, music, or novels. He evokes no historical memory of the South beyond the immediate situation of the 1950s and 1960s when he came of age. There is nothing from Penn Warren, Woodward, Steinbeck, Welty, or Conroy. He provides no insight into the civil rights movement, mentions women barely at all, has nothing on sports, the Grand Ole Opry, or Elvis Presley—that is, there is no look at the role the South played in creating modern culture. He could tell us a lot about the relationships between the various classes of African Americans and whites, but he is quiet on such issues. Carter keeps his silence because of all the media attention the South got during the civil rights movement. He is a loyal Southerner who disliked what he saw and who understood that negative press caused loss of progressive social and business climates. As a boy who learned to balance his father's racism with his mother's egalitarianism and as a political candidate in the whirlwind of change in the sixties, Carter learned to be silent except to point out calmly what was wrong and needed changing. Kenneth Morris has written that Carter is the "supreme public moralist," a conclusion that no one could miss. By 1980 we all wanted a "wizard" and so in came Ronald Reagan. Previously, America just got the kind of man that is hard to find—and thus hard to admire until he returns to the private sphere.[30]

Carter creates an image—and lived a real life—reminiscent of Jefferson, Lincoln, Roosevelt, and Kennedy. He is a Southerner who works for equality, a republican farmer, educated and political, who grew up in a simple dwelling. He is at least as honest as Abe and has worked to help heal a house divided by racism by supporting programs and voting rights. Like Roosevelt, he overcame a severe handicap; in his case the disability was being from the South. He also had an activist wife and an optimistic personality. Carter could out-tooth and match tousled hair with Kennedy. He was a military veteran and longshot political success voted in by people ready for a return to Camelot after the despair of Vietnam and Watergate, even if they were as wary of making a president of a reborn Baptist as they were of a popish Catholic.[31]

Carter became the symbolic "representative man" for the modern New South as it links most closely to the mythical American character. His books stress his sense of family and sense of place—important features in every Southern autobiography. Carter became the all-American Southern boy, with white British pioneer roots, who rose from rags to riches. He lets us imagine a collective identity in which a family grows rich by slavery with a downturn approaching the poor white class, then rises again quickly past Wilbur Cash's "man in the center" to patrician. In the sandy soil of Georgia he becomes a rich farmer, president, and best-known American advocate for human rights worldwide.[32] Southerners like him because he represents the best of what they see in themselves, an ability to overcome the past and a proof that Southern "don't mean dumb." Carter gives us a symbol of a white male challenging the Southern way of life to make the transition from racist to liberal in a New South. Charles Reagan Wilson explained that Carter overcame a racist past, was emancipated from that past, reborn in Jesus, and became a key promoter of the biracial South. James Cobb reminded us that with the election of Carter, Southern whites congratulated themselves, "we ain't trash no mo'." Skilled with a rifle, a fishing rod, and a good story, Carter proved his manhood in the navy, and even though not one American soldier died in a war during his presidency—an unglamorous claim for an American president—he openly supports the military, and even the Truman decision to drop the bomb on Hiroshima and Nagasaki.[33]

A Native Son Led the Way

Even while his father was a racist and his mother represented the cult of true womanhood—in the style of Scarlett O'Hara welded to pieces of Clara Barton and Angelina Grimke—even after he grew up poor and lived in a government housing project as an adult, Jimmy Carter overcame it through a Puritan work ethic, faith, devotion to family, and look-you-in-the-eye honesty. Carter also seems to embody the myth of the Natural Man of the frontier, whether that frontier be the dusty physical landscape of Plains, the deep-sea coldness of atomic submarines, an overheated nuclear reactor, the intellectual contact zone that "All Men Are Created Equal," the philosophical podium of religious tolerance, or as the first modern Southerner to stand astride the Mason-Dixon line in the aftermath of Watergate lies, a Vietnam defeat, the "Second Reconstruction," a generation and gender gap. Carter represents romantic love as his "love-at-first-sight" fifty-three-year-long marriage with Rosalynn attests. Not only does he love her and walk holding hands with her, but she is the hometown girl-next-door, class valedictorian who shared decision making as no other American First Lady has done until Hillary Rodham Clinton. With a strong marriage and a smart wife, Carter represents the virile yet sensitive male, and Rosalynn is the "true woman" with four children and many grandchildren. It is little wonder that James Earl Carter III is the Georgian who became the symbol of change and continuity that is the New South.

Furthermore, Carter has developed a sense of humor, something old for white Southerners that disappeared in the century between the First and Second Reconstructions, but has surged back in recent years. Humor is common in Carter's books. That may surprise some readers because of all that has been said about his pride and inability to laugh at himself. Carter's works are full of local color and reflect a heritage in "Southwestern Humor" of the backwoods.[34] In one of his poems, Carter humorously recollected when he was "Jimmy Who?"

> "Now, wait, don't tell me who you are,"
> he shouted out. I stood in dread.
> Bystanders paused. I blabbed my name.
> He frowned. "Naw, that ain't it," he said.[35]

Like the older man in the poem, academics seek to understand the New South and the Southern mind. That we will agree on what we find is not in the realm of the possible. That Carter can define himself or even know who he is, in the sense of being recognized by name and story, is too unlikely to be hoped for. The life and myth of Jimmy Carter, as invented and reinvented through autobiographies, parallels the South's contemporary hopes. Symbol, myth, and history are all intertwined in the profound and naïve recollections by Carter and the equally paradoxical portraits by biographers. Nevertheless, this native son continues to embody the growing tolerance, influence, and ambivalence of the South in the 1990s.

Notes

1. L. Frank Baum, *The Wizard of Oz*, quoted in Kenneth E. Morris, *Jimmy Carter: American Moralist* (Athens: University of Georgia Press, 1996), p. vii.

2. Cronkite, Graham, and O'Neil quoted in Peter G. Bourne, *Jimmy Carter: A Comprehensive Biography from Plains to Postpresidency* (New York: Scribner, 1997), pp. 428–29.

3. Jimmy Carter, *Why Not the Best?* (New York: Broadman Press, 1975; reprint, Fayetteville: University of Arkansas Press, 1996), p. 142. See especially James Agee, *Let Us Now Praise Famous Men* (1936); Søren Kierkegaard, *Works of Love* (1847); Dylan Thomas, *Collected Poems* (1953); Reinhold Niebuhr, *A Nation so Conceived* (1963). Niebuhr quoted in Bourne, *Jimmy Carter*, p. 508.

4. Carter, *Why Not the Best?* p. 138.

5. Orville V. Burton, "The Modern 'New' South in a Postmodern Academy: A Review Essay," *Journal of Southern History* 62 (November 1996): 775; Jimmy Carter, *Turning Point: A Candidate, a State and a Nation Come of Age* (New York: Random House, 1992), focuses exclusively on the overthrow of the county unit system.

6. The sentence beginning "Carter is the Native Son . . ." includes references to well-known books in New South historiography by C. Vann Woodward, Charles Joyner, Charles Reagan Wilson, Paul M. Gaston, Dan T. Carter, James C. Cobb, and Numan V. Bartley.

7. Jimmy Carter, *Living Faith* (New York: Random House, 1996), pp. 3, 33–35, 47, 178, 195; Carter, *Why Not the Best?* p. 2; Robert Scheer, "Playboy Interview: Jimmy Carter," *Playboy*, November 1976, p. 66; Jimmy Carter, "Faith and Public Duties," *International Herald Tribune*, January 1, 1997, p. 7; Bourne, *Jimmy Carter*, p. 466.

8. Jimmy Carter, *The Little Baby Snoogle-Fleejer* (New York: Times Books, 1995), p. 24. For further insights into Carter's belief in personal approaches to conflict resolution, see Jimmy Carter, *The Blood of Abraham: Insights into the Middle East* (Boston: Houghton Mifflin, 1985; reprint, Fayetteville: University of Arkansas Press, 1993).

9. Bourne, *Jimmy Carter*, pp. 179, 507; Morris, *Jimmy Carter*, pp. 295–305; Patrick Anderson, *Electing Jimmy Carter: The Campaign of 1976* (Baton Rouge: Louisiana State University Press, 1994), p. 161; Carter, *Blood of Abraham*, passim; Carter quoted in *International Herald Tribune*, October 21, 1997, p. 3.

10. Carter, *Why Not the Best?* p. 5.

11. Ibid., pp. 5–10; Bourne, *Jimmy Carter,* pp. 20–27, 63, 81, 105; Earl Carter and Lillian Carter, quoted in Morris, *Jimmy Carter,* pp. 25, 27, 30; Carter, *Living Faith,* pp. 49–53.

12. Jimmy Carter, *An Outdoor Journal: Adventures and Reflections: A Personal Memoir* (New York: Bantam, 1988), pp. 1, 37.

13. Ibid., pp. 6–7, 53, 262–64.

14. Carter, *Living Faith,* pp. 39–41, 76, 78, 95; Carter, *Why Not the Best?* p. xvi; Jimmy Carter, *Always a Reckoning, and Other Poems* (New York: Random House, 1995), p. 43.

15. Carter, *Living Faith,* p. 51; Bourne, *Jimmy Carter,* p. 28.

16. Carter, *Always a Reckoning,* pp. 3–5, 33–34.

17. Carter, *Why Not the Best?* pp. 12–29; Carter, *Living Faith,* p. 10; Bourne, *Jimmy Carter,* pp. 22, 93.

18. Carter, *Why Not the Best?* pp. 46, 54, 60; Bourne, *Jimmy Carter,* pp. 72–75.

19. Carter, *Living Faith,* p. 62.

20. Carter, *Keeping Faith,* p. 142; Carter, *Turning Point,* p. 17. For Southern white reaction to the 1954 *Brown v. Board of Education* decision, see Numan V. Bartley, *The Rise of Massive Resistance: Race and Politics in the South During the 1950s* (Baton Rouge: Louisiana State University Press, 1969).

21. Bourne, *Jimmy Carter,* pp. 81–84, 96, 143; Rosalynn Carter, *First Lady from Plains* (Boston: Houghton Mifflin, 1984), p. 46; Carter, *Living Faith,* p. 69; Carter, *Turning Point,* pp. 21–23.

22. Carter, *Turning Point,* pp. xxiv, 74–174, 183.

23. Jimmy Carter, *A Government as Good as Its People* (New York: Simon and Schuster, 1977; reprint, Fayetteville: University of Arkansas Press, 1996), p. 22; Carter, *Why Not the Best?* p. 106; Dan T. Carter, "Jimmy Carter," in *The Reader's Companion to American History,* ed. Eric Foner and John A. Garraty (Boston: Houghton Mifflin, 1991), p. 150; Charles R. Wilson, "Carter Era," in *The Encyclopedia of Southern Culture,* ed. Charles R. Wilson and William Ferris (New York: Doubleday, 1989), vol. 3, pp. 501–2.

24. For Watson, see C. Vann Woodward, *Tom Watson: Agrarian Rebel* (New York: Oxford University Press, 1938); David Goldfield and Paul Escott, eds., *The New South,* vol. 2 of *Major Problems in the History of the American South* (Lexington, Mass.: D.C. Heath, 1990), pp. 611–13. Carter's standing as the symbol of the New South is evident in Goldfield and Escott's inclusion of his speech over any and all other governors.

25. Numan V. Bartley, *The New South, 1945–1980: The Story of the South's Modernization* (Baton Rouge: Louisiana State University Press, 1995), pp. 399–410; Carter, *Why Not the Best?* p. 109; Carter, *A Government as Good as Its People,* pp. 15, 49–50; Bourne, *Jimmy Carter,* pp. 147, 213.

26. Dewey W. Grantham, *The South in Modern America: A Region at Odds* (New York: Harper Collins, 1994), p. 291; Carter, *A Government as Good as Its People,* pp. 48–49; Bartley, *The New South,* p. 414; Jack T. Kirby, *Media Made Dixie: The South in the American Imagination,* rev. ed. (Athens: University of Georgia Press, 1986), pp. 170–73.

27. Dickey and Wicker quoted in Grantham, *The South in Modern America*, pp. 292–94.

28. Kenneth O'Reilly, *Nixon's Piano: Presidents and Racial Politics from Washington to Clinton* (New York: Free Press, 1995), pp. 335, 342; Numan V. Bartley, *Jimmy Carter and the Politics of the New South* (St. Louis: Forum Press, 1979), p. 4.

29. Carter, *A Government as Good as Its People*, p. 123; Carter, *Turning Point*, p. xix.

30. Morris, *Jimmy Carter*, p. 19.

31. Andrew Young compared Carter to Kennedy and sided with Carter: "John Kennedy read about racism and poverty in a sociology class at Harvard, but Jimmy Carter lived it." Quoted from O'Reilly, *Nixon's Piano*, p. 337.

32. Wilbur J. Cash, *The Mind of the South* (New York: Random House, 1940), pp. 30–60.

33. Charles Reagan Wilson, "The Myth of the Biracial South," and James C. Cobb, "We Ain't Trash No More," see the essays above; Carter, *Living Faith*, p. 99.

34. Scheer, "Playboy Interview: Jimmy Carter," p. 86; Anderson, *Electing Jimmy Carter*, p. 168; Wray Herbert, "Conversation: A Georgia Farmer Takes Stock," *US News & World Report*, December 9, 1996, p. 86; John Shelton Reed, *My Tears Spoiled My Aim: And Other Reflections on Southern Culture* (San Diego: Harcourt Brace, 1993).

35. *Always a Reckoning*, p.67.

Let Us Now Praise Famous Women

Kaye Gibbons's Song for a Deceased Mother

François Pitavy

Like a mask at once concealing and revealing the persona underneath, the voice of an author can be an index of profound designs and reveal underlying strains and tensions expressing themselves in his or her work and ordering it. The texture of an author's voice often answers to the grain of his or her texts. Faulkner's deliberately flat, uninflected voice may well express his furious desire to confront the ghosts of the South other than through sheer oratory and to order them in the silence of his chosen medium. Even his reading of his all too sonorous Stockholm speech reveals his desire to control the apocalypse evoked, and his ambition to transcend the constraints of his medium may be heard in his constant overriding of the grammatical rhythm.

Despite the Carolina drawl, with which she plays in a droll way when she tells or reads a story, the flat, slightly raspy voice of Kaye Gibbons sounds much like that of a little girl who must draw her strength from her very fragility and capacity for reserve: a voice at once diffident and assured, insecure and willful, as if confidence was never given but must be gained, and victory be constantly reenacted—victory over death, as Gibbons herself said, whether death be physical or spiritual. A force drawn from surface fragility or deeper fractures, at once concealing and revealing, is what strikes one who listens to Kaye Gibbons. The combination of frailty and deliberateness, the slight tautness in a voice that seemingly never takes itself seriously, in the last analysis the undertone of suffering from a never-healed wound, such are also the strains heard in the voices of Gibbons's female narrators in the five novels she has published in the past ten years at regular intervals: *Ellen Foster* (1987), *A Virtuous Woman* (1989), *A Cure for Dreams* (1991), *Charms for the Easy Life* (1993), *Sights Unseen* (1995). These five relatively slim novels yet make up a work consistent and important enough for the reader to perceive its lines of forces, particularly since the publication of *Sights Unseen*, to me the best achieved of her novels, precisely because at last it succeeds in confronting a strain of suffering perceptible from the beginning of the first novel, *Ellen Foster*—a suffering that had been kept at bay in this novel by the obstinate, courageous, at once prematurely grave and childishly funny voice of a little girl of ten who has lost her mother and her ability to cry.

The painful cathartic passage from suffering to grief over the deceased mother, and ultimately to forgiveness and healing, makes of *Sights Unseen* the long-delayed continuation of *Ellen Foster,* after a detour through three other novels in which the suffering is contained thanks to different family and narrative structures provisionally keeping at a safe distance the ultimately inevitable confrontation with the death of the mother. One must live on, and the confrontation of one's memories and their reordering to make them livable and usable can be achieved only through language, as Gibbons wrote in *How I Became a Writer,* a short text published in 1988, the year following the publication and immediate recognition of *Ellen Foster:* "I write about what I know best. And if death and sorrow and the inexplicable joy that comes from triumph over death and sorrow, if these themes are predominant in my work, past and future, it is because they dominate my memory. . . . I believe it is under the incredible burden of memory that I write, and I cannot trade my memory, as much as I've often wanted to do so. My past is what it is. All the memory will allow me or any other writer to do is order it through language."[1] This is precisely what the five female heroine-narrators of Kaye Gibbons are committed to do, with the same obstinate willfulness, the same salubrious and saving humor, the same refusal of tragedy or, worse, self-pity. The courageous voices of these women, together with Gibbons's remarkable ear for the humorous idiosyncrasies of language, brought the author immediate recognition from the critics and the general public.

Ellen Foster received the Sue Kaufman Prize for First Fiction from the American Academy and Institute of Arts and Letters, and won Gibbons the accolade of her elders who readily welcomed her into the fold and whose influence she acknowledged, particularly Eudora Welty, who called Gibbons "a stunning new writer." Welty must have loved the younger writer's sense of the ludicrous and knack for catching the droll turns of language revealing a character's refusal to succumb to self-pity. And Walker Percy recognized in the young Ellen "a southern Holden Caulfield, tougher perhaps, as funny,"[2] and in her low-key obstinacy and backwoods endurance a minor but ultimately more effective form of courage than the bombastic and narcissistic stoicism of Aunt Emily in *The Moviegoer.*

Kaye Gibbons has remained in the foreground of the younger generation of Southern novelists, regularly appearing on best-seller lists in the United States and in Europe. All of her novels have been translated into French, and

Ellen Foster was also on a best-seller list in France. The reason for the persisting success, even though to my mind the three novels between the first and the latest are imperfectly realized,[3] is that readers have recognized the courage and the humor of these female heroines (and low-key feminists, when feminists at all, it is a trap Gibbons carefully avoids). And they have heard the undertone of suffering that can also be perceived in the author's voice, a suffering ultimately linked to the loss of the mother. The opening of *Ellen Foster* created a minor sensation on the scene of American fiction by the singular, readily recognizable ring and age of its heroine's voice, and by the quiet monstrosity of her words: "When I was little, I would think of ways to kill my daddy. I would easily figure out this or that way and run it through my head until it got easy. The way I liked best was letting go a poisonous spider in his bed. It would bite him and he'd be dead and swollen up and I would shudder to find him so. . . . But I did not kill my daddy. He drank his own self to death the year after the County moved me out."[4]

At the age of ten, Ellen loses her mother: sick, harried by a brutal, insensitive drunkard of a husband, she swallows a bottle of pills for the heart. Then the father, who seems to come directly out of an Erskine Caldwell novel, brings back home pals with whom he gets drunk on the moonshine he sells them, and then he tries to rape his daughter (hidden in the closet, Ellen overhears their conversations):

> What else do you do when your house is run over by men drinking whiskey and singing and your daddy is worse than them all put together? You pray to God they forget about you and the sweet young things that are soft when you mashum and how good one feels when she is pressed up by you. You get out before one can wake up from being passed out on your floor. You get out before they start to dream about the honey pie and the sugar plums. Step over the sleeping arms and legs of dark men in shadows on your floor. You want to see a light so bad that it comes to guide you through the room and out the door where a man stops you and the light explodes into a sound that is your daddy's voice. Get away from me. He does not listen to me but touches his hands harder on me. That is not me. Oh no that was her name. Do not oh you do not say her name to me. That was her name. You know that now stop no not my name.
> I am Ellen.
> I am Ellen.
> He pulls the evil back into his self and Lord I run. (pp. 38–39)

The force of the passage rests in the decentering induced by the apprehension of the situation from a little girl's standpoint: neither pathetic, nor even tragic, the rendering of the scene keeps within the literal interpretation of the father's

François Pitavy

mistake in using his dead wife's name instead of his daughter's. The threat appears to be directed not so much at the girl's physical as psychological integrity, even though she very well understands the possibility of rape and incest. But these words, adults' words, words that hurt by their finality, are not used. Hence the representation of the abuse is kept at bay. Moreover the identity threat addresses not only the daughter, but also the mother, whom the drunken and sexually aroused father mixes up with the daughter, which is unbearable for the little girl who must have her mother clearly identified if she herself is to retain her own identity. The verbal strategy of defense concerns both the identities of the mother and the daughter, linked before, and by, the threat of the father.

In this way the first novel of Kaye Gibbons sets itself within a clearly marked American tradition—that of the novel of education whose narrator and/or hero is a child or a teenager. One comes to think of Huck Finn, Holden Caulfield, Augie March, or Truman Capote's adolescent or childlike heroes. Ellen Foster does have the preoccupations of her preadolescent age, she thinks of her own few toys and of those she could entice other children to lend her; but she is mostly anxious about her own survival in a world in which she knows she must count on herself alone: hence her constant and funny concern with food and with money in most of the situations she describes. But her overarching concern is to be herself, to become Ellen Foster. For such is not her real name, but that of the person she has decided to become, in a family she selects for herself (aptly named Foster) with a deliberateness deriving its strength from the fact that the girl never doubts she will eventually succeed, even though she does not at once envision all the particulars of her design.

Left an orphan by the death of her mother and the demise of her all too often absent and drunken father, Ellen is first taken in by an aunt on the evening of the mother's burial, but the girl realizes with a shock that the aunt intends to drive her back to her place at the end of the weekend. Later, after the rape attempt, Ellen runs away to the house of her only friend, Starletta, a black girl a little younger than herself. But a white girl cannot make a black family into a foster family, as will be seen later. After the father's death (he is reported dead somewhat in the manner of Huck's father), Ellen goes to her maternal grandmother, a stereotypical figure, that of the "bad" cotton planter. The woman hates her granddaughter for reminding her of her no-good son-in-law. To make her pay for being her father's daughter, she has the little girl work in the cotton fields together with blacks, enslaving her in a way. Yet it is precisely there that she begins to recover her mother by reappropriating her memory, through the agency of a black woman who knew the girl's mother (another Southern stereotype): "Did you know my mama?" "Yes chile! I was raised up beside her on this farm. I knowed her as good as I know my own self. I never knowed anybody sweet like your mama. Smart as a whip too!" (p. 65). The mediated memory allows her at last to begin to recover her mother and to identify with her, to realize a spiritual inheritance, after she had been deprived of a material means of identification.

The great deprivation following the mother's death had indeed been the confiscation by the wicked grandmother of the mother's clothes, which the girl had symbolically wanted to wear: "I wore some of my mama's clothes to school.... Just some things up under my dress. She was not much bigger than me.... I decided to wear a little something every day" (pp. 23–24). Whereas the boy will look for identity in opposition or difference, in confronting the Law of the Father, to the girl *identity* is often experienced as a quest for *identicality*. Ellen Foster will wear her mother's underthings, as close to her physical being as possible. If identity is emotional and spiritual, identicality begins with actual contact, which the girl means to realize with her mother's clothes, unseen by others and hence the better appropriated. Deprived of these clothes, the girl cannot readily become her mother's daughter; she will significantly become Ellen Foster, that is, a girl who has chosen another mother, provisionally: after the shock of the mother's death and the rape attempt by the father, she must first of all try to survive, find food and shelter. *Ellen Foster* is the narrative of that obstinate, even ruthless, quest of a little girl for survival. Only in *Sights Unseen* will the daughter-narrator reappropriate her mother's identity by making herself her mother's daughter, a slow process of education that will allow her to become in turn her daughter's mother. But that is another story, which Kaye Gibbons took eight years to come around to writing.

After the grandmother's death, the girl is taken up by another aunt, from whose place she will flee after an unbearable Christmas during which she is humiliated and rejected, to take refuge at the home of the "Foster" family she had selected at church, a family she thinks will be at last the fixed point she needs to become herself—that is in fact, another one, with another name, not her mother's: so she cannot yet grieve over her deceased mother. And it is from that secure standpoint that the narrator can tell how she made herself Ellen Foster. The narrative strategy of the novel is built upon the gap of about two years' time between the narrative stance and the painful events in the girl's life story, which permits the funny counterpoints and the humorous distance necessary to avoid the traps of tragedy or melodrama, in the last analysis, of self-pity. Here are not to be heard the strains of great music, with its likely pitfalls, but rather the homely, lively beats of country music, moving without ever being emotional. Such is indeed Kaye Gibbons's own tune—her success in writing Ellen's story. The trauma of the mother's death can be gauged pre-

François Pitavy

cisely in its understatement by the child, in the verbal manipulation of the unbearable. When the mother dies of an overdose of pills for the heart, the girl does not contemplate for a second whether this be suicide. Here she is, lying with her mother on her bed: "I always want to lay here. And she moves her arm up and I push my head down by her side. And I will crawl in and make room for myself. My heart can be the one that beats. And hers has stopped. . . . I have her now while she sleeps but just is not breathing. . . . You can rest with me until somebody comes to get you. We will not say anything. We can rest" (pp. 10–11). Not saying anything is precisely one of the strategies for survival—for resting—that the girl resorts to. Saying the thing makes it be. So she juggles reality by juggling the language, by not saying the irremediable.

In *As I Lay Dying,* the boy Vardaman can survive the trauma by refusing the possibility that his mother should lie dead in a box: he makes her into a fish swimming in the river or he bores holes in the lid of the coffin so she can breathe. Either she is not in there, or if so she is not dead. The verbal manipulation allows that of facts. Slightly older than Vardaman, Ellen Foster doubtless realizes the truth, but she will not look at the evidence so she can survive it: "Close the cover. Close it down. Your mama has flown. She would not wait to see them close the cover down. I will not look. No. So why do I have to watch anymore? I saw all I wanted to see in the church. . . . Where is she? Not in the box. You cannot rest in a box" (pp. 21–22). The understatement, or unstatement, is also the effect of guilt on the girl's part. Ellen Foster probably feels responsible for a death she unconsciously thinks she might have prevented, as she knew that those pills for the heart were dangerous. Moreover, as she remained alone with her dead mother, refusing for a time to accept her death and fantasizing instead that she was sleeping, she failed to do her duty towards her mother, refraining from accomplishing the last rites as she saw them. Conversely, when the bad grandmother died, the girl prepared her body by decorating it with all the artificial flowers she could find in the house: "I am not guilty today. And even when she was so dead I could not help her anymore I made her like a present to Jesus so maybe he would take her. Take this one I got prettied up and mark it down by my name to balance against the one I held back from you before" (p. 92). She had not done to her mother what she had managed to do to the grandmother. Hence the lingering sense of guilt. Such guilt about the mother is compounded by another form of guilt, over the race question—a subtheme that Gibbons may have thought an unavoidable topos when writing her first novel in the South. It probably gives the measure of her ambition in this first attempt at laying claim to recognition, at staking her claim in the field of American fiction.

Let Us Now Praise Famous Women

Ellen Foster's first refuge was the home of her little black friend Starletta. But the white girl must then express the "innate" racial prejudices of a white girl who cannot stay in a black family's home, thinking she will be contaminated by sharing their food and their glasses: "As fond as I am of all three of them I do not think I could drink after them. I try to see what Starletta leaves on the lip of a bottle but I have never seen anything with the naked eye. If something is that small it is bound to get into your system and do some damage" (pp. 29–30). The obvious dig at the so-called scientific arguments for racism among previous generations is made effective by being put in the mouth of a little girl who can only indiscriminately imbibe, without any sense of distance, and repeat the hackneyed ideas she has inherited from adults. The consciousness of difference is once more made into a mere matter of genes, and of hygiene—an unconscious irony on the part of the girl, not lost, however, on the reader of the late 1980s and the 1990s. Yet, agreeing with some Southern stereotypes (possibly another dig, this time at the contemporary priggish liberals), the black family, complete with father and mother (the only one in the novel), welcomes her warmly and without any hesitation or restriction—almost a Faulknerian cliché. Appropriately, in the final pages, Ellen will begin to acknowledge and repay her debt.

Another instance of that linguistic normalization that makes racism a matter of incontrovertible fact occurs when Ellen is asked about the rape attempt by a prurient teacher: "She asked me how it all happened so I told her my daddy put the squeeze on me and that is how it happened. She was shocked but I told her I was used to it so do not get in an uproar over it. You live with something long enough and you get used to it. Like smelling the inside of Starletta's house" (p. 44). The off-the-cuff factual comparison ending the memory of a painful episode is somehow more telling than the event itself, as the girl's refusal of self-pity or dramatization by making child abuse an everyday fact of life is here "certified" (as Binx Bolling the "Moviegoer" would put it) by another "fact of life"—a normalizing of racial prejudices, which then can no longer be taken as prejudices since they are presented as incontrovertible facts. The seemingly extemporaneous comparison demonstrates the adroitness of Gibbons in linking the education and the race themes. In that respect, the central episode is the one in which the grandmother literally enslaves her granddaughter by making her hoe cotton. Gibbons employs the almost formulaic phrase to designate the plantation slave's work, now passed into current language: "a long (hard) row to hoe." At first, the girl remarks that she has become so sun-tanned that she could almost pass for colored. She then realizes what a slave's work must have been: "Lord how did they stand it so hot? I wondered" (p. 63). And it is in those cotton fields, doing slave work compe-

François Pitavy

tently, physically and soon spiritually identifying with the blacks, that she recovers her mother's memory, precisely when it is filtered through the blacks' own memories and she has come to realize the "burden" of racial difference (but the girl does not use the word, of course). Although at the time she does not understand the importance—or the inevitability, in a Southern context— of the black mediation in the making of identity, it unwittingly prepares her for the final recognition of Starletta's place, not just in her own individual mind structure, but in the collective identity of the South. Her education as a Southern girl must also be a racial coming of age—her own and that of the Southern psyche.

At the end of the novel, she repays her debt by realizing a long entertained desire (which, to the family-deprived girl, is at first a desire for normalcy and thus for identity), to invite her friend Starletta to her foster home for a weekend. These are Ellen's closing words, while Starletta, lying on the same bed with her, has fallen asleep: "I came a long way to get here but when you think about it real hard you will see that old Starletta came even farther. And I watch her resting now because soon we'll all be eating supper and maybe some cake tonight and I say low Starletta you sure have a right to rest. And all this time I thought I had the longest row to hoe. That will always amaze me" (p. 126). Such is the end of the novel, but not of Kaye Gibbons's story. Ellen is not yet her mother's daughter, not yet quite herself—still a Foster. Throughout the novel she speaks of her "new mama." She cannot yet really say "my mother." The neat Southern closure, with the race theme, cannot be an ending yet.

When Ellen faces her "new mama" she is indirectly revealing the incredible repression of her emotions, as she casually mentions her shaking: "There has been more than a plenty days when she has put both my hands in hers and said if we relax and breathe slow together I can slow down shaking. And it always works. And there was a day last year when she said if I didn't cry sooner or later I would bust. That is something I am still working on" (p. 121). The crying over the dead mother has been repressed for the sake of survival. But the narrator lets us know that here is something she must still work on— that there will be a return of the repressed, a song for the deceased mother. That is the subject, or the object, of *Sights Unseen*—in that sense the continuation of *Ellen Foster*. Such a reading of the two novels in connection is borne out by the fact that the narrator of the first novel, about twelve or thirteen, tells events that took place when she was ten and eleven, that is, with limited perspective. In *Sights Unseen* the narrator, a young woman with daughters already, returns through most of the book to events that took place when she was twelve. There thus appears to be a deliberate continuity from the first novel to the latest, in the heroine's age. This manner of narrative continuity—and the resuming of Gibbons's meditation on her mother—can be achieved precisely because of the sharp break in the narrative stance, the now much greater distance between narration and story. That such distance has been achieved now makes possible the reordering of memories.

The three novels between *Ellen Foster* and *Sights Unseen* may be read as narrative and thematic strategies to keep at a safe distance the unavoidable confrontation with the demise of the manic-depressive mother and her suicide-like death. In *A Virtuous Woman,* Gibbons eschews the mother-daughter relationship by centering on the wife-husband dialogue on either side of the divide of death (that of the wife). In fact, it is with themselves and their memories that husband and wife carry on their dialogues. They do not love each other so much as they both long for love, need somebody to love, telling each other the small things and the simple grief and bliss of everyday life, true life indeed, but in the shadow of foretold death: their coming to terms—moving though it be—is achieved only by a juggling of the narrative stance, as the wife speaks *out of time* with the husband, from beyond death.

In *A Cure for Dreams* and *Charms for the Easy Life,* the mother-daughter relationship is set at a safe remove, as Gibbons here tells the stories of several generations of witty, gritty women—grandmothers, however, rather than mothers. Admirable though these women may be, the relationship between grandmother and granddaughter-narrator often remains insufficiently defined or emphasized, the character tending to disappear behind the narrator in spite of the narrative frame. Whereas Denver in Toni Morrison's *Beloved* comes into her own being (and her name) through the reiterated narrative of her birth, there is no real epistemological and identity quest of the narrator in the recollection of all those voices in *A Cure for Dreams;* and in *Charms for the Easy Life,* the telling of the life and death of the admirable and forceful grandmother (a fiercely independent woman pioneer, with something of the witch in her, but an enlightened one with an unimpeachable reading list) brings little to the education of the narrator. The ending is not so much suspended as a little slick, the resurfacing of the character under the narrator not quite convincing, frustrating the reader's quest for sense. But the compassion evidenced in the portraits of those women, the low-key, joyous understanding and celebration of what Faulkner in his Stockholm speech had sonorously called "the eternal verities of the human heart," has gradually brought Gibbons to mourn and remember her mother through straightforward fictional recreation requiring no elaborate narrative frame, and to return to profoundly personal concerns. Like Agee, and with the same love and compassion, she now praises a famous woman—her mother. Here, Gibbons does away with the gender gap or the layering of generations used in the three previous novels as distancing devices:

she confronts her demons not with complex narrative strategies, but with more sober resources of language and technique, writing what may be her best piece of fiction so far.

After four novels, Kaye Gibbons indeed still had to "work on" the repressed and its return, especially as it seems in her case to be compounded by guilt, unless it be simply a profound sense of duty towards a much-admired mother. Gibbons's own mother was a manic-depressive whose death the girl Kaye, at the age of ten, may well have reproached herself with not preventing[5]—and she herself is manic-depressive. Therefore, dealing with her mother's depression may also be dealing with her own. In 1997, she had a private printing made of a short text about her condition.[6] Titled *Frost and Flower: My Life with Manic Depression So Far*, it is a candid and moving exercise in self-confrontation, something not unlike William Styron's *Darkness Visible*, though much shorter. Utterly devoid of the residual pose one still finds in Styron, it is surely meant to have the same therapeutic value—a painful exorcism through language, confirming in autobiographical form what the novels achieve on a larger scale, precisely at a fictional remove.

In *Frost and Flower*, Gibbons tells us of the relationship between manic depression and creativity (as in some of the most memorable, and hilarious, episodes in the mother's life in *Sights Unseen*, notably when she plans to invite Robert Kennedy), and of the imaginative range it allows in word associations and the internal rhythms of fiction. The novel inventiveness of language is thus related to the creativeness of manic depression. Among all manners of sprees told in this text, the verbal spree is certainly one of the most remarkable effects of manic depression. In this account of her own symptoms Gibbons quotes a passage from *Sights Unseen*, describing the mother's manic depression (precisely the Kennedy episode): a deliberate acknowledgment that the fictional mother's funny, indeed outrageous, exploits and creativity are a reflection on, and of, Gibbons's own condition and strategies of survival—through words. The confrontation with her mother is, avowedly, a confrontation with herself. The song for a deceased mother took so long to be written (and no doubt it will be written again), because it is also the song of her own battle for recovery, for "triumph over death and sorrow," as she wrote in *How I Became a Writer*.

At the same time, in *How I Became a Writer*, Gibbons constantly tells us of her admiration for a mother who proved herself equal to all the odds she had to face. An admiration touched with suffering and regret because the mother disappeared at a time when the daughter needed her to inscribe herself within a significant sequence, to be continued into her own daughters: "If I can be anything to my daughters, I wish to be a bridge from my mother to them. . . . I want my mother's strength to pass through me to them." But to do that she must accept to reflect upon her mother's death and to reorder it through language—through fiction—into a usable past: "I understand her better now, and I think by letting her memory help me I'm making my peace with her, with my own past. Any truce must come of understanding" (Sternburg, p. 59). Such is the material on which the woman-narrator in *Sights Unseen* must "work." It is a work of mourning (*Trauerarbeit*), a work of duty, a song of remembrance of and reconciliation with the mother—and with herself: a song of praise.

From her first memories to the age of twelve, Hattie Barnes, the narrator, has suffered from the absence of her manic-depressive mother, mentally absent because of her manic fits or large doses of pills, or physically because of her stays in the hospital, particularly during a two months' treatment by electrotherapy—the central episode around which the novel is structured. The mother comes out sedate, apparently cured, and during the following years the daughter completes the education of which neither the mother nor the daughter knows the gestures and rituals, which they must learn gradually. For what the daughter had missed above all rested in simple everyday gestures—to be touched and cared for, to be fed and clothed with specific attention to herself: "We never sat down and had a long, constructive and restorative talk, but that mattered less and less as I grew older. Her actions were more important. . . . We were somehow able to get at the business of living without calling up ghosts. We let the past stay in the past."[7] Then the mother dies accidentally, at a time when the narrator is expecting her first child. This sharp departure from autobiography in Gibbons's fiction shows how much she is on the way to healing through writing. In *Sights Unseen*, the mother does not die of an overdose of pills, as she had done in *Ellen Foster*, nor does she leave the daughter an orphan. *Sights Unseen* is in that respect less autobiographical than *Ellen Foster*, but certainly more profoundly personal and revealing, and more moving.

The narrative standpoint is set five years later, after the birth of the narrator's daughters. She must now create for herself a usable mother (though it can never be a definitive creation) so as to make herself into a useful mother in turn, as she explains almost at the opening of the novel:

> A girl cannot go along motherless without life's noticing, taking a compensatory tuck here and there in the heart and in the mind, letting out one seam whenever she is threatened by her loneliness. I could have lurched on to adulthood, straining to be a good girl, not ever learning what to do when my own children were placed in my arms. My instinct might have been to ignore my responsibility for them the way my mother had initially relinquished responsibility for me. The children might have had to wait for me to find my way, as I had to wait for my mother. . . . But we caught each

François Pitavy

> other just in time, right on the edge of my puberty. . . . Boys, when they finally took notice of me, had to wait for my mother and me to learn each other, to learn our habits and ways.[8]

The novel is precisely the narrative of that slow—grievous and joyful—process of education, carried on retrospectively, from the now-safe distance of motherhood, which at the same time bridges the gap between the narrator and her mother through conscious identification. The seamstress metaphors in the quotation show precisely that it is a slow, attentive work, a work of dedication and love all along. The narrator can at last let out the constricting seams of memory so as to create a space for survival. Later, when the daughter attends medical school and thus can have an inside understanding of the electrotherapy treatment, she can identify with her mother the better because of her precise knowledge of what the mother had gone through years before. In the last paragraph of the novel, the daughter fully realizes the function of the narrative—the cathartic effect of putting things into words: "Both forgiving and healing are true arts, and in telling my mother's story I have been able to forgive the past without reservation and heal myself without concern over a lapse of acute sorrow over her death. I now understand the miracle of catharsis, the value of her story" (p. 209).

Such is the "value" of story-telling, the ordering of the burden of memory through language, as Gibbons defines the function of fiction writing. With *Sights Unseen,* it appears that she has succeeded in occupying the territory she had so brilliantly claimed with *Ellen Foster:* a territory of grievous compassion and joyful celebration. Is it, however, a Southern territory? Kaye Gibbons herself has no reservations about being called a Southern writer.[9] Just listening to her would confirm it. The Gibbons voice, live or on paper, undoubtedly expresses a sense of belonging (adroitly and funnily exploited, to be sure). After all, her Southernness may very well reside in the unerring and droll sense of language, possibly the ultimate definition of the sense of place in an Americanized South. Should one go any further? Are such worn-out questions about the South, the topic of so many academic literary conferences, still legitimate in the late 1990s? Do critics and readers still need such slick and reassuring categorizing, which somehow prevents them from listening to the specificity of the individual voice?

If this is felt to be a flippant way out of the question asked, which it is *not,* what else can the reading of Gibbons tell us about Southernness? From *Ellen Foster* to *Sights Unseen,* it seems that she has gradually steered away from expected Southern topoi, except for comical effects. Her Southernness, if it must be traced at all, is not to be found in her subjects, except in the revisiting of genealogies, which are now female rather than male (as Bobbie Ann Mason also does in several stories in *Shiloh and Other Stories*). Her fiction is no exploration and deploration of the death of the fathers, but a private, intensely personal confrontation with the death of the mother. And the voice has changed, too, from the times of Faulkner and Styron, it is no longer the masculine oratory of the previous generation (which Styron has somehow given up in his most recent texts), but a sotto voce song—willfully joyful and funny—made for private recoveries from death and sorrow, for private celebrations. Hers is a quest for identity rather than heritage, yet inscribed, as it should be, within a sense of continuity, of belonging. It is noticeable that in *Sights Unseen* she has even left out the genealogies of the two previous novels, the grandmothers' generation (which had probably been a way of circumventing and delaying the only confrontation worth the grief, that of the parent), to concentrate mainly upon the immediately preceding generation, that of the mother, so as to pass on the heritage of understanding and compassion onto her daughters. Here, Southern fiction has stopped being mostly past-oriented. Significantly, it is looking both ways.

George Santayana said that those who do not remember the past are condemned to repeat it. The female heroine-narrators of Kaye Gibbons remember their often grievous past so as to come to terms with it and to transmit it in a usable form; they keep their mothers and grandmothers alive so as not to die themselves and so that their daughters can live on. A great difference from the previous generation of writers is that the past is no longer a burden, however painful; it is also a means of self-definition, and survival. Unlike the two novels preceding it, *Sights Unseen* has reduced the ranging of history through genealogies to its essentials, the mother-daughter relationship, without any of the Southern trappings and the ever-present sense of History. The burden is no longer that of History, but that of individual memory.

The Gibbons heroines do write history, but definitely with a lowercase "h." Not the children or grandchildren of William Faulkner, but rather of Eudora Welty and Flannery O'Connor, they realize a feminization and privatization of a profoundly enduring Southern concern.

Notes

1. Kaye Gibbons, *How I Became a Writer: My Mother, Literature, and a Life Split Neatly into Two Halves* (Chapel Hill, N.C.: Algonquin Books, 1988). Reprinted as an article, without the first five words in the title, in Janet Sternburg, ed., *The Writer on Her Work: New Essays in New Territory* (New York and London: Norton, 1991), pp. 52–60 (quotation on p. 60). Subsequent references are to the reprint.

2. The quotations from Walker Percy and Eudora Welty appear on the cover of the Vintage edition (see n. 4).

3. See the study of the five novels in François Pitavy, "Sostenuto e Ostinato. La Petite Musique de Kaye Gibbons," *Europe* 816 (April 1997): 175–87.

4. Kaye Gibbons, *Ellen Foster* (New York: Random House, Vintage Books, 1988), p. 1. Subsequent references are to the Vintage edition and are cited in the text.

5. For some biographical information, see Julian Mason, "Kaye Gibbons," in *Contemporary Fiction Writers of the South: A Bio-Bibliographical Sourcebook,* eds. Joseph M. Flora and Robert Bain (Westport, Conn.: Greenwood Press, 1993), pp. 156–68.

6. I have not seen the printed version; but a rough copy of the text was gracefully given to me, for which I am very grateful to Kaye Gibbons.

7. Kaye Gibbons, *Sights Unseen* (New York: Putnam's Sons, 1995), pp. 208–9.

8. *Sights Unseen,* p. 6.

9. See William Starr, *Southern Writers* (Columbia: University of South Carolina Press, 1997).

Lies as the Structural Element in the Fiction of Lewis Nordan

Marcel Arbeit

There is a myth connected with Southern literature. It says that Southern writers are interested more than others in moral problems, family, and community life, that they realize to a greater extent that our world is a place of pain, suffering, and sorrow. As Flannery O'Connor put it, Southern writers (not particular writers, but writers en masse) "have to have some conception of the whole man":[1] they are still able to recognize what the difference is between good and evil. Since it is a myth, it is impossible to trace who first came up with the idea, or better, with the story. And as it is shared by numerous Southern as well as non-Southern literary scholars and even writers themselves, it is difficult to challenge. The contemporary era is ruled by a different myth: that in an age of small narratives and lack of belief in God there is no place for morals. It is the tension between these two myths that haunts the best contemporary Southern writers. The tension is between the old community-centered Southern literary model and the new postmodern cosmopolitan writing, where the point of view is deliberately blurred. Is it possible to combine the two approaches? Lewis Nordan, a contemporary Southern writer who has been writing since the mid-1970s, but only in the early 1990s received significant critical acclaim, dismisses this putative opposition. He writes about growing up in the South in the middle of a small-town community and its moral climate. And he chose lies as the uniting principle of his fiction.

From his third book, *Music of the Swamp* (1991), Nordan has written almost exclusively about Arrow Catcher, Mississippi, which was introduced in his first two collections of stories, *Welcome to the Arrow-Catcher Fair* (1983) and *The All-Girl Football Team* (1986). It is a place famous for having invented a strange game in which one member of each team shoots arrows at his or her colleague who tries to catch them in bare hands. Arrow Catcher is not exactly William Faulkner's Jefferson or Eudora Welty's Morgana, nor is it a replica of a real place that can be translated into genealogy charts and maps. It is more like a dream image of Itta Bena, Mississippi, where Nordan was born. It is a fictitious world where the historical and the imagined are mixed in such a way that they cannot be disentangled.

Music of the Swamp, although advertised as a novel, is nothing more (but also nothing less) than a sequence of short stories inhabited with characters many of whom already appeared in Nordan's previous works. The books that followed, *Wolf Whistle* (1993), *The Sharpshooter Blues* (1995), and *The Lightning Song* (1997), are novels, but their episodic structure makes them more of a kaleidoscope than a chronicle. The first two novels and most of his stories are set in the mid-1950s. It is not history, however, that primarily interests Nordan, but the process of reinventing the self in the past. To do that, Nordan blends the stories of his own childhood with tales that never happened and, as he admitted in his essay "The Invention of Sugar: An Essay about Life in Fiction—and Vice Versa" (1991), the "true memories will seem more made up than some of my lies."[2]

What are the reasons behind the idea of mixing truth with lies? What are its consequences? Walter Sullivan, a Catholic literary scholar of Agrarian stock, claims that lies are legitimized primarily by Gnostics. Because Gnostics believe that people can modify the terms of human existence, they tell us "that weakness is strength, that license is freedom, that morality is negotiable."[3] This can result in a distortion of history, which can be very dangerous, since people are supposed to learn from the past in order not to make the same mistakes in the future. On this point he comes surprisingly to a conclusion similar to that reached later by Michael O'Brien, who deals with the topic from a strictly historical point of view and, unlike Sullivan, thinks that Southern literature and myths connected with the South abuse history from the start. According to O'Brien the whole myth of the antebellum South is nonsense, there was no "Eden of community," and social conflicts, disunity, and depression ruled the area even before the Civil War: "The South is a metaphysical construct, born of the interaction of an intellectual tradition, historicist Romanticism, with social and political history."[4] From a theological or historical point of view lies have beyond any doubt purely negative connotations and are seen exclusively as instruments of bias and moral breakdown. But, from the artistic point of view lies can join creative fantasy in the search for truth. "And out of a pattern of lies art weaves the truth,"[5] as D. H. Lawrence wrote already in 1924, in his essay "The Spirit of Place."

There is yet another problem. As Walter Sullivan points out, contemporary literature serves politics. In 1976, before the era of political correctness, he wrote in his book *A Requiem for the Renascence:* "People who would never trim their convictions or vitiate their talents for fame or money collapse under the monolithic imperative of the modern intellectual milieu. All are vanquished by the shibboleths of race, ecology, sexism, and other nonnegotiable causes of our age."⁶ Ideologies of all kinds are incompatible with creative freedom. The author should have a space for dreaming, for inventing stories, in other words, for lying. The present does not provide writers with such a space. Any deliberate distortion of the present, be it idealization or demonization, would turn into a political lie. What writers need is distance, and that is why more and more Southern authors set their books in the recent past. They do not want to escape the "here and now," for even the transformed past has links to the present; they only want to have the freedom not to follow any fashionable ideological stream. When authors plunge into the recent past, their memories play important roles: the worse these memories are, the more the authors are forced to employ their imagination. To remember is to live, but even if the memory fails completely, it is possible to invent a world of one's own: to lie is to stay alive at least.

Unlike political or historical lies, the imaginative lies are not supposed to distort reality. On the contrary, without them reality is incomplete and dull, prone to canonized versions, and the "only possible" interpretation. Lies give their authors the freedom to avoid literal descriptions of reality and to create metaphors. Then the act of deceiving as well as the act of being deceived become parts of an imaginative game that brings pleasure to all participants and helps dissolve monolithic truths. It is not a rejection of "truth," only a reminder that every truth can and should be challenged.

I would like to take a more in-depth look at how the imaginative lies are used in Nordan's fiction. Nordan often narrates a story and then retells it in a completely different way, be it in the same book or in one of his later works. In the first part of *Music of the Swamp,* two ten-year-old boys, Sugar Mecklin and Sweet Austin, meet one Sunday on a small pier. They sail in a boat to the middle of Roebuck Lake and Sweet shows Sugar "bare feet and legs sticking up out of the water."⁷ Later the boys as well as the readers receive an explanation: it was an old man who went fishing and had a seizure. The night before, Sugar had a dream in which he could see a barebreasted, singing woman rising up from water, and that image drives him to the lake. The same image appears in *Wolf Whistle,* a novel inspired by the notorious lynching of Emmett Till and centered around the killing of an African American boy, Bobo, who addressed a white woman in a local drugstore and wolf-whistled at her. In this novel, Bobo is the dead person that Sugar and Sweet find in the lake. Although this is also a third-person narrative, Sugar's feelings and thoughts are not given this time. The reflector through whom one sees the events of the moment is the dead Bobo, who imagines himself as a mermaid combing her hair and holding a mirror in her hand.⁸ It looks like a metamorphosis but it is not, even though Sugar's dream from *Music of the Swamp* becomes Bobo's death image. The dead boy transmits it in *Wolf Whistle* directly to Sugar's bed: "Bobo called out from his death to Sugar, *I am the mer-*

maid that you will love."⁹ To emphasize the link between the books, Nordan then repeats word for word the beginning of a short conversation between Sugar and Sweet.

If Nordan's books set in the town of Arrow Catcher are taken as a sequence, the different renderings of the same story might be considered an inconsistency, a major flaw. Nordan himself makes an excuse in his essay "Growing Up White in the South" where he reconstructs (or pretends to reconstruct) his train of thoughts: "The narrator reports the body to be that of an old man who had 'spells.' I knew it was not. Though I had not given a thought to any future book I might write, I knew when I wrote the chapter that this dead person was none other than Emmett Till, floating upside down at the end of a barbed wire tether that was tied at one end to a hundred-pound gin fan and at the other, around the child's neck."[10] Nordan does not talk about Bobo in his essay, he talks about Emmett Till, referring directly to the 1955 historical event. In the novel he turns once again to the imaginative lie that enables him, among other things, to keep a distance and to stay in the comic mode. Those who appreciate his wild imagination and narrative skills will be less inclined to criticize him for an insufficient characterization of the young victim who appears throughout the novel more like a ghost than a three-dimensional character. Nordan's antiracist viewpoint is always clear, but his method allows him to avoid political commentaries as well as phrases and clichés. At this point, he is moral without being moralistic.

The method of gradual remembering or forgetting (one can never be sure which) is also used in the description of the key events in the life of the Mecklin family and with the families of other Nordan characters. In the stories from the Sugar Mecklin cycle, the reader is offered, for instance, several accounts of Gilbert Mecklin's suicide. In one version, Sugar's father sticks an ice pick in his own chest while Bessie Smith is singing "Muddy Water" on the phonograph (*Music*, p. 17); in another, the suicide attempt takes place many years later, one year before Sugar joins the army. At that time Sugar's father stabs himself in the stomach with a kitchen knife and then drives to the hospital. Sugar, who is a witness to all this, is asked to hand him a towel, not to wake the mother, and to clean up the mess. Are there two suicide attempts, or just one, the timing and form of which changed due to the author's forgetful mind? In "The Cellar of Runt Conroy" from the same book a blend of the two versions can be found: the night rain washes out from under the Mecklins' house "the ice pick my father once stabbed himself in the chest with while I watched him, the towels he bled into as his face turned white while my mother closed the window shades so that no one else would see" (*Music*, p. 113). What is completely new in this version is the presence of Sugar's mother, but from a short story, "The Sears and Roebuck Catalog Game," in which the family members did not even have names, the reader knows that the mother had tried to kill herself as well: she played "a pantomime of suicide"[11] with a razor blade and then, in the presence of her son, she opened an artery.

Why does Nordan tell different versions of the same story again and again? The important point is not the truth itself but the search for it and the challenge it presents. After reading all the stories, the reader is not even sure who Sugar's father is: Sweet Austin looks almost like his twin, but does that mean that Gilbert Mecklin seduced Sweet's mother, or that Mrs. Mecklin spent a night with Mr. Austin who later left his family? In "Creatures with Shining Scales," Sugar struggles to carry his father's dead body from the living room to the bathroom to save it in a hurricane. His mother comments on this: "You have always been a good boy. Your daddy loved you so much, even if he wasn't your real daddy" (*Music*, p. 179). A few minutes later she pretends that she had not said anything. Was this what had been on Sugar's mind all these years? Was his mother lying? In "Owls," the last story of *Music of the Swamp*, the adult Sugar confesses to his lover: "I think I made the whole thing up." Still, the invented father was with him "in a way he could not be in life" (*Music*, pp. 190–91). It is tempting to consider Sugar Mecklin as the writer's alter ego, but Nordan does his best to warn us against the identification of writers with their protagonists. The reluctance of the author to answer from his double distance the questions of truth and untruth, and his urge to invent new and newer lies, can also be explained as an effort to retain the state of innocence as long as possible. Innocent people cannot be immoral, and their innocence can help maintain the optimistic tone of the story, even in scenes of moral breakdown, violence, and chaos. Even when Gilbert and his wife become separated, there is not a single word about a divorce, and it is obvious that sooner or later they will give their life together another try. Sugar Mecklin lives in a complete family and his parents care for each other, although depression, alcoholism, and bad luck make their lives difficult, and many other Arrow Catcher families follow their example.

Nordan's ability to see the most undesirable state of affairs as an idyll sometimes gives the stories a touch of the absurd. In "Field and Stream," Sugar and his father save a drug addict from suffocation, only to have Gilbert Mecklin give him a shot of morphine which kills him. Even in this case the effect is optimistic: Sugar comes to the conclusion that the death was painless and in addition to that, the corpse is warm and comfortable to lean against. It looks like cynicism, but it is only innocence shown through a well-structured protective lie. The same method is used when Sugar is not merely a witness or a victim, but an active performer in a crime. Then the lie can be shared by the whole community in order to protect him. When he shoots at his father through the window and misses him in "Sugar, the Eunuchs and Big G. B.," everybody in Arrow Catcher takes it as evidence of Sugar's growing independence. The father becomes the most celebrated person in the town because he was the only citizen who was worthy to be shot at. And even Big G. B., Sugar's surrogate father, tells a grand lie to save Sugar from lifelong trauma: "Shooting to kill is what a boy is supposed to do to his daddy, Sugar-man."[12]

Nordan is not the only contemporary Southern writer who uses lies as structural elements. A good example would be Fred Chappell and his *I Am One of You Forever* (1985), a collection of short stories disguised as a novel, set in the early 1940s, one decade earlier than Nordan's books.[13] The parallels are numerous: the main protagonists are a ten-year-old boy and his father, the story is focused on family life, and there is an obvious mixture of reality and fantasy. In the story "Telegram," a whole family pretends not to have received a telegram announcing the death in a military training camp of a young orphan, who is almost a member of the family. One after another, they try to hide the ominous piece of paper in various places, but it reappears every day on the dining table. The merciful lie does not work, the cruel truth forces its way to the surface, and this is something unheard of in Nordan's books.

In Fred Chappell's *I Am One of You Forever,* there is nothing reality can be transformed into; if you try to escape to an alternative world of imagination, it can be even more dangerous than staying where you are. The story that best illustrates this is "Storytellers," where the family is visited by Uncle Zeno who tells stories almost round the clock. But his listeners can never be sure whether they will be lucky enough to hear the endings, as the narrator sometimes chooses to change his audience and begins to talk to animals and trees. When the father tries to find out the conclusion to one of the unfinished stories through investigation among the neighbors, he becomes a subject of the narration himself, which is ominous since all the people in the stories seem to vanish without a trace. The story can be considered a tale of horror, but only when published separately, for the father is alive and well in the next story, and another crazy uncle comes to visit and teaches him and his son another lesson. Like Nordan, Chappell starts the same story again and again, but its different versions are not interconnected. Although the whole atmosphere of Chappell's book seems to be more playful than that of *Music of the Swamp* and the other stories of the Sugar Mecklin cycle, it is actually less optimistic, as lies are not only challenges to invent new worlds that can help you survive, but also dangerous weapons that can never be protective and can turn the magic of the narrative into black magic. Lies are not the center here, they are just a means for creating the magic.[14]

There is probably no other contemporary Southern author who shapes characters so consistently by piling lies up around them as Lewis Nordan does. An illustrative example may be the central character of *The Sharpshooter Blues*

Hydro Raney, a hydrocephalic with an enormous head and weak brains. He appears for the first time in one of the stories from *Welcome to the Arrow-Catcher Fair* as a "gawky young boy with a broom and a large head" sweeping the floor in a bar while interrupting the local storyteller with his comments.[15] In "Sugar, the Eunuchs and Big G. B." he is introduced as a son of the local sheriff nicknamed Big'un. He is among those who saw Sugar shooting at his daddy, but nobody believes him, including his own father. In *Music of the Swamp* he is the only child of Mr. Raney, the owner of the fish camp on Raney's Island, and he "often chased cars and howled when the fire truck turned on the siren and had to be given ice cream so that he would stop" (*Music*, pp. 13–14). Nobody would believe such a person could ever work as a shop assistant, but in *Wolf Whistle* Nordan makes him a man of thirty and an employee of the Sims and Hill drugstore. In *The Sharpshooter Blues* he miraculously grows ten years younger, the Sims and Hill drugstore becomes William Tell's, and the town is invaded by two perverse gangsters, brother and sister, who look and behave as if they just came out of one of David Lynch's films. Hydro proves to be extremely handy with a gun and shoots them both dead, but nobody believes him and another person is investigated. Hydro commits suicide; feebleminded or not, he feels that a man who is not taken seriously under any circumstances has no reason to live.

As in Chappell's "Storyteller," the truth is not what really happened, but what became a part of oral tradition. The citizens of Arrow Catcher share the story about a midget sharpshooter shooting his way out of jail and do not care that in reality he shot a refrigerator only and never tried to escape: "As long as there was a story, that's all that really mattered. It didn't have to be true, or to make much sense."[16] Nobody challenges the story of a local mortician who is said to have been resurrected by Aunt Lily, a local voodoo woman and fortune-teller, but the mortician denies the rumor with statements like "My flesh had started to decay a little. Just in patches, you know, not all over" (*Sharpshooter*, p. 228). Stories are even more important than prophecies. "Facts don't mean the first thing to that worthless crystal ball," complains Aunt Lily (*Sharpshooter*, p. 149).

The Sharpshooter Blues is Nordan's first book in which a character invents a vengeful lie. Morgan the sharpshooter is its victim. The liar is ten-year-old Louis who wishes him behind bars because Morgan is his mother's lover. When Louis, an eye-witness, accuses Morgan of the killing, everybody believes him (although he speaks the language of his favorite comic book). But Louis matures early enough to disclaim his words. In addition, Morgan gets away with his own lie, a story about his murder of a Mexican which was supposed to make him more admired and mysterious. The use of lies as both the leading theme and the creative principle could come about only in a postmodern age. In *The Southern Writer in the Postmodern World* (1991), Fred Hobson argues that Southern literature is generally not postmodern because "the contemporary southern writer . . . essentially *accepts,* rather than invents, his world, is not given to fantasy, does not *in his fiction* question the whole assumed relationship between narrator and narrative, does not question the nature of fiction itself."[17] Hobson's characterization of postmodern writing is convincing; numerous Southern authors would appear to comply with his specifications. Nordan is one of them, he does not challenge the nature of fiction. But he is closer to the oral tradition than most of the contemporary Southern writers. The examples from Nordan's books demonstrate that he really invents a world of his own, a world where imaginative lies are the basic building units. His approach to the narrative is the approach of a liar who aims at producing the version of a story that is neither canonical nor final, and can be rewritten any time he manages to generate a better lie. This is not a new factor in American literature, as it can be seen as far back as in Mark Twain's works.[18] Nordan is closer to Twain than to Faulkner or Welty. Twain's tall tales, sketches, and, above all, his Tom Sawyer—Huck Finn novels use lies as their structural elements. This does not mean that Nordan could avoid the influence of Faulkner completely; his second collection of stories even includes a Faulkner parody. The Faulkner books that influenced him the most are, however, those greatly indebted to the Twain tradition: *The Unvanquished* (1938) and *The Reivers* (1962).

Of the two Faulkner books, *The Unvanquished* is the better example, because lies and their consequences represent one of its major themes and penetrate the very structure of the book. Bayard Sartoris, the central character of this novel or collection of stories, remembers the times when he and his African American friend Ringo were twelve and "Granny had never whipped us for anything in our lives except lying, and . . . even when it wasn't even a told lie but keeping quiet."[19] After a lie the ritual punishment followed: children had to wash out their mouths with soap. Rosa Millard, "Granny," is allowed to lie if it is for the good of the community, or if she at least persuades herself that it is for that reason. In the course of the story Rosa herself becomes the victim of a political lie. While on the surface she is a good Christian who asks the Lord on her knees to forgive both her and the boys, her soul becomes poisoned by Gnosticism. She believes that with her charisma she can stop the evil development of the region, bring it back to the good old times, and introduce the rituals and manners she grew up with. Bayard also lives with a lie. To his son, Colonel John Sartoris will never be an arrogant and selfish horsethief, but will always remain a Confederate hero and esteemed citizen. And in the background there is the omnipresent myth of the idyllic antebellum South, the exploitation of which can lead to a historical lie.

In modernist Faulkner, lies, whatever their reason and nature, can have tragic consequences. In contrast, Nordan, who flirts with postmodern arbitrariness, comes to the conclusion that imaginative lies cannot be harmful. The bridge between the period when his books are set and the 1980s and 1990s can be found in the central arrow-catching metaphor. The South is seen as a place where everybody must be alert and any innocent game can turn deadly. Among the rubber-tipped blunts, a real blade of solid sharp steel may appear any time. School excursions to funeral parlors, girls having sex with feeble-minded shop assistants before killing them, and children attempting to kill their parents are representations of a Southern world full of skepticism. But Nordan is not pessimistic about the future. He believes the imagination will enable people to extricate themselves from the torpor and overcome their feeling of alienation.

The perspective in Nordan's books is essentially Southern, optimistic, and comic. The comic often springs from the characters' evaluation of each other. According to Sugar Mecklin, those who display personal and family problems in public are "white trash," which is for him not a social, but a moral category. Sugar condemns the manners of the family of his best friend Roy Dale Conroy, as well as other people he encounters, but he pretends not to realize that if he applied his moral criteria to his own family, he would have to label it "white trash" as well. He gradually takes a liking to such people, and he does not reject the idea of becoming one of them: "There was a prophet's voice in the rain. It said: *You will grow up to marry a white-trash girl*" (*Music,* p. 104). This does not mean that he cannot tell good from evil any more. On the contrary; he knows that alcoholism is bad. He must admit that when he grew up, he also had to attend "Don't Drink" meetings. He still considers it immoral to break up a family although he admits that he also did it once. His lies influenced everything in his life but his moral center.

No characters in Nordan's fiction claim that they are moral, but they do believe in certain moral standards of the Southern community. The line has remained the same for generations, no matter how the stories and their author develop and change. Nordan does not have a conception of the whole man, but he has a conception at least of an imaginative man, who is imperfect and who may be seen as a little immoral, but who is never indifferent to human suffering. A good imaginative lie can always send people on another hunt for a truth that can never be attained, but always must be searched for.

Notes

1. Flannery O'Connor, *Mystery and Manners* (New York: Farrar, Straus and Giroux, 1969), p. 44.
2. Lewis Nordan, "The Invention of Sugar: An Essay about Life in Fiction—and Vice Versa," Advertising Folder (Chapel Hill, N.C.: Algonquin Books, 1991), p. 7.

3. Walter Sullivan, *A Requiem for the Renascence* (Athens: University of Georgia Press, 1976), p. 22.

4. Michael O'Brien, *Rethinking the South: Essays in Intellectual History* (Baltimore: Johns Hopkins University Press, 1988), p. 166.

5. D. H. Lawrence, *Selected Literary Criticism,* ed. Anthony Beal (London: Heinemann, 1956), p. 297.

6. Sullivan, *A Requiem,* pp. 23–24.

7. Lewis Nordan, *Music of the Swamp* (Chapel Hill, N.C.: Algonquin Books, 1991), p. 11. Subsequent references are to this edition and are cited in the text.

8. See Franz K. Stanzel, *Theorie des Erzählens* (Göttingen: Vandenhoeck and Ruprecht, 1979).

9. Lewis Nordan, *Wolf Whistle* (Chapel Hill, N.C.: Algonquin Books, 1993), p. 183. Nordan's italics.

10. Lewis Nordan, "Growing Up White in the South: An Essay," Advertising Folder (Chapel Hill, N.C.: Algonquin Books, 1993), [3] unpaginated.

11. See Lewis Nordan, *The All-Girl Football Team* (Chapel Hill, N.C.: Algonquin Books, 1986), p. 53.

12. Nordan, *The All-Girl Football Team,* p. 40.

13. See Fred Chappell, *I Am One of You Forever* (Baton Rouge: Louisiana State University Press, 1985), pp. 93–96, 97–118.

14. Chappell explores various aspects of the magic both in his poetic novels, especially in *It Is Time, Lord* (1963), and in his horror fiction; most of all in his novel *Dagon* (New York: Harcourt, Brace and World, 1968), but also in his short stories.

15. Lewis Nordan, *Welcome to the Arrow-Catcher Fair* (Baton Rouge: Louisiana State University Press, 1983), p. 63.

16. Lewis Nordan, *The Sharpshooter Blues* (Chapel Hill, N.C.: Algonquin Books, 1995), p. 238.

17. Fred Hobson, *The Southern Writer in the Postmodern World* (Athens: University of Georgia Press, 1991), p. 9. Hobson lists among Southern postmodern writers only Barry Hannah, Richard Ford, and James Alan McPherson.

18. The controversial ending of *Adventures of Huckleberry Finn* can be also seen as a deliberate imaginative lie, one of the versions of a story told again and again.

19. William Faulkner, *The Unvanquished,* in *Novels 1936–1940,* ed. Joseph Blotner (New York: Library of America, 1990), p. 338.

Dancers and Angels

Communication in the Fiction of Josephine Humphreys

Danièle Pitavy-Souques

What marks Josephine Humphreys as a major writer is the dominance of her concern for writing, over a concern for themes. Humphreys's fiction has been considered by perceptive critics, like Fred Hobson, who sees *Dreams of Sleep,* Humphreys's first and best novel so far, as "a novel of conscious social commentary of the sort usually associated with southern male authors, from Mark Twain through Percy to Richard Ford, it contains the same sort of semi-serious, sometimes hilarious self-conscious regionalism, southern and otherwise, we find especially in Percy,"[1] and like Kathryn B. McKee, who reconsiders the characters of Will and Alice Reese.[2] But whatever the critics claim, if themes and fine characterization alone were to be considered, Humphreys would have no claim to rank among the great Southern writers of the postmodern tradition. Her message is to be read in her technique rather than in the themes themselves, which are as old as fiction itself, for what must be new is the writer's imagination, her ability to invent narrative rules and categories to tell old stories in a fresh way.

The power to invent Welty calls vision; Humphreys calls it surprise. As she told Southern Forum scholars in Columbia, South Carolina, in 1993, "The principle I believe in is this: no surprise for the writer, no surprise for the reader."[3] True surprise, of the kind she talks about, the kind that draws admiration for a writer, does not come from contents or plot, but from aesthetic daring and inventiveness, which is the artist's own, something unique, identifiable as his or hers. In this respect, if one influence can be traced, it is Eudora Welty's. Like her, Josephine Humphreys possesses that supreme gift of the artist: vision. Not just insight or perceptiveness, which are primary requisites for all fiction writers, but vision as the revelation, or truly inspired invention, of the aesthetic mode appropriate to the age in which he or she writes, the mode that best expresses the philosophical and sociological interrogations of an age and is

Danièle Pitavy-Souques

often in correspondence with new scientific discoveries or preoccupations. Eudora Welty puts the emphasis on the visual and on images; Humphreys puts it on movement and transformations. In her best stories or novels about the South, Welty hits upon devices that become both theme and technique: the puppeteer in "Old Mr. Marblehall," the stereopticon in "Kin," or a catoptric stage with mirrors placed *en vis à vis* in *Delta Wedding,* in order to present her brilliant narrative exposure of fraud and imposture in family portraits and photographs. As she deconstructs the myth-making process that sustains family life and social status in the South, Welty exploits the aesthetic field of photography as well as the cinematic possibilities of visual distortion and special effects.

In an age more preoccupied with movement, fluidity, and free-flowing information, Josephine Humphreys fictionalizes new relationships or their absence through other aesthetic and philosophical devices that best embody this constant change. She is not preoccupied with disintegration as critics would have it, but with the biological and sociological process of transformation.[4] In a deceptively simple sentence, of the kind only great artists use to state what they do when they paint or write, Humphreys said in an interview: "I write mostly about families, in long-term relationships. . . . We see them as static, but they always change."[5] In this statement about both theme and technique in her work, she is very much of her time, a time mathematically interested in seeing form "not as it affects our sight, something static, definitive, solidified in a way, but form as something that tells of movement, of evolution, hence of time," as Jean Dhombres redefines form in "Qu'est-ce qu'une forme?"[6] I mention this branch of mathematical research, because it can have applications in literary criticism, as it provides analogies that enable us to see the functioning of the structure of Humphreys's novels and their meaning. Their congruence proves, once more, that all innovative artistic processes in this century spring from a desire to "make visible that there is something that can be conceived and can neither be seen nor made visible," or to use another definition by Jean François Lyotard in "What Is Postmodernism?": "I shall call modern the art which devotes its 'little technical expertise' *(son 'petit technique'),* as Diderot used to say, to present the fact that the unpresentable exists."[7]

The unpresentable in Humphreys's novels is the necessity to disrupt the present myth of order, which is in fact destructive disorder, and to revert to an older form of disorder, a subversive, richer, and more creative one. In direct relation with Humphreys's fiction is the idea of movement, of a dynamism linked with form, and its corollary: a form is interesting only inasmuch as it belongs to a group. *Through deformations, in time and space,* morphogenesis determines how forms are affected by the deformations, and how they can be classified. More interestingly for us, it determines what remains unchanged, what resists change—the singularities of the forms.[8] To put it more simply, I will argue that Humphreys fictionalizes those deformations as they affect Southern society, and poeticizes what resists change, for there lies hope for the future of the South: the secret awe and worship of violence, the supreme love of beauty and the beau geste thriving on dire reality and unexpected reversals, and that never-ending dialogue with the invisible.

This purely mental process throws light on the singular coherence of Humphreys's fiction, on her preoccupation with the abstract (something she shares with Welty) not only as it affects her research on fictional form, but also as it affects the dominant theme of her fiction: communication. "Our subject," she writes, "is the concert of human lives."[9] I will not define it as the way people relate to one another in a changing world, something that has been at the heart of Southern fiction and life for decades just as it is a postmodern worldwide preoccupation at present, nor simply as an antagonistic static process, but as a dynamic Protean process. These fluid transformations in time and space are together theme, poetic pattern, and the governing principle of Humphreys's work. The depth and width of her reflection, combined with a rare moral quality, give her fiction its hallmark and transform it into texts that will last.

Each of her three novels, *Dreams of Sleep* (1984), *Rich in Love* (1987), *The Fireman's Fair* (1991), reads like a new art of thinking, an urgent invitation to reconsider the way we relate to place, history, and others. And the reader's pleasure comes from the unexpected dialectics of questions and answers: ontological questions and fictionalized answers, since the true questions raised by reading the first book are answered, or partly so, in the second one, which in its turn raises more questions that will be answered in the third volume. This is neither a saga, nor a trilogy, but something new in Southern literature, which in a way evokes Plato's dialogues and requires active reading. Nothing moralizing or didactic is in these novels, where permanent surprise is caused by shifts in point of view and this reader-response activity. There is nothing conventional either: known situations, incidents common in the South, all are seen in their strangeness, as irruptions of the uncanny and create, while we wait for the irrational to invade the scene, an opening to knowledge. In this respect Humphreys stands alone among her contemporaries. Far from lamenting the mutability of the world, she sees it as the ineradicable, perhaps even hopeful, sign of life itself.

In his general appreciation of Humphreys's work, Joseph Millichap combines the views of early reviewers and critics, especially women, when he writes that her fiction is well regarded for "a unique balance of traditional methods and contemporary interests. Though contrasting in many ways, all her novels combine her major themes—the dislocations of history, particularly Southern history, and the disintegration of the family, particularly Southern family. Perhaps her most intriguing contribution is the persistent suggestion of renewal and reintegration that pervades her fiction" (Millichap, p. 246). This restrictive judgment labels Humphreys's fiction as banal and conventional, when it is less concerned with rewriting, or parodying as Hobson argues, the traditional modes of representation of such pillars of Southern fiction as family and history, than with exploding known forms of representation and inventing new ones to present her vision of the South. There is renewal of some sort as I will try to show, but no reintegration that implies closure. It is precisely because the surface themes of her fiction put on the mask of naturalism and tradition that her creative disorder is so powerful.

Humphreys builds her vision of the South like a battlefield where two kinds of arcadia contend for dominance: the more recent kind of established order institutes peace and harmony on a severely controlled hierarchy, which tames instincts and life-giving forces, and the older darker kind, which is "a place of primitive panic," according to Simon Schama's distinction between two kinds of arcadias in *Landscape and Memory*.[10] In this other myth, nature is wild and shaggy, filled with disorder and misrule; clear distinctions such as between men and animal do not exist, yet its forces are those of life and creativity. Although it seems, Schama argues, that the rough myth was established first, specialists agree on the coexistence of both myths in Western thinking. Humphreys rewrites this coexistence as a parable of the present state of things while offering a new version: the myth of the happy arcadia is enforced with the violence attributed to the mythic dark arcadia; the result is not peace, harmony, and graceful order, but a destructive chaos bereft of inventive possibilities. She departs from traditional Southern orthodoxy, which superimposed the myth of the happy South to correct the initial mistake of slavery; instead, she shares Eudora Welty's ontological vision of time and the artist in "A Still Moment," when the preacher Lorenzo reflects: "He could understand God's giving Separateness first, and then giving Love to follow and heal in its wonder; but God had reversed this, and given Love first and then Separateness, as though it did not matter to Him which came first. Perhaps it was that God never counted the moment of Time."[11]

Another distinction must be made between the mood of the fiction, the prevalent sadness of nearly all male characters, and the mood of the creative artist herself, a jubilation, which has been mistaken for theme sometimes when it reflects the creative mind's attitude towards creation. In his discussion of postmodernism, Jean François Lyotard distinguishes two modes, to use the musician's language:

> The emphasis can be placed on the powerlessness of the faculty of presentation, on the nostalgia for presence felt by the human subject, on the obscure and futile will which inhabits him in spite of everything. The emphasis can be placed, rather, on the power of the faculty to conceive,

on its "inhumanity" so to speak (it was the quality Appollinaire demanded of modern artists), since it is not the business of our understanding whether or not human sensibility or imagination can match what it conceives. The emphasis can also be placed on the increase of being and the jubilation which results from the invention of new rules of the game, be it pictorial, artistic, or any other. (pp. 79–80)

Thus Lyotard places the German expressionists on the side of melancholia, Braque, Picasso (and Joyce) on the side of *novatio*. Although the nuance that distinguishes these two modes may be infinitesimal, "they testify to a difference [un différend] on which the fate of thought depends and will depend for a long time, between regret and assay" (p. 80). Obviously Humphreys is on the side of *novatio*. She allows the unpresentable to become perceptible in her writing itself, in the signifier, in order to impart a stronger sense of the unpresentable. Among others, her signifiers are dancers and angels and place revisited to make visible that the present social order in the South is as much a myth as ever—white supremacy, sanctity of the white family, with miscegenation as fear and reality, ghost families, and dark doubles. It turns forces into destructive ones, which if allowed to flow freely could bring about positive change. In her aesthetic postmodern treatment, Humphreys uses structure and plot to dramatize the emptiness of myths and creates the characters of angels to establish a network of new relationships.

There is no real communication where it should begin—in the family. All the subtlety of Humphreys's strategy is to qualify the common view presented by young Lucille's saying in *Rich in Love:* "All around me I saw the American family blowing apart, as described in *Psychology Today* " (p.15). The novelist does not present a degrading process at work, but the unreality of the myth of the closely knit Southern family. The fallacy of representations over the years, oral or written, is exposed through the device of theatricality that is by representing family relationships like a ballet, with a modern fluid choreography in the style and spirit of Martha Graham's, down to mythic overtones. Humphreys builds her novels as she would write a choreography relying on mirroring effects, the interchangeability of couples, arrivals on the stage and departures into the wings. Intertextuality sends back ironic echoes from Strindberg's *Dance of Death* and further away in time from medieval frescoes. Although present in all three novels, this ballet effect is most visible in the first novel, *Dreams of Sleep,* where the principal male character, Will Reese, reflects: "Marriage is a wordless dance" (p. 172).

Humphreys's characters are in this way caught in a whirl, couples are made then unmade, as they exchange partners and move along in altered ever-changing pairs. The narrator's voice, third person or first person with neurotic Lucille in *Rich in Love,* creates a distancing effect, an atmosphere of unreality as the recording of actions is doubled by voyeurism. The reader is invited to see the original couples, the official ones, as the shadows of newer couples, which appear more authentic in the end. In *Dreams of Sleep* Humphreys plays on doubles that are not quite identical in order to deconstruct the myth of the Southern family; thus the surface structure of the novel puts into parallel two families, a rich one and a poor one, the patrician Reeses and Iris's good-for-nothing parents. Everywhere mothers and fathers fail to do their duties as spouses and parents. Nervous breakdown is the symbol of the absent mother—a sign of reality (Roland Barthes's "effet de réel") to mirror the present state of women's difficulties in adjusting to a changing world where the desire for personal fulfilment and a career is in conflict with family duties, and more interestingly it is a sign of unreality that turns the characters into mere shadows, dancing shadows.

The cruel, sadistic game of domination over children is played by everyone, men and women, rich and poor. The fathers are weak and despicable and refuse to endorse their responsibilities. In an ironical way they represent the Southern man, self-centered and pleasure-loving, averse to change and a great talker. In the aristocratic family, Will Reese is a learned man fond of reciting lines from the metaphysical poets with his friend and partner, Danny Cardozo; in the lower-class family, Owen is a good-for-nothing, a great womanizer and a swindler, always ready to take advantage of women and despoil them. In a variation on the pattern that stresses the characters' indecisiveness and their refusal to settle down for good, Robert and Louise, the heroes of *The Fireman's Fair,* play at being in and out of love with each other, as they come closer and draw apart with another partner. At one stage Rob Wyatt wittily sums up the failure of his romantic life: "He tried not to think of the old days when he'd counted on marrying Louise—but made the mistake of not letting her in on the plan, and had to abandon it altogether when one starry night, in a green silky dress, she announced—without prior notice—her impending marriage to his partner" (*Fireman,* p. 33).

A second structure, richer and more varied, amplifies the general demise of mothers and fathers by tracing it back to older generations, as each character reflects on his or her parents' and grandparents' general failure in their family relationships. In so doing Humphreys demythifies family pride, exposes the hollowness of family trees and of Charleston's obsession with "placing people." As she says: "I grew up in a town where the most important thing was to know who your grandfather was."[12] In *The Fireman's Fair,* a novel about drifting—drifting characters surrounded by sea drifts after the hurricane—Maude's "genealogical obsession" takes an ironical twist when the old woman declares she is not studying the family's genealogy to trace glorious ancestors but because she "is looking for something interesting," namely the connection with a pirate, whose name was "a little different." On hearing Billie's report:

"She said nobody would admit there was a family connection, but she thinks she can find it." Her son Robert, who like her believes in the right to choose one's ancestors among disreputable but inventive citizens—those adventurers who disrupted rules and establishment—retorts: "But why didn't she say so? I'm the one who always wanted Stede Bonnet for an ancestor" (p. 160).

At the same time, the interchanging of roles within the plot establishes a series of fatherly and motherly relationships no longer founded on social institutions like marriage, but on Darwinian laws. The sanctity of the white family rooted in rigid patriarchy is "blown apart" as Lucille would say, when the survival of the fittest implies a necessary redistribution of roles. Displacements, reversals, or pure creations imply a truer, vital order, as when in *Dreams of Sleep,* Queen, the generous African American grandmother of Emory, substitutes for the irresponsible mothers of Emory and Iris. Iris herself becomes her mother's mother at seven and the two little Reeses' mother at seventeen. In *The Fireman's Fair* Billie also finds a substitute family with Carlo at thirteen. In this exchange of traditional roles there is an indictment of a society that has forfeited its duties and responsibilities as educator and protector and betrayed the ideals of solidarity among pioneers. Derision is the mode, functioning like a very thin garment that would expose characters rather than adorn bodies. The sheerness of the social fabric discloses the harsh reality of chaos beneath the superimposed order.

Just as a provocative choreography shows the violence of the world through the bodies of the dancers, words rather than scenes broaden the picture to reveal the brutality of social relationships in the South. Verbal blows create a background of racial violence, social injustice, and blindness to the fate of the other, since they come as fact rather than comment, unexpectedly making sense of "slanting" or refused gazes. They function like the *punctum* that moves Roland Barthes so deeply in photographies, the unexpected detail that suddenly alters our perception of the world represented in the photograph.[13] The dry summary of the family story of Estelle, Alice's mother's black maid, is such an instance: Alice "knew Estelle had high blood pressure and diabetes, and that of her own six children one was killed in Korea, one robbed of eight dollars and stabbed on a Bayside street, and one fatally shot in the back by an off-duty policeman who mistook him for a suspect, when he was really only peeing against a wall. But those weren't reasons not to look *Alice* in the eye" (*Dreams,* p. 134).

"My Real Invisible Self" is a fine story-essay about photography that discloses Humphreys's narrative technique and method. It must be read as her *ars poetica*. It tells how the grandmother would organize the photographing of her granddaughters by an itinerant photographer to illustrate Christmas cards. Humphreys emphasizes the total effect that comes from an accumulation of the Christmas cards representing herself and her two sisters; by describing varied costumes and scenes over the years she stresses the artistic efficiency of the staging imposed by the grandmother, who would invent new plots to reveal the invisible about her granddaughters. For the present viewer of those photographs, Humphreys notes that they function as signs, not as records, *signs for the future:* "I have come to doubt the validity of photography as historical record. Instead, it occurs to me that these pictures tell our fortune. They reveal something that is normally not visible: how the future lies curled and hidden in the present. It may be that we ourselves have a good chance at the future happiness our cards wish others. These pictures predict it in spite of my current despair."[14] In the same way her fiction provides signs for the future, in spite of the present pessimistic panorama. Alice muses that since the great hope of the sixties things have not changed much: "What will happen to all these black people, now the movement is dead, their heroes tucked away in public offices? Was the whole civil rights movement nothing but a minor disturbance in the succession of years?" (*Dreams,* p. 134).

The signs for the future are to be deciphered in her treatment of space, along with signs that tell of stasis or regression, signs fraught with history. In Columbia, S.C., Humphreys spoke of her difficulties with history, of her refusal to write it along the lines of historians, and of her decision to use it freely: "When I was writing *Dreams of Sleep,* I found that I *needed* history, and not knowing the kind I wanted, I made it up. This is what happens with fiction, things that are presented as history are actually fiction." Humphreys uses history as a painter uses *tone and coloring* in order to enhance effects, as is obvious with her treatment of space. The same pattern of the betrayal of old hopes and the assertion of present failure organizes space in all three novels. Yet, there are hopeful signs, which are still little visible and must be deciphered. Humphreys's fictional Charleston reads like a book of hieroglyphs telling of desire. In her fiction the Southern landscape becomes the language of desire, an objective correlate for those other languages that few understand: the language of marriage, of interracial relations, of love. Thus, with its two rivers and their confluence, with the many interconnected waterways and modern bridges bringing islands closer, with its long tradition of shipping and overseas trade and its well-known history, geographical and historical Charleston is turned into a blueprint under Humphreys's pen, a blueprint for a vast project about communication.

At first, obstacles only are visible; the roads that would lead to older roads and in this way make the past meaningful and significant for the present are blocked. Twentieth-century inhabitants have lost directions as the past has become meaningless: "This new section of highway had been laid out with no regard to pre-existing roads, and some of the new roads came up to the highway and dead-ended in striped barricades. . . . Out in the developments, some of the new roads curved back upon themselves, and I sometimes lost my sense of direction trying to get somewhere" (*Rich,* p. 3). The urban space is in this way both fragmented, to suggest incommunicability, and unsafe: everybody spies on everybody, privacy is threatened. The patrician architecture meant for the ostentatious display of power and respectability, now serves the morbid jealousy of inheritors, espying their lovers in galleries and formerly well-tended gardens. The degradation is less social than moral. Signs of consumerism become new icons for jealousy as when the window of a supermarket serves as a spying mirror for Alice Reese, the betrayed wife. Yet, the hopeful sign is that the compartmenting imposed by class and prejudice is disappearing. Proud mansions formerly glorifying the wealth and comfort of one family alone, now provide good living to several middle-class families.

The formerly revered statues of the city's great men become iconic signs of derision, as when Lucille reports gossips about Calhoun as Lincoln's illegitimate father. The many monuments, plaques, and historical signs in Charleston become signs of derision, which topple the city's pride in its past. Charleston is no longer the sanctified place of Southern pilgrimage, because facts and figures alone are preserved in the tour offered to tourists. Emptied of their contents, old historical places are restored to their original function as places where to live ordinary lives. What is at stake is less history itself, whose message must remain alive, than the freezing effect of misunderstood respect. Too much allegiance to proprieties and decorum kills life, public and private, as it imprisons within false and forced roles. Paths and roads must lead to life, just as William Reese realizes that a symbolic new path has just opened before his mother to liberate her from the proprieties of good middle-class marriage and widowhood. Marcella, who had been a prisoner of her husband's social circle even after his death, launches into a new career as she participates in the desacralization of Charleston's urban space, marries again, and finds a new life:

> Marcella is living proof that unexpected things can happen, fast. Only two years ago Marcella was old. She was in the same house she'd been in all her adult life, her husband long dead, her pastimes the little amusements offered to widows in Charleston. . . . One morning fifteen years after Edmund's death, widowhood lost its hold on her. She cut an ad from the paper, and within a month she was selling houses. It turned out she had a gift for selling houses. The first year she sold four of them, for a total of $570,000. The next year she sold "a million-four," including one to the man from Ohio who wanted to live in a house with columns.
>
> She sold Duncan Nesmith a monster overlooking the harbor and the Battery, built in 1953 on landfill—on garbage, in other words—but it had columns. Then she married him. (*Dreams,* p. 143)

Danièle Pitavy-Souques

    Despite appearances, the truly subversive move out of a dead-ended life is Alice's decision to walk through the black neighborhood to go shopping, at Iris's suggestion. It is far more of a change to establish some communication between two urban areas historically separated by race and class, than it is to "desecrate" sites marked by a questionable past by superimposing new signs that duplicate older ones. Alice's walk is emblematic of the whole message of *Dreams of Sleep:* in a key passage about black gardens, Humphreys shows vitality versus death and "predicts" what must be done: "The little gardens are different from white people's boxwood-and-bulb gardens. The flowers overflow, bend out onto the sidewalks, climb fences. After blooming they are allowed to die in their own beds. . . . Occasionally a thick wistaria winds up the side of a porch, a fibrous wooden snake, ridged and rough. A big one can pull a beam down or lift sewer pipes out of the earth, nothing but root above ground and below, *undiversified and therefore of magnificent strength.* Its bloom is always a surprise when it comes" (*Dreams,* p. 133, my italics). To the static picture of a white garden symbolizing the stereotyped reproduction of Elizabethan order and hierarchy, Humphreys opposes the freedom, change, and exuberance of a true Southern garden.[15] The emphasis is on the dynamics of space, with the profusion of verbs of movement: unbridled nature and the natural cycle of birth and decay are fully respected. If the "untidy" gardens symbolize the exuberance of both the garden of Eden and the Promised Land, they can also be seen as miniatures of the original virgin land of America protected in national and state parks. This conventional symbolization is renewed by Humphreys's innovative treatment of the wistaria as an emblem of the South. She does away with the brooding vindictive atmosphere of Miss Rosa's room filled with the smell of wistaria in *Absalom, Absalom!* as she does away with the snake as a symbol of evil; with its ridged and rough trunk the wistaria becomes the older symbol of fertility, renewal, and life. The surprise comes from the adjective "undiversified" allied with "magnificent strength." I read the passage as the vibrant reassertion of the original common root for all human beings, of the moment before race diversification brought war. It is a return to that original wild Arcadia where distinction did not yet prevail. What is destructive, the garden implies, are distinctions of race and hierarchy.

    Humphreys reestablishes the South as wilderness, not what she describes as "our original home, the Eden of the great forests, swamps, rivers, islands, mountains" ("Disappearing," p. 215), but wilderness in towns, "the natural setting of Southern fiction." It is wilderness seen in a positive way because it superimposes a new vitality over the tragic traces of slavery, *without erasing them* as the duck-hunting scene in the marshes shows. True to its original vocation as political and religious asylum, Charleston offers the Jewish doctor and his Anglo-Saxon friend a moment of higher intensity as both men together recite lines from the metaphysical poets, but the intellectual height and distance are precisely what is needed to hand down the message of history—betrayal and exploitation—and it is their responsibility to do so: "The broken dikes impounding the wetlands looked like ancient earthworks built by a design that could be seen only from a spaceship; but he knew the dikes were built by slaves in an expanse of human labor greater than what it took to build the Great Wall of China. He began to feel uncomfortable" (*Dreams,* p. 105).

Signs of former distinction and separateness are thus blurred, to enable life to bloom again. They represent the mutilating traces of an order imposed by the myth of a well-ordained, hierarchized arcadia over primitive wilderness. By a metaphorical translation, Humphreys further deconstructs the myth, just as Alice Walker will demystify the African American myth of a return to an idealized Africa in *Possessing the Secret of Joy* (1992). The design traced on the surface of the land is not unlike the scarifications and genital mutilations inflicted by men and tradition on the bodies of women and children in traditional African societies. Humphreys invites us to read the virgin land of the South as female body, once subjected to the domination of patriarchal society. The result is destructive chaos. Far from bringing harmony, distinction separates and opposes, it establishes inequality, oppression, and exploitation. Paradoxically, Humphreys advocates that natural chaos outside man's responsibility, such as the natural violence of hurricanes that too often devastate the South, has its benefits since it brings people together in order to face common disaster. The old pioneer solidarity is restored, for all class and race distinctions are of no avail. This is why Humphreys partly rewrote *The Fireman's Fair* after the destructive passage of hurricane Hugo. Chaos may be a symbol of shattered lives and hopes, but out of chaos comes a new life in the South with gestures of interracial solidarity.

In this manner Humphreys urges a correct deciphering of signs, which requires some visionary power, as the danger is to misread them, to give importance to false signs and overlook authentic ones. Depressive Alice, for instance, internalizes omens and signs as a degenerate form of mathematics when she feels tempted to believe in fate: "Fate is what people blame when they give up" (*Dreams,* p. 207). She will need the imaginative perceptiveness of Iris to decipher the good signs, such as the luxuriant black garden, in order to walk toward recovery and a new understanding of interracial communication. The role of Iris in *Dreams of Sleep,* and of her avatars in the next novels, Lucille and Billie, has not been properly identified so far, yet it is capital and further manifests Humphreys's breaking new fictional paths in her exploration of the "singularities of the form." The recurrence of the character of the unusual, odd adolescent girl gives Humphreys's fiction a mythic dimension. What could have been mistaken for unusually good social comedy becomes a timeless reflection on the invisible made visible. Those three girls must be read as modern avatars of angels, and as such they are the other signifier, or narrative device, that stamps Humphreys as a postmodern writer. With them, Humphreys does not attempt to represent the sublime, which pertains to God, but true love, agape, which pertains to human beings: true relationship between races, sexes, and people in the South.

Humphreys provides clues to identify these teenagers as angels—modern instances of characters as old as literature. Like the old beggars in Eastern literature or in Greek mythology or folk tales from all over the world, they go about in disguise, bearing messages that teach us how to relate in the modern world, provided we are able to decipher them. In *La Légende des Anges,* Michel Serres suggests that today's beggars and hoboes are also avatars of angels, as we come across them they tell us of dereliction, hunger, and loneliness.[16] In Humphreys's fiction, angels belong to a marginal world of broken families or broken minds, a world in between, and because they live in the margin, their acuteness of perception enables them to see what other people are too blinded by selfishness and self-centeredness to perceive. The reader is invited to take hints about the extraordinary that surrounds those girls quite seriously. The hint can be just a name borrowed from Greek mythology as in *Dreams of Sleep,* since Iris was the messenger of the gods. Or the reader is sent back to old beliefs about twins in *Rich in Love,* with Lucille as the surviving twin, miraculously rescued from her mother's abortion: "'Well,' she said, 'there were two. Twins. It got one. You were the other one. They didn't know you were in there'" (p. 50). As for Billie, she was sold at thirteen by her parents to a vagrant gypsy.

With these characters, Humphreys's novels dramatize a reappropriation of the supernatural, the haunting motif of Southern fiction, especially feminine Southern fiction. Whereas in her best short stories Elizabeth Spencer plays with the literality of the motif to displace it from external manifestations to the sudden awareness of the self, Josephine Humphreys reactualizes the supernatural by transforming it into a major component of communication through the device of angels. The adolescent girls, especially Lucille in *Rich in Love* with her voice and humor, can be seen as female counterparts of that great American character, Huckleberry Finn, as they provide an indirect moral commentary on the corrupt society of their time. The difference, and this is where Humphreys can be defined as the avant-garde of post–civil-rights-movement writers, is that her characters *act* as much as they observe. Because Iris, Lucille, and Billie have been battered by life and given an awareness of tensions between people and races above their age, they are able to act towards establishing communication. They are less agents of moral awareness or self-awareness, than agents of true relationships with the other. The uncanny with which they play is of a subtle and modern kind. "The long repressed suddenly surfacing," as Freud defines the *Unheimlich,* is no longer the fear of sexuality or the fear of the other or a death wish—the thanatos syndrome—but the temptation of inertia as the end of creative imagination—another name for the revolutionary spirit.

The actions of the angels may seem derisory, almost pathetic, because they are so simple, yet this very simplicity is what is lacking in true communication. It always implies an imaginative reversal of attitudes in the necessary step towards the other. As in any true love relationship, we must value the other enough to receive from him or her rather than to give him or her a feeling tainted by self-satisfaction. Iris teaches how *to learn from* the other. In order to cure Alice of her numbing fear of the black community, she gives her the simple advice to walk across the black neighborhood when she goes shopping. In so doing, Iris teaches Alice how to renew herself with her old ideals—her possible commitment to the civil rights movement when "she held on to her own girlish trust in a trend for the better, certain for example, that by the time she grew up there would be no more maids. People like Estelle would all get master's degrees in counseling, their children would go to medical school" (*Dreams,* p. 135).

In the same practical way, Iris is the one who sees clearly through Alice's ill-prepared and unrealistic flight from home and drives the mother and her two daughters back to Charleston. The fine moment for Iris is when she realizes her own mother cannot mature into a responsible human being as long as Iris mothers her. Playing God's angel, after wrestling with Fay, as Jacob did with the angel, Iris allows her mother not to be defeated by calling for help mentally and directing her thoughts at Fay: "Then, slowly, across the room, for she is hurt, Fay walks to Iris's side and sets her hand on her daughter's rich, shining, brown head. Iris lifts her head and Fay holds it close to her in an awkward embrace, as unsure of herself as a mother with her firstborn . . . Iris wraps her arms around Fay at waist level. From here they can start. She can teach Fay how to love a child. . . . She starts by letting Fay stroke her hair" (*Dreams,* pp. 226–27). Iris had learned this action from her black "double," Emory, the young black artist in love with her. He decides to help his mother by letting her help him find a job in Atlanta, a precarious arrangement dictated by love just as Iris accepts Emory's priceless ephemeral presents to her—the magnificent gardens he draws for her in chalk on the pavement. Lucille, so clear-sighted in her neurosis, listens to people, establishes communication between the two communities, and restores her mother's mental health. The third angel, Elizabeth Poe, is a seer of another kind. Her great gift to people is time. She gives time to time, literally, as when she allows Rob's father to speak his marital difficulties publicly, when she decides the time for a trip to bring together the members of the family, or more dangerously, when she runs away from the man whom she loves in order to give him the time of her absence as reflection-time over his true feelings for her.

Because they are surprisingly present and absent, of this world and of another one, the angels become the messengers of the country that lies beyond death and is but the reverse of the figure, as the myths of Eurydice and Persephone tell us. Can we then construct the last page of *The Fireman's Fair* as an imaginative positive rewriting of Gluck's opera? Doubling the fragile figure of Billie-Eurydice, who has returned to Bob and stands unseen behind him, there is another figure, that of triumphant Persephone; the moment no longer speaks of love versus life, but of love and life, as one woman symbolizes love and the other life. The fine ambiguities of Humphreys's fiction lie in this moment—in this "Dance of the Happy Shades" urging and pushing Eurydice towards hope, light, and life, the precarious moment when everything is possible.

Humphreys's South is full of surprises, if we know where to look for them. The writer does not dig the past in order to trace layers of culture through folk tales and music; she does not analyze contemporary teenage culture in depth, as other female Southern writers do. Her attitude is the opposite of nostalgia, as it would imply inertia. Just as Ellen Glasgow puts her novel into perspective in the last pages of *Virginia* and clearly shows that for all her brilliant and often sympathetic portrayal of the Southern lady, she clearly condemns her, Humphreys clearly indicts Will Reese in *Dreams of Sleep,* just as she indicts his avatar Robert Wyatt in *The Fireman's Fair*.[17] The true gentleman of the South, her fiction implies, is not the learned self-centered William Reese who imprisons people, his mother and mistress included, in conventional categories, but that other gentleman, equally learned, equally fond of reciting the metaphysical poets, the Jewish doctor Danny Cardozo. Out of true love and respect he marries Claire, Will Reese's former mistress, the nurse forced to abort by her inefficient selfish lover, and yet, when Alice runs away with the children, Cardozo does not hesitate to leave his bridal bed to answer Will Reese's call for help.

Humphreys suggests that we have to look for the Southern gentleman in unexpected places, in "the secret towns. . . . the poor towns like Tchula, or Indian towns like Pearl River, in Mississippi . . . towns hidden within cities. . . . Nothing picturesque or festive or quaint or even comfortable here" ("Disappearing," p. 220). Here are to be found marginal characters who somehow epitomize the true ideal of the Southern gentleman, men like Carlo in *The Fireman's Fair,* who, in a rewriting of *The Mayor of Casterbridge,* "buys" Willie to save her from an unworthy family, in order to give her a true childhood, to which any human being is entitled. He is the one who understands her best and knows where to look for her when she runs away. In a plea to "our better writers" Humphreys advocates on the same page that far away from the picturesque unreal settings of romance or the privileged grounds of rapacious and destructive developers, there lies a true South that must be written about, because "these are real places, with more force and more story and more community than any of our developed places. *We are here.*" She is vastly present in those margins with her fiction filled with lesser figures of angels, black doubles, and unsuccessful yet kindly friends, subtly weaving a network of warm rejuvenative relationships. If everyone would accept help of the other, then the hopes raised by the civil rights movement could just begin to be realized.

It seems to me that just as Robert Scholes could write about the new fabulators some thirty years ago, using allegories and new modes of fiction departing from both realism and pure deconstruction and gratuitous games, we could write about the new romantics, who produce fine new imaginative works throughout North America, for this innovative fictional trend is just as present in Canada, with Jane Urquhart, for instance, as it is in the South of the United States—two regions whose landscape, history, and literary production have much more in common than it would seem at first. This new trend is marked by its going away from the restrictive study of family relationships or ordinary violence, and its concern for the ontological, the "unpresentable" understood as that margin where "the mystery of human communication and the mystery of non-human beauty touch." The New South would then be the territory where people gifted with imagination and sensitiveness must in Humphreys's words "stand there awhile, where you can see both town and no-town, and you will know something about life on Earth. You will know enough for a novel" ("Disappearing," p. 218).

The Fireman's Fair, which ideally realizes the true community, comes once a year. It is the emblem of the permanence of the South, a South rejuvenated by its very idiosyncrasies as well as its deep allegiance to the values of the American democracy. In her novel, Humphreys draws as doubles the present shipwrecked American community and the old wild communities of early pioneering, when their wilderness was truly creative, and in so doing she may be the first novelist to write about the "secret towns, those that are still real because no one wants to develop them or even lay eyes on them," which are the future of Southern fiction.

Notes

1. All quotations from Josephine Humphreys's books are from the first editions by the Viking Press. Humphreys, "My Real Invisible Self," is in *The World Unsuspected,* ed. Alex Harris (Chapel Hill: University of North Carolina Press, 1987), pp. 1–13. Fred

Danièle Pitavy-Souques

Hobson, "Richard Ford and Josephine Humphreys: Walker Percy in New Jersey and Charleston," in *The Southern Writer in the Postmodern World* (Athens: University of Georgia Press, 1991), p. 59.

2. Kathryn B. McKee, "Rewriting Southern Male Introspection in Josephine Humphreys' *Dreams of Sleep,*" *Mississippi Quarterly* 66 (Spring 1993): 241–54.

3. During the European Southern Studies Forum conference held at the University of South Carolina in Columbia, November 8–10, 1993, Josephine Humphreys gave a splendid lecture as guest writer of the conference.

4. Joseph Millichap, "Josephine Humphreys," *Contemporary Fiction Writers of the South,* eds. J. Flora and R. Bair (Westport, Conn.: Greenwood Press, 1993).

5. Quoted by Millichap, "Josephine Humphreys," p. 247.

6. Jean Dhombres, "Qu'est-ce qu'une forme?" *Les Sciences de la forme aujourd'hui* (Paris: Seuil, 1994), p. 14, my translation.

7. Jean-François Lyotard, "What Is Postmodernism?" *The Postmodern Condition: A Report on Knowledge* (1979; Minneapolis: University of Minnesota Press, 1993 edition), pp. 79–80.

8. See Jean Dhombres, "Qu'est-ce qu'une forme?" p. 17.

9. Josephine Humphreys, "A Disappearing Subject Called the South," *The Prevailing South,* ed. Dudley Clendinen (Atlanta: Longstreet Press, 1988), p. 216. Subsequent references are cited in the text.

10. Simon Schama, *Landscape and Memory* (New York, Alfred A. Knopf, 1995), pp. 526ff.

11. Eudora Welty, *Collected Stories* (New York, Harcourt and Brace, 1980), p. 198.

12. European Southern Studies Forum conference in Columbia, S.C., November 1993.

13. Roland Barthes, *La Chambre claire* (Paris: Gallimard, 1980), p. 148.

14. Humphreys, "My Real Invisible Self," p. 5.

15. One more proof, it seems, of Hawthorne's influence on Southern writers, as this black garden reads like an echo of Phoebe's discovering a wild garden in *The House of the Seven Gables,* with the same overtones of liberation.

16. Michel Serres, *La Légende des Anges* (Paris: Flammarion, 1993).

17. See Danièle Pitavy-Souques, "De quelques stratégies de la libération chez Glasgow et Cather," *Femmes Ecrivains au Tournant du XIX ècle, Revue Française d'Etudes Américaines,* ed. Danièle Pitavy-Souques, vol. 34 (June 1996), pp. 67–76.

Part IV

Looking West and Back

Westward, Ho!

Contemporary Southern Writing and the American West

Robert H. Brinkmeyer, Jr.

One of the most intriguing developments in contemporary Southern fiction is that a number of Southern writers have been writing about the American West, both in fiction of the contemporary West (particularly Montana) and in fiction that we typically think of as "westerns"—that is, stories set on the range with cowboys, gunfights, and Indians. This development raises a number of issues about the nature of Southern fiction—and more generally of cultural regionalism—in contemporary America and suggests a remarkable break in the history of Southern literature. Writers who have turned their eyes to the immoderate West include Richard Ford, Barry Hannah, Clyde Egerton, Rick Bass, Doris Betts, Cormac McCarthy, Barbara Kingsolver, Madison Smartt Bell, James Lee Burke, Frederick Barthelme, and Chris Offutt. Certainly Southern writers of previous generations have written about the West—one thinks most significantly of Mark Twain—but the earlier writers came few and far between and rarely expressed an allegiance to the West. In their enthusiasm for and commitment to the Western territories, contemporary Southern writers have charted new paths and opened up a new territory of "Southern" fiction, if we can still call it that.

Traditionally, Southern literature has been grounded in a strong sense of place—and that place has been the South, particularly the small town and the countryside. The Southern literary imagination's emphasis on place has characteristically celebrated settledness and rootedness: one celebrates place when one is "in place," not when one is roaming about. In her classic essay, "Place in Fiction," which explores not only how place shapes literature but also more generally how it shapes consciousness, Eudora Welty writes: "Focus . . . means awareness, discernment, order, clarity, insight—they are like the attributes of love. The act of focusing itself has beauty and meaning; it is the act that, continued in, turns into mediation, into poetry. Indeed, as soon as the least of us stands still, that is the moment something extraordinary is seen to be going on in the world."¹ Standing still, staying put: such are the means to engage the mystery of place. The mystery of existence characteristically opens up for Welty in still moments, in moments where all motion stops. While there are plenty of journeys in Welty's fiction, the most significant of these are internal, with people coming to terms with themselves not in motion but in place, rooted rather than uprooted. Welty, I believe, speaks for most Southern writing up through the late 1940s.

But since the end of World War II, and particularly since the 1960s when the South evolved from the Cotton Belt into the Sun Belt (a much more prosperous and urban—and suburban—region), the significance of place appears to be losing ground in the Southern imagination. In an age of shopping malls and high-rises, it is harder to find places that nurture and nourish in traditional ways. As Binx Bolling in Walker Percy's *The Moviegoer* puts it, places get used up—that is, their distinctive identity and history (what Binx characterizes as "the sense of place, the savor of the genie-soul of the place, which every place has or else is not a place") become lost amidst the malaise of modern existence.² Binx and other Percy characters are always attempting to recertify a place, to rediscover a place's unique character and to ground themselves there. In Percy's world such grounding is necessary for a person's recognition of his or her uniqueness; without the grounding, an individual loses individuality and becomes merely Anyone living Anywhere. Percy's depiction of a Southern landscape bled dry of a sense of place speaks for the situation in much of contemporary Southern writing.

Besides manifesting the Southern literary imagination's recognition of a widespread diminishment of place, Percy in his second novel, *The Last Gentleman* (1967), looks forward to the later turn to the West that Southern writers in the 1980s and 1990s would take. In that novel the protagonist, Will Barrett, embarks on a journey of self-discovery and spiritual enlightenment that takes him through the South and finally into the desert Southwest. Barrett's quest for fundamental answers in a stark desert landscape represents the most compelling motive for contemporary Southern writers' later interest in the West. To go West, a move from place into space, represents an attempt to step free of both the traditional burdens of Southern history and identity and the contemporary anxieties of the suburban and corporate Sun Belt. The desire of the protagonists in James Dickey's *Deliverance* (1970) to leave behind the responsibilities of home and work, in their weekend escape to the wilderness, becomes for the later Southern writers of the West the desire to step free of Southern identity altogether—to light out for the wilderness, maybe to return, maybe not.

Dickey's first novel ends with the flooding and taming of the Cahulawassee River, suggesting the closing of the wilderness in the South.

Later writers, working with patterns similar to Dickey's, will look farther west to find wilderness spaces, untamed and untouched by civilized culture. *Deliverance* can be understood as a "western" set in the South, a novel that looks to the West and its literary traditions without geographically going there. Similar invokings of the western can be seen in the work of other Southern writers, particularly in Larry Brown's *Joe,* which bears striking resemblances to Jack Shaeffer's *Shane*. To move West in the contemporary Southern literary imagination means, metaphorically if not literally, stepping free of history and leaving behind a world rapidly becoming standardized and mechanized. It means moving into a world stripped of civilized conventions where a person, standing alone rather than enmeshed in the web of culture, creates himself or herself through ordeal and action.

The contemporary Southern writers who have looked West represent a broad spectrum of Southern writing, from the feminist to the macho, from the traditional to the postmodern. But African American writers, as far as I can tell, have for the most part kept themselves rooted in the South or have depicted the northward migration of African American Southerners. It could be suggested that, in contrast to socially responsible Southern African American writers, those who go West shirk the responsibility of exploring the problems and burdens of Southern culture. Whether or not one agrees that artists bear a social responsibility and should be judged accordingly, such an objection seems misguided with regard to the writers focused on in this essay. Their turn to the West almost always involves an elaborate critique of Southern culture. And the fictional flights West are mostly shadowed by the culture left behind. The characters in flight may think they jettison the workings of Southern culture, but typically they discover that the South remains painfully alive and kicking in their consciousness, as Quentin Compson did on his journey to Cambridge. What shapes the Southern fugitive's experiences and understanding is less the West itself than it is the interplay between the West and the South, a historically troubled tradition informing and being informed by the vast and open Western landscape.

Although the group listed at the beginning of my paper includes two women writers—Barbara Kingsolver and Doris Betts, whose 1982 novel *Heading West* is the first Western novel from the group—the writers are, not surprisingly, predominantly male. After all, literature about the West, and most particularly westerns, as Lee Clark Mitchell observes, has traditionally been "deeply haunted by the problem of becoming a man" and has explored "the construction of masculinity, whether in terms of gender (women), maturation (sons), honor (restraint), or self transformation (the West itself)."[3] Two writers, whose fiction I want to discuss, Rick Bass and Cormac McCarthy, cer-

Robert H. Brinkmeyer, Jr.

tainly address issues of male identity and masculinity, but the focus of my discussion will be less on the *construction* of gendered identity than on the *destruction* of culturally constructed identities, gendered and otherwise. Both writers explore the wilderness within the self, and both portray characters descending to the "natural" in their Western sojourns. But despite these similar narrative patterns, Bass and McCarthy present totally different worlds and worldviews. Their startlingly different takes on the Western experience point to the rich, diverse, and volatile creative expression erupting from the interplay between the Southern and Western literary imaginations.

There are few Southern writers—or American, for that matter—who exhibit such a complete affinity with the wilderness as Rick Bass. Although Bass has characteristically identified himself as a Southerner—he grew up in Houston and worked for a while in Jackson, Mississippi—his imaginative development, beginning with his first book, *The Deer Pasture* (1985) and extending up through *The Sky, the Stars, the Wilderness* (1997), shows a progressive movement away from a Southern to a Western sensibility—his imaginative grounding moves from a predominantly Southern understanding of place and tradition to a predominantly Western one, grounded in the wilderness of Montana, where Bass now lives. Southern, perhaps, in his respect for and grounding in a specific place—he finds the mysteries of place that become visible when one stands still every bit as wondrous as Eudora Welty—Bass nonetheless is quite un-Southern in his looking to the wilderness for inspiration and transfiguration. Southerners traditionally celebrate the cultural and historical (a Southern sense of place always bristles with history); Bass instead looks to the Montana wilderness to free him from all that, to provide the means to purify his imagination from the anxiety and fragmentation of modern—and Southern—life.

The tension between the South and the West is most obvious in Bass's *Wild to the Heart* (1987), a collection of autobiographical essays centering on his life in Jackson, Mississippi. For Bass, Jackson represents the worst of the New South, a world of corporate bureaucracy and concrete cityscapes; he lights out to his beloved Western mountains whenever he can, to rejuvenate himself and ground himself in the natural world. Here and elsewhere in his work Bass depicts modern life as incarceration with people living in "high-rise jails" and entombed in death-in-life routine.[4] The South is particularly death-dealing, because not only has it embraced New South corporatism but it is also shackled by an overwhelming sense of history that still dominates the present. "Nothing is forgotten," Bass writes in his story "Mississippi"; and in another story, "Government Bears," he describes how the history of the Civil War still permeates the Mississippi landscape: "I don't care if it was a hundred and twenty years ago, these things still last and that is really no time at all, not for a real war like that one, with screaming and pain. The trees absorb the echoes of the screams and cries and humiliations. Their bark is only an inch thick between the time then and now: the distance between your thumb and forefinger. The sun beating down on us now saw the flames and troops' campfires then, and in fact the warmth from those flames is still not entirely through traveling to the sun. The fear of the women: you can still feel it, in places where it was strong."[5]

Opposed to the confinement of the South is the possibility of the West. If the South represents enclosure—with the confining walls of tradition, history, and New South boosterism—the wilderness West represents unbordered space where a person can start over anew, freed from the constraints of the past and tradition. In all of his work Bass stresses the need for letting go, for getting past the past, for acting spontaneously and instinctually, of acting, as he puts it in "Mahatma Joe," "wild like animals, and happy."[6] Not allowing oneself to act so freely is to be trapped in stultifying routine and stunted by the demands of the past. Escape to the West is Bass's primary metaphor for this healthy spontaneity, and characters who break free from their old lives to embrace new ones in the West typically characterize their experience as the bracing immersion in a frigid lake or stream, from which they emerge reborn—or at least ready to be, now that the dirt and grime of their previous lives have been washed away.

Moving to the West can be understood as a shedding of the modern self and an acceptance of humanity's "natural" state of being. To live in the Western wilderness is to reorient one's life according to nature and its cycles, what Bass calls "the blood rhythms of the wilderness."[7] Masked and repressed by modern culture, these rhythms live deep in the hearts of all of us. In *Winter: Notes from Montana* and *The Book of Yaak,* two meditations on his life in the West, Bass portrays the transformations he undergoes as a positively configured devolution, a move toward the primal state of the animal. "I'm falling away from the human race," he writes in *Winter.* "I don't mean to sound churlish—but I'm liking it. It frightens me a little to recognize how much I like it. It's as if you'd looked down at your hand and seen the beginnings of fur. It's not as bad as you might think."[8]

Bass's falling away from the human does not, of course, carry him completely into a world of pure instinct, as he still maintains his self-consciousness and his loyalties to family and friends. Nonetheless, he progressively looks to the woods and animal world, rather than to human community, for the models by which to structure his life. He comes to see the natural world not as an unstructured chaos but "a constantly changing state of unrelenting order and complexity, unrelenting grace" (*Yaak,* p. 191). He sees the natural world as a self-supporting community, one imaged in a triple-trunked larch tree that has survived only through the help of its neighbors. "Trees of different species formed a circle around it—fir, aspen, lodgepole, even cedar," Bass writes. "Their branches, as it was growing, must have helped to shelter and stabilize it, hold it up, as though they were friends, or at the very least—and in the sense of the word that I think we must turn to the woods to relearn—like community" (*Yaak,* p. 181).

That the wilderness ultimately suggests to Bass the nurturing power of community in part explains his fascination with wolves, particularly their ferocious loyalties to kin and pack. For Bass, wolves have much to teach humans about commitment and culture. "All wolves are tied together," writes Bass. "It's a brotherhood, a sisterhood. You can't help it. They—the wolves—remind us of ourselves on our better days, our best days. They teach us splendidly about the overriding force of nature, too—about the way we've managed to suppress and ignore it in ourselves, or judge it."[9] Theirs is a life, Bass observes, grounded in a spirituality at one with the natural world, and it is precisely this spirituality that he strives to discover in himself as he sheds his modern self in the wilderness depths. His most intensely spiritual moments come during snowstorms when the world becomes a "blank infinity" and Bass its sole inhabitant. "Anything I am guilty of is forgiven when the snow falls," he writes. "I feel powerful. In cities I feel weak and wasted away, but out in the field, in snow, I am like an animal" (*Winter,* p. 90). Here is the transformation Bass looks for in the West: the shedding of the modern self and the emergence of the primitive self, an emergence that lets him, as he puts it in *Oil Notes,* think like the earth. To think like the earth is to follow joyfully nature's rhythms and cycles. It is to feel wondrously alive and free, aglow with the feeling that one will live forever, if not in body then in spirit, coursing through the endless cycles of the natural world.

The Judge in Cormac McCarthy's *Blood Meridian* also dreams of immortality, and at the end of the novel he is naked and dancing in a satyrean frenzy saying that he will "never die." But while the Judge has, in a motion similar to that found in Rick Bass's work, fallen away from humanity to become more primal, his is a very different descent, one that carries him to a world of murder and mayhem. Unlike the fragile balance of community and fellowship that shapes Bass's wilderness world, the state of nature to which the Judge devolves is a chaotic battlefield of death and destruction. The everyday life-and-death struggle to survive dominates and overshadows everything, including the ethical and spiritual. As the Judge puts it: "Decisions of life and death, of what shall be and what shall not, beggar all questions of right. In elections of these magnitudes are all lesser ones subsumed, moral, spiritual, and natural."[10] Welcome to the West of Cormac McCarthy.

McCarthy's West is a frightening mirror image of Bass's, though on the surface there are a number of similarities. Like Bass's, McCarthy's Western wilderness stands opposed to the "civilized" world of the East; it's a space where the constructions of the "civilized" self fall away to allow unmediated confrontations with the natural world. It is a space for elemental passions and actions, for primal human nature to emerge unrestrained by social constraints. It is a space for people to act instinctually, like animals. But while Bass finds spiritual wonder in the natural and animal world, McCarthy finds violence and bestiality—a world not of spirit but of blood. In *Blood Meridian* people are "bleeding westward like some heliotropic plague" into the "bloodlands of the West" (pp. 78, 138). To be "wild to the heart," returning to Bass's words for the essential goodness and joyfulness of human nature, is in McCarthy's world to be an unrestrained and unforgiving killer. That is McCarthy's primal self. In all four of McCarthy's Western novels, *Blood Meridian, All the Pretty Horses, The Crossing,* and *Cities of the Plain,* characters who roam the West are described as creatures who appear to be from an age long past, as men from precivilized time. McCarthy's point is that we all still carry within us these murderous instincts from our ancient forbears, even if we think we do not. In McCarthy's world the boundary separating civilized from uncivilized is paper thin and easily crossed. Civilization totters tenuously over the abyss.

Although McCarthy's West appears to be a world of infinite potentiality and possibility, that is only because it is a vast void that can be imaginatively configured into any pattern a person wishes—until someone bigger and stronger comes along to impose a different order upon things. As the Blind Man tells Billy in *The Crossing,* the effort to find a bedrock of order to oppose the disorder of evil is finally fruitless. There is, in the end, no order and lineage in the world. The imposition of order is precisely that—an imposition, the desire for order rather than order itself. Nor is there any mystery to creation, much as people want to believe there is. "Your heart's desire is to be told some mystery," the Judge in *Blood Meridian* tells his recruits. "The mystery is that there is no mystery" (p. 252). McCarthy's West is thus a mirage, an "incoordinate waste" and "shoreless void" (*Blood Meridian,* pp. 148, 50) that at first glance may appear to human eyes as hopeful space for renewal and rebirth. To enter this realm is to wander about ceaselessly, enmeshed in an endless repetition of death and destruction. So vast and empty is the landscape that, as a character in *Blood Meridian* feels, it seems to swallow up the soul. Eventually, people lose themselves in their wanderings, no longer aware of their origins, purpose, or future. Movement through the wasteland becomes all there is; when two parties of men pass each other, they are described as each riding back "the way the other had come, pursuing as all travelers must inversions without end upon other men's journeys" (p. 121). There are no rebirths, no wondrous renewals in McCarthy's West: *Blood Meridian* ends with the protagonist's murder in an outhouse, and *All the Pretty Horses* and *The Crossing* conclude with their protagonists about to set off wandering again, their circles out and back into the wilderness having brought them little but suffering and hardened sensibilities. The sun always rises in McCarthy's West, but daylight announces merely another in the endless procession of days, rather than a transfigured new world. Here's one of McCarthy's daybreaks: "In the morning a urinecolored sun rose blearily through panes of dust on a dim world and without feature" (*Blood Meridian*, p. 47).

As death-dealing and doom-filled as McCarthy's Western landscape is, there are suggestions that not all is totally lost and forsaken. Sprinkled throughout McCarthy's bloodlands are a few messengers of hope and wisdom, people who act out of and/or counsel a generosity of spirit and a code of individual integrity in the face of chaos. There are countless impoverished families, for instance, who offer McCarthy's wanderers food and shelter, seeking nothing in return; they possess a quiet and generous dignity, as do those other skilled practitioners who also offer aid and counsel, such as the doctor who treats Boyd and the Judge who counsels Billy in *The Crossing*. (There is a great respect in McCarthy's world for those who do their jobs well, who master a craft that they then selflessly share with others.) Perhaps the most striking messenger of hope and humanity in McCarthy's West is the old man in *The Crossing* who counsels Billy to quit his journey and to move back into the human community: "He told the boy that although he was huerfano still he must cease his wanderings and for himself find some place in the world because to wander in this way would become for him a passion and by this passion he would become estranged from men and so ultimately from himself. He said that the world could only be known as it existed in men's hearts."[11]

The Old Man's advice echoes not only the observations of Eudora Welty about the significance of place and standing still (rather than moving about), but also those of Rick Bass concerning the human need for bonding and community that he finds manifested in the fragile ecosystem of the Yaak Valley. In the celebration of place and settledness, we are back to the Southern literary imagination and to its continued presence in the work of contemporary Southern writers, even those who forsake the home place. It seems, finally, that although both Bass and McCarthy have literally and imaginatively moved out of the South and into the West, and into Wests so different as to be almost unrecognizable to each other, they carry with them significant traces of a Southern sensibility profoundly aware of and nourished by the power of place and community. This should not be all that surprising, since clearly the origins of a writer's imaginative life and sensibilities run deep, and are the product of all his or her experience, particularly that from childhood. Relevant here is Flannery O'Connor's observation in "The Catholic Novelist in the Protestant South" that her imaginative life was fundamentally Southern rather than Catholic, a statement suggesting the staying power of a sensibility marked by a Southern upbringing: "The things we see, hear, smell, and touch affect us long before we believe anything at all, and the South impresses its image on us from the moment we are able to distinguish one sound from another. By the time we are able to use our imaginations for fiction, we find that our senses have responded irrevocably to a certain reality."[12]

The literature about the West by contemporary Southern writers—a literature of regional border crossings—ultimately embodies a rich confluence of the Southern and the Western literary imaginations. In *The Book of Yaak*, Rick Bass observes that he sees "more and more the human stories in the West becoming those not only of passing through and drifting on but of settling in and making a stand" (*Yaak*, p. 13). What better way to think about this imaginative confluence that I believe is profoundly reshaping both the Southern and the Western literary traditions?

Notes

1. Eudora Welty, *The Eye of the Story* (New York: Random House, 1977), p. 123.

2. Walker Percy, *The Moviegoer* (1961; New York: Fawcett Columbine, 1996 edition), p. 202.

3. Lee Clark Mitchell, *Westerns: Making the Man in Fiction and Film* (Chicago: University of Chicago Press, 1996), p. 4.

4. Rick Bass, *In the Loyal Mountains* (Boston: Houghton, Mifflin, 1995), p. 114

5. Rick Bass, *The Watch* (New York: Norton, 1989), pp. 126, 172–73.

6. Rick Bass, *Platte River* (Boston: Houghton, Mifflin / Seymour Lawrence, 1994), p. 17.

7. Rick Bass, *The Book of Yaak* (Boston: Houghton, Mifflin, 1996), p. 13.

8. Rick Bass, *Winter: Notes from Montana* (Boston: Houghton, Mifflin / Seymour Lawrence, 1991), p. 73.

9. Rick Bass, *The Ninemile Wolves* (New York: Ballentine, 1992), p. 39.

10. Cormac McCarthy, *Blood Meridian, or, the Evening Redness in the West* (New York: Random House, 1985), p. 250.

11. Cormac McCarthy, *The Crossing* (New York: Knopf, 1994), p. 134.

12. Flannery O'Connor, *Mystery and Manners: Occasional Prose,* eds. Sally Fitzgerald and Robert Fitzgerald (New York: Farrar, Straus and Giroux, 1961), p. 197.

Post-Reconstruction Periods Compared

1890s and 1990s

C. Vann Woodward

It is not as if I undertake this comparison in blind innocence of the risks involved. In 1965 I compared the First Reconstruction with what I called the "Second" and find myself writing that "the Second Reconstruction has already scored up more achievements of durable promise than the First ever did."[1] Of course I was thinking of *promises* when I wrote *achievements*. I only hope that I shall be more cautious with hindsight than I was then with foresight. My comparisons between the 1890s and the 1990s will be limited to racial disfranchisement and segregation in each period.

The disfranchisers of the 1890s were predominantly upper-class whites of the Black Belt who had both partisan and economic interests at stake. In order to evade prohibitions of racial disfranchisement in the Fourteenth and Fifteenth Amendments they resorted to violence, intimidation, and gross fraud. That failing, they developed in the 1870s and 1880s a great number of voting restraints that fell not only upon freedmen but many lower-class whites as well. Most common were those aimed at illiterates, such as the secret ballot and multiple ballot-box laws, and laws directed at the poor, such as cumulative poll taxes and fees for registration, which were required months in advance of voting. By such means the total of votes cast by blacks and whites was sharply reduced by 1890.[2]

What then remained to be done in the 1890s by way of ending the legacy of the First Reconstruction? The 1890s witnessed a severe depression, a mounting militancy of farmers and workers, and the most powerful third-party revolt the ruling Democrats had faced. The Populist Party combined farmers, workers, and as many black voters as they could attract. These circumstances shaped the changes brought about by the Democrats. In the first half of the decade, however, racial disfranchisement was reversed or delayed by competition between the two parties for black votes. The Democrats won that contest by their own methods, and the Populist Party subsided. Meanwhile white disfranchisers hesitated to follow the example Mississippi set in 1890 when that state held a constitutional convention to legalize disfranchisement. Other states hesitated for fear white radicals might incorporate wild Populist notions into fundamental law.[3]

Then quite suddenly the way opened to complete and legalize racial disfranchisement. The Spanish-American war of 1898 endowed the whole country with a large assortment of "inferior races" in the Pacific and the Atlantic that Americans found it unthinkable to enfranchise. Quaint notions of white supremacy and Southern ways gained national respect. The U.S. Supreme Court by its 1898 decision in *Williams v. Mississippi* (170 US 213 [1898])passed favorably on the Mississippi plan. Already by 1895 Booker T. Washington joined other black leaders who seemed to suggest renunciation of political aspirations for their race. The way at last appeared to lie open.

Between 1895 and 1902 six more states wrote disfranchisement into their constitutions. Encouraged by the Supreme Court decision of 1898 the remaining states relied upon the poll tax and other devices already in use. Even more effective after party supremacy was assured was the Democratic white primary election, invented by Louisiana in 1892. Even though black voters had already been thus rendered politically ineffective or helpless, this whole disfranchisement crusade was fought in the name of white supremacy. It was waged with skillful racist propaganda, acts of organized racist mob brutality, lynching, murder, and terror by shrewd Democratic leaders. The fact is that the real issue was not about white supremacy, but about which whites would be supreme. The disfranchisers used the racist slogans to confuse the voters and weaken their opponents, Black Belt against whites of the Uplands, upper class versus lower class. It was bitterly fought and settled grudgingly only by compromises such as the "understanding clause" for illiterate whites and the "grandfather clause" enfranchising all who had voted in 1857 as well as their sons and grandsons. After that, New South politics became little but intraparty contests between aspirants for nomination by one party, with little or no public consequence—the solid South lasted for some six decades.[4]

In turning to the Second Reconstruction it is well to remember that it was national rather than regional and faced new as well as old problems. Black disfranchisement was not seriously threatened until the Voting Rights Act of the Second Reconstruction was passed by Congress in 1965, which outlawed the old poll taxes, registration fees, and confusing ballot boxes. Federal registrars were dispatched to the Black Belt where compliance with the new law was most doubtful, but withheld in hopes of voluntary compliance by the very white Democratic officials long responsible for black disfranchisement in nearly 90 percent of Southern counties. To the surprise of all, these hopes proved justified. Within a year a majority of the blacks of voting age had been registered, and in less than twenty years some three-fifths of them had reentered Southern political life. Simultaneously came an upsurge of white registration that left them with an 83 percent majority.[5]

These changes illustrate and characterize an era of ironic reversals and paradoxes that still persists. Blacks had already reversed their historic party alignment from Republican to Democratic during the New Deal. White voters of the South had begun their experiment with Republican presidential politics, but still remained largely Democratic in state and local elections, where black Democrats were more acceptable. The complex consequences include a marked decline of old-style racism, but very little evidence of increased liberalism. Democratic candidates must take care not to lose essential white votes by the way they gain black support. Some of the old devices of black voter dilution were still available and used to keep minority power under some restraint. Nevertheless, the number of black state and local officials, a mere 72 in 1965, nearly quadrupled in the next two decades. Virginia seated the first black state governor in its history, and cities with majorities or near equal numbers of black voters elected black mayors. Even so, with 20 percent of the Southern population, blacks held only one-third of that percentage of state legislators and rarely more than that in local and minor offices. Significant changes there were, but as in the old days the fundamental political question was not whether blacks or whites shall vote, but which whites shall rule.[6]

By 1990 white voters in the South were fairly equally divided between the two major parties, but with a distinct advantage to the white Democrats so long as they could count upon the black vote. By 1992, however, the black vote had begun to decline. Explanations differed, but many, including several scholars, attributed the decline in part to a decision of the Supreme Court in 1986 implementing the revised Voting Rights Act by requiring "the creation of a maximum number of minority districts" where blacks were a majority (*Thornburg v. Dingles,* 478 US 30 [1986]). Before the redistricting so ordered, the South had only four congressional districts with a majority of black voters, but afterward there were fourteen. With a corresponding increase in the number of black congressmen, they and their supporters were delighted with the redistricting. They do seem justified in assuming at the time that the intended consequence of the new black districts was belated justice for an underrepresented minority.[7] Challenges and criticisms of this view nevertheless multiplied in the 1990s. Some critics see racial segregation of voters as being at odds with the spirit of the civil rights revolution, denounce the rise of racial gerrymandering to aid a minority that was long the victim of the same white strategy. Others contend that the gain in safe seats in congress for blacks came at the expense of minority influence on Democratic state politics. These criticisms are often combined with the contention that by draining off strong Democratic votes from surrounding districts black gains in redistricting are linked to Republican gains, though they do not account for all of them.[8]

As if to intensify and complicate the debate, in 1993 a sharply divided Supreme Court reversed the decision of 1986 requiring the redistricting on the ground that it adversely affected white voters. To Justice Sandra Day O'Connor, who wrote the majority opinion in *Shaw v. Reno*, the redistricting plan of North Carolina seemed to segregate voters by race and bore "an uncomfortable resemblance to political "apartheid" and "resembles the most egregious racial gerrymandering of the past" (*Shaw v. Reno*, 113 S.Ct. 2827 [1993]). Inspired by the decision, four Southern states quickly filed suits to rid themselves of the new minority-majority districts. Black opponents, on the other hand, were outraged by the Court's reversal on redistricting. The Black Caucus in Congress enlisted the support of ten national organizations for civil rights to join their struggle. Their council compared the *Shaw* decision with *Plessy v. Ferguson* (16 US 537 [1896]) a century before for its "devastating racial consequences."[9] Like the nineteenth-century struggle for political equality, the twentieth-century sequel, similarly plagued with litigation, was threatened with defeat.

Now to racial segregation in the 90s of the two centuries. In the slave states it was a relatively new idea at the time of emancipation. Slavery made constant contact a necessity. It was rather impractical to segregate slaves, especially in the rural life that the vast majority lived. There were no busses, restaurants, theaters, hotels, or hospitals to segregate. Slaves were in and out of white masters' homes, grew up, played, and worked together, and served not only as nurses but often as mothers of the owners' offspring. Between the best, W. E. B. DuBois wrote, existed "bonds of intimacy, affection, and sometimes blood relationship." Racism of the sort that bred Jim Crow segregation began in Yankeedom. Alexis de Tocqueville, who traveled in both North and South in the 1830s, was astonished at the extremes of racial bias in the free states and wrote that "nowhere is it so intolerant as in those states where servitude has never been known." In the West, several states blocked admission of blacks or required them to post bond, and in the East, Boston had her "Nigger Hill," and New York and Philadelphia their ghettoes, for which Richmond, Charleston, and New Orleans had no counterpart.[10] The first edition of my history of segregation has been criticized for neglect of city life in the South. By 1860, however, only 2 percent of slaves lived in cities, along with most of the South's free blacks. They were subject to exclusion and discrimination of various kinds. But urban blacks, free or slave, mingled with lower-class whites more or less freely in bars, balls, and religious groups. Even so, fewer than 8 percent of the total population of the slave states lived in towns as large as 4,000, and those slaves who did, usually lived in compounds with their owners, while free blacks were not confined to segregated living areas.[11]

C. Vann Woodward

The collapse of slavery brought some voluntary racial separation on both sides: freedmen separated from old masters and plantations and from white churches to found their own; whites withdrew from old intimacies and responsibilities. Three states passed laws excluding blacks from first-class railroad cars, though mixing them with whites in other cars. The First Reconstruction disallowed or repealed these laws, but not the practice of segregation in public schools or separate quarters for blacks in jails, hospitals, or asylums. More evidence of such early racial separation continues to appear. Northern radicals came to the South from states more segregated than those under reconstruction, states in which blacks enjoyed few if any of the rights the radicals sought for the freedmen. The new constitutional amendments and laws supposedly guaranteeing those rights were ambiguously written and very indifferently enforced against the Ku Klux Klan, and in 1874 the Supreme Court cast sufficient doubt upon the enforcement acts as to make them virtually useless. By 1877 the North had lost interest in the First Reconstruction and was ready to make peace with Southern whites at the expense of the freedmen and abandonment of their cause.[12]

The new regime in the South bore the names of "Home Rule" and "White Supremacy," but the transition was not accompanied by any immediate changes in segregation. Separation of the races in schools, churches, and the military continued, and without the force of law, as did established custom elsewhere. But under the rule of conservatives, who had little to fear from blacks and framed the Compromise of 1877 accordingly, race relations appeared little changed to Northern visitors in the 1880s. They witnessed in the South an acceptance of blacks in public accommodations that they had never seen in New England. Others were impressed by the amount of interracial unionism, particularly that organized by the Knights of Labor, which had more than 500 locals in the South that defied the color line. Black and white labor joined in bargaining for wages and hours, in local politics, and in strikes.[13]

This was not, however, an era of racial peace and harmony. The very thing that impelled white labor unions to recruit black members was that white wages and hours were often determined by the miserable pay blacks received. At its worst that was no pay at all, the plight of black convicts leased by states to corporations all over the South. Their plight was clearly worse than that of slaves, who were at least property of considerable value. A legislative investigation reported that the stockades in which a Tennessee mining corporation confined its leased convicts were "hell holes of rage, cruelty, despair and vice." When the Tennessee Coal Mine Company sought to replace its free labor force with leased convicts in 1891 the discharged workers freed the convicts, allowed them to escape, and burned down the stockades. Discharged free labor used the same tactics at two other mining companies, freed in all some 500 prisoners, and took back their jobs. When the mining companies sought to return to convict labor in 1892 free miners laid siege to the militia in Fort Anderson, sent to guard the convicts, and killed some of the troops. Convict labor was briefly reinstated but the lease system was abolished in Tennessee the following year. In 1892 radicalism of Southern workers paralleled the radicalism of Southern farmers.[14]

It is an apparent paradox of Southern history that waves of democratic upheaval coincide with waves of extreme racism. We have seen one example in the history of disfranchisement, and we have a second in the history of Jim Crow segregation. The common misreading lies not in the existence but in the causes of the paradox, that is, in attributing the ugly outbursts of racism to lower-class whites. But in 1892 that class of white farmers was striving to make common cause with black farmers in the Populist Party, and white workers were recruiting black members for their unions. It was not this class of whites but the whites who feared and opposed such interracial alliances as farmers and workers were then trying to make, and who raised the storm of racist fears, hatreds, phobias and violence in the 1890s. The racist propaganda had the support of the conservatives who ran the Democratic Party, their governors, judges, legislatures, and police forces. From these officials a terrified black minority could expect little or no protection from murderous white mobs, Red Shirt terrorists, Ku Kluxers, or lynchers, whose atrocities set new records in the early 1890s.[15]

Segregation had begun without resort to laws until the Jim Crow car laws for trains, and only three Southern states had adopted them before 1890. In the meantime precedents for such law began to accumulate in the North. A Republican Congress had adopted a law segregating the public schools of the District of Columbia, and several Northern states had passed Jim Crow car laws of some kind, upheld by a host of state courts. The Supreme Court had yet to speak, but eventually a case challenging the constitutionality of such a law adopted by Louisiana in 1890 reached the court, and its historic opinion in *Plessy v. Ferguson* was handed down on May 18, 1896. Written by Justice Henry B. Brown, a native of Massachusetts, it upheld the "separate but equal" doctrine as constitutional, maintained that "established usages, customs, and traditions" should be respected, and held that law is "powerless to eradicate racial instincts." That decision remained the law of the land for fifty-eight years, confidently cited to uphold the flood of Jim Crow legislation that followed.[16]

That was not a flash flood finished in the 1890s, but it was that decade during which the floodgates were opened for the deluge that lasted more than half a century. The last resistance of Southern conservatives was a broadside ridiculing the fanatics by the editor of the South's oldest newspaper, the

Charleston *News and Courier* in 1898. "If there must be Jim Crow cars on the railroad," he wrote, "there should be Jim Crow cars on the street railways. Also on all passenger boats. . . . Jim Crow waiting saloons at all [railway] stations, and Jim Crow eating houses. . . . Jim Crow sections of the jury box . . . and a Jim Crow Bible for colored witnesses to kiss." Within a very short time all the editor's sample of absurdities, down to and including the Jim Crow Bible, were in practice—all save the Jim Crow jury box, rendered useless by disqualifying all blacks for jury service. The printed signs "Whites Only" and "Colored Entrance" appeared in profusion at places specified by law or at the whim of an officer or private individual. As for the law, a sample of the South Carolina code of 1915 will suggest its uses in working conditions: factories were prohibited from permitting black and white employees from working in the same room, using the same entrances, pay windows, doorways, or stairways at the same time, or the same "lavatories, toilets, drinking water buckets, pails, cups, dippers or glasses" at any time.[17] By such means fellow citizens, who had been assured equal rights that cost a war and had used those rights to vote, hold offices of authority, and win respect for thirty years, were reduced to virtual outcasts of a status and circumstance for which it is difficult to find anything comparable short of the one-time status of India's Untouchables.

On May 17, 1954, fifty-eight years after *Plessy v. Ferguson,* the Supreme Court reversed that decision in *Brown v. Board of Education* (347 US 483 [1954]), declaring school segregation unconstitutional for denying equal protection of the law and later applying the same rule to other Jim Crow laws. When decrees implementing the decision came a year later a panic of rebellions seized the white South. Organized, determined resistance continued for five years. All states of the South and border states passed measures nullifying or evading the law and local violence often stopped integration. President Eisenhower reluctantly used troops to integrate the Little Rock high school in 1957 and kept it open the rest of the year. But Governor Orval Faubus closed down the schools for 1958–59 and declared they would never reopen if integrated. A small percentage of public schools were integrated, but neither the *Brown* decision nor President Truman's successful integration of the military could be regarded as the beginning of the Second Reconstruction. They were only fortunate precedents. It began in 1960 and was led by young native blacks of the South in massive demonstrations.

Martin Luther King, Jr., set a precedent in 1956 with the Montgomery bus boycott, but the mass movement began early in 1960 with the black sit-ins and marches, nonviolent demonstrations that spread to all the states. These youths faced constant insult and frequent violence with firm display of courage. One of them, James Meredith, risked his life in efforts to register at the University of Mississippi; that precipitated the Battle of Oxford, in October

1962, an insurrection that proved the most serious clash of federal and state troops since the Civil War. Casualties included two killed and 375 injured, 166 of them federal marshals, 29 by gunshot wounds. Of the 30,000 Union troops committed, 300 remained ten months after Meredith was registered. The worst of many violent explosions the year following occurred in Birmingham, where Dr. King and other black leaders launched a campaign for limited desegregation goals with many forbidden marches of demonstrators through the city. They were beaten, attacked by police dogs, and hundreds were packed into prisons after their arrests, Dr. King for the thirteenth time. After a truce that supposedly ended the demonstrations, their headquarters and four homes, including that of Dr. King's brother, were bombed or burned, and fifty people were hospitalized after an ensuing riot. The worst incident yet was the bombing of a black church the following Sunday that killed four children and injured fourteen. In the ten weeks that followed, the Justice Department counted a national total of 758 racial demonstrations.[18] In the midst of all this President Kennedy committed his administration to the most sweeping civil rights legislation up to that time. Immediately after Kennedy's assassination his successor Lyndon Johnson made the cause his own and pushed the 1964 civil rights bill through a stubborn Congress in a seven-month struggle. In the presidential election of 1964 Johnson won even though he carried only one Southern state, his own. After another year of violence, North and South, and more black demonstrations, the Voting Rights Act was passed. Nothing comparable in legislative programs and executive will to enforce them occurred in the First Reconstruction, or ever before.

Whatever remained to be done, there can be no doubt that the black minority made substantial gains in the Second Reconstruction. It swept away the legal foundations of segregation in schools, housing, employment, and the ban on Jim Crow in hotels, motels, theaters, restaurants, and public accommodations went into effect immediately. The old Jim Crow signs over hundreds of places took longer, but their days were numbered. And instead of the expected defiance, peaceful compliance predominated in much of the South. Cities such as Birmingham built museums to memorialize civil rights leaders and atrocities they suffered. For one thing, all these whites had seen blacks risk and sometimes give their lives for their cause, a type of courage that commanded a peculiar respect in their culture. This made it more difficult for them to express their traditional racism—at least for the generation of witnesses.

The black minority had its ups and downs nationwide over the next two decades, but in that period a growing black middle class made unprecedented gains. These were registered in savings accounts, purchasing power, insurance policies, clerical and professional jobs, along with advances in education. As for political gains, the new black voters accounted not only for the many state, local, and congressional officials elected, but also for the pressure that brought the appointment of black federal judges and U.S. ambassadors. It is no wonder that optimism briefly soared, as it had after the legal end of slavery. The optimists in both instances shared two false assumptions: that the legal end of an institution meant the end of the abuses outlawed, and that the institution outlawed had been responsible for all the abuses.

The failure of those hopes is not to be blamed on the blacks, but their reactions are part of its tragic history. Coinciding with the peak of optimism a split widened in the black ranks between those who sought integration and those who sought separation, between assimilationists and nationalists, between those who shared and those who scorned King's "Dream," those who used peaceful means and those who resorted to violence for Black Power. The flaming cities, looted stores and homes, and the carnage resulting from the 150 major black riots that occurred during the four summers from 1965 through 1968 cannot be entirely attributed to black nationalism. But the Black Panthers, Black Muslims, and other minority nationalists played a significant part in the riots, nearly all outside the South. The President's Commission on the riots reported the nation "moving toward two societies, one black, one white—separate and unequal."[19]

From the start it was school desegregation that triggered most white opposition and virtually the only type of desegregation to provoke some black opposition, which nevertheless welcomed the downfall of Jim Crow elsewhere. The states with the most extreme school segregation for black students are New York, Illinois, Michigan, and New Jersey. This is mistakenly attributed to white withdrawal from integrated schools to suburban homes and private schools. The basic cause was a dramatic decline in white birth rates in the 1970s and 1980s and a retreat to suburbs (not to private schools) by all middle-class people, white and black, who could afford it. This left central city ghettos crowded with impoverished minorities, school-age children in one-parent families, and unmarried and unemployed men. Single young males, whether in the wild West with booze or in the wild slums with drugs, are notorious producers of violence.

If for no other reason, the shortage of white children made desegregation and integration of schools more and more difficult. The use of busing to overcome this difficulty was ordered by the Supreme Court in 1971. After a few years of opposition, busing gained in both white and black support until in 1989 some two-thirds of the families using the system found it very satisfactory. In the meantime, however, Supreme Court opinion was moving in the opposite direction toward resegregation. President Nixon appointed four justices to the Court, one of whom, Justice William Rehnquist, appointed in 1971, was made chief justice by President Reagan in 1986. Many years earlier while a clerk of the court Rehnquist had written in a memo: "I realize that it is an unpopular and unhumanitarian position . . . but I think *Plessy v. Ferguson* was right and should be reaffirmed." That case had reversed a previous decision, and *Brown* in 1954 reversed the "separate but equal" opinion of 1896. A third reversal was on the way, the three of them occurring roughly half a century apart. By 1991 the Rehnquist court was prepared with a majority for a series of opinions all favoring resegregation. These came in 1991, 1992 and 1995, with the last and most remarkable one, *Missouri v. Jenkins* (115 S.Ct. 2038 [1995]) prohibiting the improvement of city schools to attract white students from suburbs. Justice Clarence Thomas, appointed by President Bush, became the deciding vote in the decision that outdid *Plessy* a century before by support of separate but *un*equal rights. Desegregation thus became a lost cause save for one more seeming paradox: it lasted much longer where it had been most extensive—in the South.[20]

It is not to be assumed that Justice Thomas stood alone among the black people for resegregation. Support for such a position had grown since the rise of black nationalism, its rejection of assimilation and Dr. King's dream of integration in the 1960s. In 1963 some 200,000 blacks and whites stood facing the Lincoln Memorial enraptured by Dr. King's message of peaceful integration. In 1995 more than twice that number, this time all black and male, stood at the same scene but facing the opposite way—in more than the literal sense. They listened to Islamic Minister Louis Farrakhan who had organized this so-called "Million Man March" and used it skillfully to spread his gospel of nationalism, separatism, racism, and hatred.

The global fever of ethnic nationalism that convulses and divides countries all over the world seems to have infected the one country that assumed that a creed of assimilation for all, *e pluribus unum,* guaranteed immunity. The remarkable thing is how long the one minority least assimilated clung to that creed— from David Walker in the 1820s to Dr. King, who declared, "The Negro is American. We know nothing of Africa." Back-to-Africa had been a white man's idea for ridding the country of free blacks in slavery times. Now blacks suddenly became African Americans, exchanged old family names for African names, learned African dialects, wore African costumes. In universities appeared African departments and dormitories, African faculties to teach Afrocentric studies. In secondary schools across the country appeared an Afrocentric curriculum that included "black English" and history teaching that Africa is the mother of Greece, Rome, and all Western civilization. As Arthur Schlesinger has said, "If some Kleagle of the Ku Klux Klan wanted to devise a curriculum

C. Vann Woodward

for the specific purpose of handicapping and disabling black Americans, he would not be likely to come up with anything more diabolically effective than Afrocentrism."[21] These may be passing fads. It is impossible to guess the percentage of converts or the durability of their faith. By no means are all black intellectuals, writers, and professors converts, but the large number who strive to keep in step, in style, in fashion, from Los Angeles to Cambridge, had best manifest strong sympathies. Most ominous was what was happening to the National Association for the Advancement of Colored People, which for some ninety years has led the fight against segregation and for integration. In 1994 the association dismissed its director Rev. Benjamin F. Chavis, Jr., who promptly joined Farrakhan to direct his march. In 1997 a confused NAACP was debating a reconsideration of its historic mission.

I am not dismissing the lasting achievements of the Second Reconstruction as unimportant. And I am certainly not placing the chief blame for its failures upon the shoulders of blacks themselves. Their nationalists and separatists are still a minority of the black minority and seem likely to remain so for some time. It is harder to be so optimistic about the shift to the right in the courts and in the American electorate.[22]

Notes

1. C. Vann Woodward, "From the First Reconstruction to the Second," *The South Today: 100 Years after Appomattox,* ed. Willie Morris (New York: Harper & Row, 1965), p. 12.

2. J. Morgan Kousser, *The Shaping of Southern Politics: Suffrage Restriction and the Establishment of the One-Party South* (New Haven: Yale University Press, 1974), pp. 45–62, 71–82.

3. C. Vann Woodward, *Origins of the New South* (Baton Rouge: Louisiana State University Press, 1971), pp. 235–65.

4. Kousser, *Shaping of Southern Politics,* pp. 138–74.

5. Earl Black and Merle Black, *Politics and Society in the South* (Cambridge, Mass.: Harvard University Press, 1987), pp. 135–45.

6. Chandler Davidson, *Minority Vote Dilution* (Washington, D.C.: Howard University Press, 1984), pp. 4–20.

7. L. Marvin Overby and Kenneth M. Cosgrove, "Unintended Consequences: Racial Redistricting and the Representation of Minority Interests," *Journal of Politics* 58, no. 2 (1996): 540–50.

8. Kevin A. Hill, "Does the Creation of Minority Black Districts Aid Republicans?" *Journal of Politics* 57, no. 2 (1995): 348–401.

9. A. Leon Higginbotham, Jr., "*Shaw v. Reno:* A Mirage of Good Intentions with Devastating Racial Consequences," *Fordham Law Review* 62 (1994): 257–64.

10. Leon F. Litwack, *North of Slavery: The Negro in the Free States* (Chicago: University of Chicago Press, 1961), pp. 91–98.

11. Howard Rabinowitz, *Race, Ethnicity, and Urbanization* (Columbia: University of Missouri Press, 1994), pp. 23–41, 37–38; C. Vann Woodward, *The Strange Career of Jim Crow* (New York: Oxford University Press, 1973), pp. 18–29.

12. Eric Foner, *Reconstruction: America's Unfinished Revolution* (New York: Harper & Row, 1988), pp. 512–63; C. Vann Woodward, *American Counterpoint: Slavery and Racism in the North-South Dialogue* (Boston: Little, Brown, 1971), pp. 163–83; Joel Williamson, *The Crucible of Race: Black-White Relations in the American South since Emancipation* (New York: Oxford University Press, 1984).

13. Frederic Myers, "The Knights of Labor in the South," *Southern Economic Journal* 6 (1939–40): 479–85; Daniel Letwin, *The Challenge of Interracial Unionism: Alabama Coal Miners, 1878–1921* (Chapel Hill: University of North Carolina Press, 1997).

14. David M. Oshinsky, *"Worse Than Slavery": Parchman Farm and the Ordeal of Jim Crow Justice* (New York: Free Press, 1996), pp. 57–67, 81–82.

15. Woodward, *Origins of the New South,* pp. 235–82.

16. Kousser, *Shaping Southern Politics,* pp. 139–71.

17. Williamson, *The Crucible of Race,* pp. 184–209.

18. David J. Garrow, *Bearing the Cross: Martin Luther King, Jr., and the Southern Christian Leadership Conference* (New York: William Morrow, 1986), pp. 24–32, 225–64.

19. *Report of the National Advisory Commission on Civil Disorders* (Washington, D.C.: U.S. Government Printing Office, 1968), usually called "the Kerner Report."

20. Gary Orfield and Susan E. Eaton, *Dismantling Desegregation: The Quiet Reversal of Brown v. Board of Education and the Harvard Project on School Desegregation* (New York: New Press, 1996), pp. 9–45.

21. Arthur M. Schlesinger, Jr., *The Disuniting of America: Reflections on a Multicultural Society* (Knoxville: University of Tennessee Press, 1991), pp. 21–60.

22. In revisions of my original views of the First and Second Reconstructions over the years I have profited from the views of my critics. Many of these are represented in John Herbert Roper, ed., *C. Vann Woodward: A Southern Historian and His Critics* (Athens: University of Georgia Press, 1997).

Afterword

Rereading *The Southern State of Mind*, I have been delighted to find that the voices speaking on its pages of Southern history, fiction, and social change are still audible and necessary. Arranged primarily around the notions of race and identity, the book has survived into a new decade and into a new cultural climate. Its subject is the Southern and American experience as recorded by historians and literary historians. The quality of the contributions was exceptional; their depth and breadth made it possible to corral such an untamable beast as "the Southern state of mind."

As the essays demonstrate, the South is a region that continues to wrestle with its heritage and identity. There is nothing far-fetched about the approach in the essays as they explore the ontological and emotional implications of Southern identity. The topics illustrate the main problems of an interracial society and register important changes in contemporary attitudes toward the region. The contributors respond to the way issues, such as cultural commodification and globalization, challenge Southern identity. Some of the writers, such as Walter Edgar and Paul M. Gaston, may seem alienated, sometimes even haunted by their region, but they are also intellectually and emotionally unable to separate themselves from the South.

The success of the essays is rooted in their focus on the changing state of the Southern mind, which provides the volume with, as Bertram Wyatt-Brown wrote of the hardcover edition, "a coherence often lacking in collections." The juxtaposition of historical and literary dimensions offers insight into the origin and the future of debates on race and identity. By studying the Southern state of mind through essays by representative historians and literary critics, the old discussion of the relationship between changes in society and their expression in fiction is brought to life. Robert H. Brinkmeyer, Jr., Richard Gray, and other critics show the privatization in contemporary Southern fiction of enduring regional concerns as well as how Southern fiction helps us grasp a larger picture. The dialogue between historians and literary historians remains rewarding.

The contributors to the book attempt to understand the life and times of the region. The main discussion is about the impact on the region—and on America—of two races living side by side, and the focus is steadily on race relations and the mythology surrounding the notion of a biracial community. The changes in the culture are mirrored in its history and literature, and a distilled

Afterword

version becomes apparent through essays that invoke the hopes and possibilities of the region's emergence into national prominence. What becomes explicit is that old values, problems, and contradictions have survived modernization—and that they include racism.

It is perhaps worth asking whether racism distinguishes Southerners from other Americans, even today. It is not obvious to me that it does; in fact the difficulty in determining what exactly is Southern may stem to some extent from the ongoing "Southernizing" of the nation. Moreover the persistent misperceptions of racial issues and the continued strength of racial oppressiveness are concerns that remain important, not only nationally but globally. The essays make us ponder where, in terms of race and identity, Americans have been and are now heading. With a meaning that resonates beyond the region, South Carolina novelist Dori Sanders describes her region as an integrated culture in which people still live separate racial lives.

The late C. Vann Woodward's essay on one hundred years of the region's racial history provides a fitting end to the collection. He suggests there is continuity in the Southern mind and shows parallels in segregation and disenfranchisement between the 1890s and the 1990s. In his essay, one of the last he saw in print, the celebrated historian found it hard "to be optimistic about the shift to the right in the courts and in the American electorate."

The Southern State of Mind is not a conventional collection of scholarly essays: the continued relevance of its subject matter and the immediacy of the opinions voiced have made its reissue desirable, and I want to thank University of South Carolina Press for seeing this. We still speculate about the future of the regional identity, and we are still engrossed in the history and imagination of a South that seems fated to become a nationally encompassing state of mind.

Jan Nordby Gretlund
February 2010

Index

African Americans (of the South): blues, 122; conservative ideas, 58–60, 63n. 32; disfranchisement, 51, 212–15; elected officials, xi, xvi, 7, 14, 28, 32–33, 45, 102, 148, 153, 214, 217, 220; history of, 121–28; identity, x, xiv, 14, 17; in-migration, ix, xiv, 13, 14, 28, 32, 125; interracial friendships, xiii, 107–20; migration, ix, xiv, 13–14, 32, 125, 144, 205; nationalism, 220–21; as nurses, 124, 215; resegregation, 221; Southern culture, 143; voter registration, x, 24, 27, 32, 54, 212–13; the West, 205
Afrocentric studies, 221–22
Agee, James, 37, 147, 169
Agrarians, 8, 114
Albee, Edward: *Who's Afraid of Virginia Woolf,* 85
Alexander, Will, 7
American literature, child narrators, 164
Andersonville Prison Camp, 155
anticommunism, 25; crusaders, 56; the labor movement, 53
Applebome, Peter, 17, 137; *Dixie Rising,* 106n. 27
Armey, Dick, 52
Arroyo, Elizabeth Fortson, 144
Ashe, Arthur; monument, 16
Ashmore, Harry, 103
Askew, Reuben, 10, 11, 28
Atlanta Journal-Constitution, 115, 143
Attenborough, Richard, 42–44
Ayers, H. Brandt, 8

Badger, Anthony, 54
Baker v. Carr, 148

Bakhtin, Mikhail: *The Dialogic Imagination,* 113
Barnwell, William H., 103; *Richard's World,* 99
Barthes, Roland, 190, 191
Bartley, Numan, 24–25, 26, 54, 58, 59, 148, 153, 155; *The Rise of Massive Resistance,* 54
Bass, Rick, xv, 205–11; *The Book of Yaak,* 207–8, 211; *The Deer Pasture,* 206; "Government Bears," 206; "Mahatma Joe," 207; "Mississippi," 206; *Oil Notes,* 208; *The Sky, the Stars, the Wilderness,* 206; *Wild to the Heart,* 206; *Winter: Notes from Montana,* 207, 208
Bearden, Romare, 9
Beasley, David, 96, 141
Beckwith, Byron de la, 43
Bell, Madison Smartt, xiii, xv, 107–18; "An Essay Introducing His Work in Rather a Lunatic Fashion," 118; "Literature and Pleasure: Bridging the Gap," 117; *Soldier's Joy,* 110–18; violence, 115, 117, 118, 120n. 26
Berendt, John: *Midnight in the Garden of Good and Evil,* 81
Betts, Doris, xv, *Heading West,* 203, 205
Bierce, Ambrose: "Chickamauga," 83
Biko, Steve, 42, 43
biracial South, viii, ix, x, xiii, 3–20, 23–33, 95–103, 107–18, 166–68, 194–95
Birmingham, Alabama, 4, 28, 44, 49–50, 58, 142, 219
Black Belt, 23, 25, 50–51, 212, 213; elite, 51

Index

Black Power movement, 39; outside the South, 220
Black, Charles L., 3, 18
Bond, Julian, 39, 40
Boston school desegregation, 11
Bourne, Peter, 149, 152
Boyd, Blanche McCrary, 74
Boyd, Malcolm, 126
Brewer, Albert, 27
Brown v. Board of Education, 7, 24, 25, 36, 44, 45, 53, 152, 218, 221
Brown, Larry, xiii, 71, 73, 107–18; *Dirty Work,* xiii, 108–13; *Joe,* 205
Bruce, Steve: *The Rise and Fall of the New Christian Right,* 59
Buckley, William, 39; *God and Man at Yale,* 56
Bumpers, Dale, 10, 28
Burke, James Lee, xv
Burton, Orville, 148
Busbee, George, 10
Bush, George, 221; civil rights, 30

Caldwell, Erskine, 76, 163
Calhoun, John C., 77, 90, 91, 193
California anti-affirmative action referendum, 38
Campbell, Carroll, 97
Campbell, Jessie, 13
Campbell, Will, 95
Capote, Truman, 75, 164
Carr, Jr., Oscar, 19
Carter III, Hodding, 143, 144
Carter, Dan, xi, 30, 32
Carter, Jimmy, xiv, 10, 12, 28–29, 52, 135, 147–58; characterized, 148, 157; Civil War, 155; family history, 150; favorite authors, 147; fundamentalists, 149; humor, 157; integration, 152, 153; intelligence, 147; navy career, 152; *An Outdoor Journal,* 150; poetry, 151, 157; political books, 155; popular Southern culture, 155; Project Atlanta, 29; public image of, 149; recent books by, 149; reinventions of, 148; representative New Southerner, 156; the South, 148; *Turning Point,* 152, 155; wealth, 152; *Why Not the Best?,* 149; wizard, 147
Carter, Rosalynn, 150, 151, 155, 157
Cash, W. J., 12, 156
Cat on a Hot Tin Roof (film), 103
Chadwick, Vernon, 137
Chappell, Fred, 180–81; *I Am One of You Forever,* 180; "Storyteller," 181; use of imaginative lies, 180
Charleston News and Courier, Jim Crow laws, 218
Charleston, South Carolina, 89, 90, 96, 97, 99, 102, 139, 190, 192, 193, 194, 197, 215
Charlotte Observer, 128
Chavis, Jr., Benjamin F., 222
Chiles, Lawton, 32
Christian Right, x, 31
Civil Rights Act of 1964, 14, 31, 41, 50, 52, 53, 55, 219
Civil Rights Movement, ix, xiii, xv, xvi, 15, 16, 30, 36–46, 50, 66, 192, 199, 218–20; courage of, 219; historians and, 44–45; Hollywood and, 39–46
Civil War, vii, xii, xiii, 5, 12, 13, 15, 16, 17, 18, 51, 80–92, 107, 115, 123, 125, 141, 155, 176, 206, 219
Clark, Rachel, 151, 152
Clark, Septima Poinsette, 99
Clinton, Bill, 10, 33, 38
Clinton, Hillary Rodham, 157
Cobb, James C., xii, xiv, 67, 135, 156
Coles, Robert, 45
Colmer, William, 23
Commission on Interracial Cooperation, 6
Compromise of 1877, 216
Confederate States, xi, 52
Connerly, Ward, 38
Connor, Eugene, 10, 50

Index

Cooke, John Esten: *Surry of Eagle's Nest*, 83
Crane, Stephen: *The Red Badge of Courage*, 83
Crews, Harry, xi, 74–76; *A Childhood*, 75; *Karate Is a Thing of the Spirit*, 74; *The Gospel Singer*, 75; *The Mulching of America*, 75–76
Cry Freedom (film), 42–43
Culture of Contentment, 29

Dabbs, James McBride, 97–99, 103
Darrow, Clarence, 56
Davidson, Charles, 30
Davis, Thadious M., 14–15
Davis, Thulani, 76
Delaney, Paul, 15, 16, 17
DeLaughter, Bobby, 43
DeLay, Tom, 52
Democratic Party, x, xvi, 9, 23, 28, 29, 32, 33, 50, 51–52, 53, 54, 55, 97, 101, 135, 149, 153, 212, 213, 214, 217; African American voters, 214; conservatives, 217; middle-class disenchantment, 54
desegregation, 3, 11, 12, 24, 25, 27, 28, 31, 59, 95, 102, 219, 220, 221; a lost cause, 221
Dhombres, Jean, 186
Dickey, James, xvi, 154; *Deliverance*, 204–205
Dixiecrat revolt, 51
Dollard, John, 28
Douglass, Fredrick, 121
Dr. Strangelove (film), 85
DuBois, W. E. B., 215
Duke, David, 17, 30–31
Dunbar, Leslie, 3

Economist, 69
Edgerton, Clyde, xii, xv, 76, 81, 83, 91, 92; *Raney*, 81, 83, 85, 87
Edwards, Edwin, 10
Egerton, John, 51, 58

Eisenhower, Dwight, 55, 126, 218
Encyclopedia of Southern Culture, 138
European Southern Studies Forum, the, 185
Evangelical Protestantism: Christian schools, 57; fundamentalism, 56; integration, 57; Internal Revenue Service, 57; politicized, 55; religious right, 62n. 21; televangelists, 56
Evers, Medgar, xi, 43; monument, 16
Eyes on the Prize: America's Civil Rights Years (TV series), xi, 44; viewers of, 48n. 26

Falwell, Jerry: "Moral Majority," 57, 149
Farrakhan, Louis: "Million Man March," 101, 221, 222
Fascell, Dante, 26
Faubus, Orval, 27, 218
Faulkner, William, xi, xii, xiv, 73, 74, 77, 81, 88, 89, 161, 167, 169, 173, 175, 182; *Absalom, Absalom!*, 80, 83, 194; *As I Lay Dying*, 76, 166; conference, 70, 137; *The Mansion*, 76; masculine oratory, 173; *The Reivers*, 182; *The Sound and the Fury*, 74, 205; *The Unvanquished*, 107, 182
Faust, Drew, 144
Federal Bureau of Investigation, 40, 41, 42, 43
Ferris, William, 137
Fields, Cleo, 31
Finney, Ernest, 102
Finster, Howard, 137
Flynt, Larry, 57
Folsom, Jim, 24, 26, 27
Foote, Shelby, 140
Ford, Gerald, 154
Ford, Richard, 72, 185, 203
Ford, Robert, 101
Fordice, Kirk, 19, 31
Fort Anderson, 217
Foster, Mike, 31
Foxworthy, Jeff, 139, 144

229

Index

Franklin, John Hope, 128
Freud, Sigmund, 143, 197
Fulbright, William, 26

Gaines, Ernest J., 15, 76; *The Autobiography of Miss Jane Pittman,* 83; *A Gathering of Old Men,* 113
Galbraith, John Kenneth, 29
Gandhi, Mohandas, 54
Gantt, Harvey, 29
Genovese, Eugene: *The Southern Tradition,* 69
Gerolmo, Chris, 40, 41, 42
Ghosts of Mississippi (film), xi, 43
Gibbons, Kaye, xiv, xv, 161–73; autobiography, 170; *Charms for the Easy Life,* 169; *A Cure for Dreams,* 161, 169; *Ellen Foster,* 161–69; feminism, 163; *Frost and Flower,* 170; guilt, 166, 170; history, 173; *How I Became a Writer,* 162, 170; humor, 162, 163; identity, 165; memory, 162, 172, 173; mother-daughter relationships, 169, 173; narrators, 164; race, 167–68; *Sights Unseen,* 161, 162, 164, 168, 170–73; *A Virtuous Woman,* 169; voice of, 161, 172
Gibson, James William: *Warrior Dreams: Paramilitary Culture in Post-Vietnam America,* 116
Gilligan, Carol, 112
Gingrich, Newt, 30, 38, 52, 60
Glasgow, Ellen, 76; *Virginia,* 198
globalization, 69, 80, 92
Gluck, Christoph Willibald von: opera, 198
Goldwater, Barry, 30, 55
Gone with the Wind (film), 45
Gore, Sr., Albert, 24
Grady, Henry W., 5
Graham, Billy: anticommunist rhetoric, 56, 62n. 20
Graham, Frank Porter, 23
Graham, Katherine, 147

Graham, Martha, 189
Grantham, Dewey, 148, 154
Graves, Curtis M., 14
Gray, J. Glenn, 110; *The Warriors,* 107
Gray, Richard, xi, xii, 6
Greenberg, Paul, 16
Groom, Winston, 115

Hackman, Gene, 40–41
Hackney, Sheldon, 68
Haley, Alex, 9, 15; *Roots,* 83
Hampton, Henry, 44
Hamsun, Knut: *Growth of the Soil,* 92n. 6
Hannah, Barry, xii, xv, 73, 74, 91, 92, 203; "Bats Out of Hell Division," 87–89
Hansberry, Lorraine: *A Raisin in the Sun* (play), 131
Hardy, Thomas: *The Mayor of Casterbridge,* 198
Harris, Richard, 25
Harris, Roy, 28
Hawthorne, Nathaniel, 200n. 15
Heady, Robert, 60
Heale, Michael, 25
Helms, Jesse, 23, 30, 52
Hemingway, Ernest, 73
Herrnstein, Richard J.: *The Bell Curve,* 49, 123
Hill, Anita, 131
Hine, Darlene Clark, 100
Hobsbawm, Eric, 143
Hobson, Fred, 4–5, 67, 185, 188; *The Southern Writer in the Postmodern World,* 181–82
Hodgson, Geoffrey, 57
Holmes, Stephen, 32–33
Holton, Linwood, 30
"Hootie and the Blowfish" (band), 101
Hoover, J. Edgar, 41
Horwitz, Tony, 142
Humphreys, Josephine, xi, xv, 77, 76, 89, 90, 91, 92, 185–99; communication, 187, 192; and the critics, 185; "A

230

Disappearing Subject Called the South," 199; *Dreams of Sleep,* 189–97; *The Fireman's Fair,* 187, 190–91, 195, 198; interchanging roles, 191; Mark Twain, 196; "My Real Invisible Self," 191–92; race, 100, 197, 199; *Rich in Love,* 76, 77, 89, 90, 91, 92, 100, 187, 189, 192–94, 196, 198; the Southern male, 190, 198; technique, 185; time, 188; and the unpresentable, 186, 189, 199; William Faulkner, 194

Hunt, James, 28, 29, 32

Intelligence Report: Klan Watch and Militia Task Force, 120n. 28

James, Forrest, 10
Jameson, Fredric, 71
Jefferson, Thomas, 131
Jim Crow segregation, xvi, 4, 6, 7, 37, 39, 42, 44, 45, 46, 215, 217; banned, 95, 219; Northern racism, 215; South Carolina, 95, 100
John Birch Society, 56
Johnson, Frank, 30
Johnson, Lyndon, 38, 148, 219
Jordan, Winthrop, 4
Joyner, Charles, 18, 96, 103

Keats, John: "Ode on a Grecian Urn," 88
Kefauver, Estes, 24
Kennedy, John F., 30, 126, 148, 156, 219
Kester, Howard, 6–7
Key, V. O.: *Southern Politics in State and Nation,* 24, 23, 50–52
Kierkegaard, Søren, 147
King, Jr., Martin Luther, x, xvi, 7, 10, 16, 36, 37–39, 40, 43, 126, 127, 148, 153, 154, 218–22; federal holiday, 16, 141
King, Larry L., 11, 135

King, Sr., Martin Luther, 153, 154
Kingsolver, Barbara, 203, 205
Kirby, Jack Temple, 139
Knights of Labor, 216
Koinonia, South Georgia, 6
Ku Klux Klan, 4, 7, 9, 30, 40, 111, 115, 117, 125, 140, 142, 151, 153, 216, 217, 221; Shelby Foote on, 140

Lawrence, D. H.: "The Spirit of Place," 176
Lee, Robert E., 10, 16
Lerche, Charles, 68
Lewis, John, 29
Limbaugh, Rush, 38
Lin, Maya, 15–16
Lincoln, Abraham, 123
Little Rock, Arkansas, 126, 218
Loewen, James, 45
Lost Cause, x, xii, 4, 8, 12–13, 15, 17, 18, 85, 87, 88, 89, 148; deconstruction of, 85, 88–89
Lott, Trent, 23, 52
Lyotard, Jean François, 188, 189; "What Is Postmodernism?," 186

MacCannell, Dean & Juliet Flower, 89
Maddox, Lester, 27, 28, 148, 153
Marquez, Gabriel Garcia, 73
Marsalis, Wynton, 70
Marx, Karl, 56
Mason, Bobbie Ann, xii, 91, 92; "Shiloh," 84–87; *Shiloh and Other Stories,* 172–73
May, Larry, 112
Mays, Benjamin, 98
McCarthy period, 25, 52–53
McCarthy, Cormac, xi, xv, 72–74, 203, 205, 206, 208–11; *All the Pretty Horses,* 73, 209, 210; *Blood Meridian,* 208–10; *Child of God,* 73; *Cities of the Plain,* 209; *The Crossing,* 209, 210
McClinton, I. S., 26

Index

McCullers, Carson, 75
McGill, Ralph, 7
McKee, Kathryn B., 185
McKinney, Cynthia, 33
McLaurin, Melton: "Rituals of Initiation and Rebellion," 98
McMath, Sid, 24
McNair, Robert E., 100
Mebane, Mary E., 13–14
Medlock, Travis, 97
Mencken, H. L., 4, 89
Meredith, James, 218–19
Miller, Zell, 32
Millichap, Joseph, 187–88
Mississippi, 7, 13, 19, 25, 31, 108; 1890 disfranchisement, 212
Mississippi Burning (film), 40–45; unfavorable reviews, 47n. 14
Missouri v. Jenkins, 221
Mitchell, Lee Clark, 205
Mitchell, Margaret, xii, 10; *Gone with the Wind*, 80, 87
Montgomery, Alabama, 16, 26, 43; bus boycott, 27, 43, 45, 218
Morgan, Robert, 30
Morris, Kenneth, 156
Morris, Willie: *You Can't Eat Magnolias*, 8
Morrison, Toni, ix; *Beloved*, 169; *The Bluest Eye*, 119n. 14
Murray, Albert, 19–20
Murray, Charles: *Losing Ground*, 49; *The Bell Curve*, 49–50, 123
music, 70, 122, 136, 137, 138, 144, 165, 188
Myrdal, Gunnar, 58–59

NAACP, 44, 53, 125, 126, 142; confused, 222
Naipaul, V. S., 140
National Review, 56, 58
neo-Confederate hero, 142
neo-Confederate magazines, 17–18
Neshoba County, Mississippi, 4
New England abolitionism, 11

New Republic, 3
New York Times, 15, 154
Newsweek, 101
Niebuhr, Reinhold, 147
Nixon, Richard, 39, 147, 220–21
Nordan, Lewis, xv, 175–83; *The All-Girl Football Team*, 175; Arrow Catcher, 175, 178; "Growing Up White in the South," 178; "The Invention of Sugar," 176; Itta Bena, Mississippi, 175; *The Lightning Song*, 176; Mark Twain, 182; *Music of the Swamp*, 175, 177, 179, 181; optimism, 183; race, 178; *The Sharpshooter Blues*, 176, 180–81; short stories, 175; suicide, 178, 179; use of imaginative lies, xv, 177, 179; *Welcome to the Arrow-Catcher Fair*, 175; *Wolf Whistle*, 176, 177, 181
Norris, Clarence, 53

O'Brien, Michael, 176
O'Connor, Flannery, 73, 74, 76, 89, 173, 175; "The Catholic Novelist in the Protestant South," 211
O'Connor, Sandra Day, 215
Olympic Games, Atlanta, 138
O'Neill, Tip, 147
O'Reilly, Kenneth, 154, 155
Oxford Eagle, 138
Oxford, Mississippi, 4, 70, 74, 218–19

Page, Thomas Nelson, 5–6
Panic in the Streets (film), 82
Parker, Alan, 40, 41, 42, 43, 44, 45
Parks, Rosa, 27, 126
Pearson, T. R., 76
Percy, Walker, 114, 162, 185; American West, 204; *The Last Gentleman*, 204; *The Moviegoer*, 81, 82, 162, 167, 204
Perry, Matthew, 100
Peterson, Richard, 139
Phillips, Kevin, 63n. 28

Plessy v. Ferguson, 36, 215, 218; Justice Henry B. Brown, 217; outdone in 1995, 221
Pollak, Susan, 112
Populist Party, 212, 217
Presley, Elvis: conference on, 138; course on, 137; Graceland, 138
Promised Land, South Carolina, 98, 103
Providence Cooperative Farm, Tchula, Mississippi, 6
Public Broadcasting System, 43, 44
Puddington, Arch, 38

Ramphele, Mamphela, 42–43
Raspberry, William, 19
Reagan, Ronald, 37, 38, 57–58, 59, 156, 221; administration, 16, 59; unions, 60
Reaganomics, income decline, 59–60
Reconstruction, xvi, 6, 33, 36, 45, 212–22
redistricting, xvi, 32–33, 55, 214; reversed, 215
Reed, John Shelton, xi, 68–69, 81, 135; *The Enduring South,* 68–69
Reese, Frederick, 13
regionalization, 80
Rehnquist, William, 221
Reissman, Leonard, 67
religion, ix, x, xi, 4, 6, 7, 12, 13, 18, 19, 31, 50, 56, 57, 58, 59, 74, 100, 128, 147, 149, 151, 156, 166, 175, 176, 188
Republican Party, x, xi, 18, 23, 29, 30, 31, 32, 33, 49, 51, 52, 54, 58, 60, 61, 97, 101, 141, 214, 217; abortion, 31; "Contract with America," 55; South Carolina, 96; Southern conservatives, 52; white party, 30
right-wing foundations, 58
right-wing publications, 58
Robertson, Pat: "Christian Coalition," 58, 149
Rockefeller, Winthrop, 30

Rogers, Jr., George C., 100
Roosevelt, Theodore, 147, 148, 156
Rose, Willie Lee, 36

Sanders, Dori, ix, xiii; *Clover,* 128–30; *Her Own Place,* 99
Santayana, George, 36, 175
Savage South, 3–20, 148
Schama, Simon: *Landscape and Memory,* 188
Scholes, Robert, 199
school desegregation, Northern states, 220
Scopes trial, 56
Scott, Kerr, 24, 26
Scottsboro Case, the, 4, 53
Selma, Alabama, 4, 44, 149
Serres, Michel: *La Légende des Anges,* 196
Shaeffer, Jack: *Shane,* 205
Shaw v. Reno, 215
Simpson, Lewis, 19
Smith v. Allwright, 53
Smith, Al, 50
Smith, Bessie, 178
Smith, Frank, 31
Smith, Lee, 114; *Oral History,* 69–70
SNCC, 46, 152
Sobel, Mechal, 18
Sosna, Morton, 6
South Carolina, ix, xii, xiii, xv, 10, 11, 17, 23, 31, 52, 95–103, 121–31; Abbeville, 98, 102; church burnings, 96, 141, 104n. 7; Columbia Kiwanis Club, 99; integration of schools, 105–6n. 20; interracial socializing, 99, 100, 101; Jim Crow laws, 95, 218; Kosmos Club, 99, 100; Ku Klux Klan, 125; late segregation, 96, 97, 128
South Carolina Conference of Black Mayors, 27
South, the: Americanization of, 99, 172; antebellum wealth, 122; classes, 60; commodification of population, 68;

233

Index

cultural differences, 68; globalization of, 92; identity, 80; masculine conventions, 107–18; as moral problem, 59; per capita income, 29; popular bands, 138; popular culture, 136; popular films about, 70; racial segregation, 215; redneck culture, 139, 144; solid South, 213; suburbia, 140; unions, 68, 137; violence, 120n. 30
Southern Conference for Human Welfare, 6, 24, 25
Southern cultures, 71
Southern Cultures, 136
Southern Exposure, 9, 136, 137
Southern Growth Policies Board, 9
Southern heritage, 80–92
Southern Journal, Lamar Society, 9
Southern Journal, University of Mississippi, 9
Southern League, 18, 142, 143
Southern literature, 13; American West, 203–11; contemporary characters, 72; cultural regionalism, 203; destruction of cultural identity, 206; established authors, 89; Gothic, 75–76; myths about, 175; postmodernism, 91; race, 127; regionalism, 83; sense of place, 203, 210; use of imaginative lies, 177, 181; white supremacy, 93n. 8; writers of the small town, 76
Southern Living, 91, 135, 136, 138, 145
Southern Partisan, 17
Southern poor whites, 135–45; race, 217
Southern Poverty Law Center, 16
Southern public symbols, 15–17, 32, 96, 101, 102, 104n. 5, 130, 140, 141, 142
Southern whites, xiii, 7, 12, 14, 17, 23, 50, 135–45, 147–58, 216
Southern writers, American West, 203–11
Southernization, xii, xiv, 58, 69, 82, 143, 154
Sparkman, John, 24

Spencer, Elizabeth, 196
Sproat, John C., 95
Strikwerda, Robert A., 112
Strindberg, August: *Dance of Death* (play), 189
Styron, William, 173; *Confessions of Nat Turner,* ix; *Darkness Visible,* 170
suburbanization, 55
Sullivan, Walter, 176; *A Requiem for the Renascence,* 176
Sun Belt, xvi, 4, 32, 84, 204; Sunbelt South, 148, 154
Supreme Court, 26, 33, 53, 126, 213, 214, 215, 216, 217, 218, 220; resegregation, 220
Swaggart, Jimmy, 31

Talmadge, Eugene, 150
Talmadge, Herman, 30
Tannen, Deborah, 109
Tate, Allen, 114; "A Southern Mode of the Imagination," 108
Taulbert, Clifton, 15
Tennessee Coal Mine Company, 216
The Long Walk Home (film), 43
The Man Who Shot Liberty Valance (film), 40, 41
Thomas, Clarence, 221
Thomas, Dylan, 147
Thornburg v. Dingles, 214
Thornton, Mills, 26
Thurmond, J. Strom, 23, 27, 30, 52, 102, 141
Till, Emmett, 177, 178
Time (magazine), 12, 153
Tindall, George Brown, 5, 67, 144; "Mythology: A New Frontier in Southern History," 4
Tocqueville, Alexis de: Northern racial bias, 215
Truman, Harry S, 156, 218
Tunica, Mississippi, 29
Tuscaloosa, Alabama, 142
Tuttle, Elbert, 30

Twain, Mark, xvi, 75, 164, 182, 196

United Daughters of the Confederacy, 86, 89
University of Alabama, 10; Center for Southern History and Culture, 136
University of Mississippi, 16, 17; Center for the Study of Southern Culture, 9, 136, 137
University of North Carolina at Chapel Hill, Center for the Study of the American South, 136
University of South Carolina, Institute for Southern Studies, 136

Vietnam War, xiii, 8–9, 107, 108, 109, 110, 111, 112, 113, 114, 115, 116, 117, 154, 155, 156, 157; interracial friendships, xiii, 109–10
Voting Rights Act of 1965, xi, 23, 27, 44, 45, 54, 55, 213, 214, 219

Walker, Alice, ix, 15, 129; *Possessing the Secret of Joy*, 195
Walker, David, 221
Walker, Margaret, 15; *Jubilee*, 83
Wallace, George, 10, 11, 17, 27, 28, 30, 54, 58, 148, 154
Warren, Robert Penn, 141, 155
Washington Post, 19, 147
Washington, Booker T., 213; *Up from Slavery*, 121
Washington, Denzel, 43
Watkins, Sam R.: *Co. Aytch*, 83
Watson, Tom, 153

Weisbrot, Robert, 38
Welch, Joseph, 56
Welty, Eudora, 9, 89, 121–22, 155, 162, 173, 175, 182, 185–86, 187, 203–4, 206, 210; *Delta Wedding*, 186; "Kin," 186; "Old Mr. Marblehall," 186; "A Still Moment," 188
West, John, 10
Westerman, Michael, 141, 142
White, Hayden, 72
Whitman, Walt: *Drum-Taps*, 83
Wicker, Tom, 154
Wideman, John Edgar, 97, 98, 102, 103
Wilcox, James, 72; *Polite Sex*, 72; *Sort of Rich*, 72
Wilder, Douglas, 32
Will, George, 38
Williams v. Mississippi, 213
Williams, Raymond, 71
Wilson, Charles Reagan, 156
Winter, William, 10, 28
Winton, Tim, 73
Wisdom, John Minor, 30
Wiseman, Frederick, 40
Wolfe, Thomas, 76
Woods, Donald, 42–43
Woodward, C. Vann, xvi, 32
Workman, Jr., William D., 103; *The Case for the South*, 98

Yoder, Edwin M., 138, 143, 144
Young, Andrew, 9, 13, 29, 148, 153, 154